The Shell Book of the Home in Britain

Other books by the author
BRITISH FOLK ART
ENGLISH NAIVE PAINTING 1750–1900

Wrought-iron fitting used as a door knocker on the Priest's House at Muchelney, Somerset—14th or 15th century. *Photograph by the author*

Wrought–iron fitting used as a door knocker on the Priest's House at Muchelney, Somerset — 14th or 15th century. *Photograph by the author*

The Shell Book of the Home in Britain

Decoration, Design and Construction of Vernacular Interiors, 1500–1850

JAMES AYRES

FABER & FABER
London · Boston

First published in 1981
by Faber and Faber Limited
3 Queen Square London WC1
Printed in Great Britain by
BAS Printers Limited
Over Wallop, Hants
All rights reserved

Although sponsoring this book
Shell (U.K.) Ltd would point out that
the author is expressing his own views.

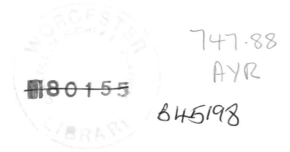
British Library Cataloguing in Publication Data

Ayres, James
   The Shell book of the home in Britain
   1. Interior decoration—England
   I. Title
   747'.8'80941   NKZ043
   ISBN 0-571-11625-6

For Annabel

Contents

*All line drawings are by the author
except where otherwise indicated*

Colour Plates

1. The hall of Plas Uchaf, LLANGAR, NEAR CORWEN, CLWYD. This interior may date from 1400 or even earlier and is a rare survival of the aisled hall in a domestic building, a common feature in barns in Britain. Despite its relatively small size this house was of palatial significance in relation to its time and place. *Photograph by courtesy of the Landmark Trust*

Introduction

If the peasant can be satisfied with his establishment, and the gentleman could not tell how to live without his, one would be almost persuaded that they could not be of the same class of animals.

William Howitt, *The Rural Life of England*, 1837[1]

This is a book about vernacular interiors. That is to say, it is concerned with interiors which may sometimes be quite large but in their arrangement and construction draw from tradition. Today many small houses have reverted to their original middle-class status, but in the past housing has tended to descend the social scale as expectations of comfort and privacy have risen. Many so-called cottages were intended for the yeoman class just as many farmhouses were built for the lesser gentry. The last traces of the Saxon hall [1] once suitable for kings and princes may be seen in many a timber-built barn: such a transition was no doubt caused by the ancient tradition for man to cohabit with his domesticated animals [2a, b]. Thus we may view the stone-built beehive pigsties of Wales [3] as being related to the ancient and primitive houses of similar construction found in Scotland and Ireland.

It is exceedingly rare for small houses in Britain to be 'listed' for preservation *because* of their interiors, and fairly common for them to be listed without knowledge of their interiors. Although existing legislation theoretically makes provision for the statutory protection of interiors in all listed buildings, in practice it is not effective. This matter demands further exploration and debate. To admire the external elevations of architecture is for most people a cerebral activity, whereas to be within an historic building, to be enveloped by history, is an important emotional and physical experience.

The fragmentary condition of the interiors and decoration of many small houses is to some extent reflected in the form of this book which gives an account of a succession of details. That approach should make reference easier. Some consideration is given to the practical details of construction in wood and stone, as well as to paint and painting, in the hope of assisting those concerned with the restoration and maintenance of similar buildings.

The vernacular interior was not designed on paper in an office; it evolved on carpenter's bench and mason's 'banker' and was built *in situ*. In other words, vernacular building is arrived at either by individuals constructing shelter for themselves or by trained craftsmen, both categories of builder drawing upon the traditions of the culture at large, inspired and disciplined by local materials and climate. Until the late sixteenth

3. Pigsty, PENDDEUCAE FACH, BEDLINOG, GWENT. The beehive construction was used in many of the early single-cell houses of Celtic Europe. The transition from human to animal occupation is a recurring theme. *Photograph: Welsh Folk Museum*

century all those who designed buildings were trained craftsmen: masons or carpenters. In the seventeenth century and afterwards architectural craftsmen often had little understanding of the basic thinking behind the classical orders, whilst architects sometimes had little appreciation of materials or craftsmanship. The technical proficiency of the master craftsman, dominated by the architect with his aesthetic manifestos, reached its height in the late nineteenth century. The position of the architect as master is now threatened by the structural engineer and, according to *The Times*, architecture is considered to be 'a profession and not an art'.[2]

Buildings surviving from before 1600 tend to belong to the upper levels of society. The mud shelters of the peasants have been dissolved by the action of rain and time. Nevertheless, there are examples of features long since rejected by the aristocracy that continued in use in houses built for the gentry. An example of this is the persistence of the king post in lesser buildings down to the Reformation despite the fact that it had not been fashionable with the élite for a hundred and fifty years.[3] The emergence of the middle classes following the Reformation gave rise to more substantial homes for lesser

2a, b. (*left*) Byre dwelling (two views) from MAGHERAGALLAN, ULSTER. The tradition of man cohabiting with his domesticated animals is well illustrated in this nineteenth-century example. The 'house part' is separated from the byre by an open drain. *Re-erected at Ulster Folk and Transport Museum*

4. Greive's Farm, NORTHUMBERLAND, water-colour drawing by S. H. Grimm, late eighteenth century, 12 × 9.5 in (30.5 × 24.1 cm). This drawing conveys the effect of such domestic scenes as they were lived. Note the open half-door, the washing line and the niddy-noddy behind and to the left of the fire. *Kaye Collection, British Library, Department of Manuscripts*

5. A 'third-rate house' and a 'fourth-rate house' from Peter Nicholson's *New Practical Builder. British Library.*

men [4]. Inevitably much of this book is concerned with the middle classes as represented in the engravings of 'Third and Fourth Rate Houses' illustrated in Peter Nicholson's *New Practical Builder* of 1823–5 [5]. By the time of the 1851 Exhibition the vernacular traditions were dying as a result of the mass culture brought about by industrialization and the concomitant improvement in communications. After 1851 the rich were not so easily recognized as an élite by the quality of their surroundings so much as by the quantity of objects in those surroundings.

Many of the features with which this book is concerned are more important than architecture or decoration, and even more fundamental than craftsmanship. In 1963 after a fire at Lauderdale House, Highgate, London, builders discovered bricked up in a wall near a first-floor fireplace a basket containing two shoes, a candlestick, a goblet, two strangled chickens and two chickens that had been walled-up alive. This miscellaneous collection had been ceremonially incarcerated as a builder's offering circa 1600,[4] a religious and mystical approach to building that declined with the emergence of the architectural profession. Its extinction has been confirmed by planning regulations. The concept of the home as a near holy place with its lares and penates is ancient. Indeed, for the liturgy of daily life the threshold and the hearth may be seen as equivalent respectively to the church porch and altar. Such a reverential attitude to man's shelter produced an outlook that regarded comfort as a proper but subordinate consideration. Health, as defined by government edict and imposed by local officials, was yet to be invented. Before houses were 'designed' they evolved, with a sensitivity towards their environment that may be seen as truly organic. It is such values that we have lost today and thus it is that we so cherish them.

> I see the barns and comely manors planned
> By men who somehow moved in comely thought,
> Who, with a simple shippon on their hand
> As men upon some godlike business wrought.
>
> John Drinkwater

Freshford 1979   JAMES AYRES

Notes to Introduction

1. William Howitt, *The Rural Life of England*, London, 1837, 1840 edition.
2. Letter from *The Times* to the author dated 7 June 1978. See Astragal, *The Architects' Journal*, London, 28 June 1978, p. 1237, which quotes this letter.
3. Eric Mercer, *English Vernacular Houses*, HMSO, London, 1975, p. 91.
4. Now exhibited at the Museum of London. This was by no means an isolated example. See J. M. Swann, 'Shoes Concealed in Buildings', *Journal No. 6* of the Northampton Museum and Art Gallery. In Ireland it was customary to bury a horse's skull under the floor of a house as a builder's sacrifice.

1 · The Vernacular Interior

House: a building wherein to shelter a man's
person and goods from the inclemencies of the
weather and the injuries of ill-disposed persons.

Anon, *Builder's Dictionary*, 1734[1]

Decor: The keeping of due Respect between the
Inhabitant and the Habitation.

Richard Neve, *The City and Country Purchaser*, 1726[2]

The main sources of reliable information on small domestic interiors are contemporary descriptions[3] and pictures [J]. In general only the grander houses were considered valid subjects, but travellers often had to accept accommodation where they could find it and if particularly primitive it was just as worthy of record as the nobleman's seat. The growing number of open air museums which exhibit reconstructed and furnished houses provide an interesting picture of the past, but as they necessarily involve some speculation they should be treated with caution. In the present state of knowledge so many issues are unresolved. How widespread was the use of wire-gauze window blinds, floor cloths or fire boards in eighteenth-century England? In the grand houses these questions are less difficult to answer. The larger the house, the more easily rooms could be left unchanged for a century or more, particularly if they were state apartments used only on formal occasions. In small houses the clutter of human occupation and activity had greater effect and as each successive innovation was introduced so it either overlaid or destroyed earlier decoration or previous ways of life. There is almost a case for including here a history of costume and even a history of agricultural and fishing implements as these often strayed indoors [6, 7].

In the reconstruction of a small interior the degree of speculation involved very much depends upon period and geographical location. An interior of circa 1750 could be reconstructed with reasonable accuracy if it came from the south-east of England, but in many parts of the British Isles it could not be assembled with confidence unless dating from the mid-nineteenth century or later. So long as, and wherever, the basics of the mediaeval tradition [8] persisted the use of paint for colour and pattern was probably more pungent than we would now suspect, although textiles which are so often today's vehicle for colour and pattern were exceedingly scarce until after the Industrial Revolution.

The Reformation brought with it effects that were to prove more far-reaching than a shift of power (from mason to architect) or style (from Gothic to Classicism). It introduced the middle classes.[4] Later, one hundred years elapsed between the appear-

6. An ORKNEY living-room in about 1930. In peasant communities the home was a place of work as much as a refuge for relaxation. Note the fishing floats visible in the top left of the picture. *Photograph by Bryce Wilson: National Museum of Antiquities, Edinburgh*

7. Interior of a croft on FOULA, SHETLAND. Note the fish hanging up to dry over the fireplace. *Photograph c. 1900, National Museum of Antiquities, Edinburgh*

8. Reconstruction of the
hall of the Priest's House,
MUCHELNEY, SOMERSET

ance of a prophet like Inigo Jones and a disciple of Palladianism like Lord Burlington, that 'Apollo of the Arts' whose 'proper Priest' was William Kent. In the intervening years the Dutch influence and the use of brick made possible the emergence of a new vernacular which contrived to unite the seemingly irreconcilable by acknowledging the influence of both the English climate and the Italian Renaissance. The simple brick town houses devised after the Great Fire of London under the supervision of Wren were the basis of British domestic architecture for over two hundred years. Even the nineteenth-century stucco-clad houses of Nash and his Victorian followers conform in their internal planning to these seventeenth-century origins in what the late Sir Albert Richardson, rejecting that vague term 'Georgian', sensibly dubbed 'the English Style'.

The development of towns in the sixteenth century resulted in a division between the character of life in town and country which was confirmed by the spectacular growth of urban centres in the nineteenth century. The late mediaeval gable facing the High Street and possibly the jettied storey were early manifestations of the effects of urban congestion. The use of dormer windows made attics more useful and the provision of a roof with a double pitch created more headroom. This feature is known in England as a 'curb roof' but the old English word 'gambrel' is still used in America.[5]

Before the coming of the railways the self-sufficient economy of many villages was still sustained. In the towns a degree of specialization in the manufacture of some products developed in the late seventeenth century on the basis of locally available materials. Nevertheless, in much of the country conditions had scarcely changed for three hundred years. William Cobbett's description of a farm sale near Reigate in October 1825 shows that even in the Home Counties a farmhouse of basically Tudor character would have but one room that was of its time:

> Every thing about this farm-house was formerly the scene of *plain manners* and *plentiful living*. Oak clothes-chests, oak bedsteads, oak chests of drawers, and oak tables to eat on, long, strong, and well supplied with joint stools. Some of the things were many hundreds of years old. But all appeared to be in a state of decay and nearly of *disuse*. There appeared to have been hardly any *family* in that house, where formerly there were in all probability, from ten to fifteen men, boys, and maids and, which was the worst of all, there was a *parlour*! Ay, and a *carpet* and *bell-pull* too! One end of the front of this once plain and substantial house had been moulded into a '*parlour*'; and there was the mahogany table, and the fine chairs, and the fine glass, and all as bare-faced upstart as any stock-jobber in the kingdom can boast of. And, there were the decanters, the glasses, the 'dinner-set' of crockery ware, and all just in the true stock-jobber style. And I dare say it has been '*Squire* Charington and the *Miss* Charingtons; and not plain Master Charington, and his son Hodge, and his daughter Betty Charington, all of whom this accursed system has, in all likelihood, transmuted into a species of mock gentlefolks, while it has ground the labourers down into real slaves. Why do not farmers now *feed* and *lodge* their work-people, as they did formerly?
>
>   *   *   *
>
> When the old farm-houses are down (and down they must come in time) what a miserable thing the country will be! Those that are now erected are mere painted shells, with a Mistress within, who is stuck up in a place she calls a *parlour*, with, if she have children, the 'young ladies and gentlemen' about her: some showy chairs and a sofa (a *sofa* by all means): half a dozen prints in gilt frames hanging up: some swinging book-shelves with novels and tracts upon them: . . .[6]

Such a description is of great value, emphasizing little-known details like the rarity and high social status of carpets and the better-known issues of changing social organization. Because standards varied so much, descriptions of interiors are only of value if their approximate date is known together with their geographical location. Celia Fiennes described the occupants of the old timber houses of Goudhurst, Kent, in 1697: '. . . they are a sort of yeomanly Gentry, about 2 or 3 or 400 £ a year and eate and drink well and live comfortably and hospitably; the old proverb was a Yeoman of Kent with one year's Rent could buy out the Gentlemen of Wales and Knights of Scales and a Lord of the North Country.'[7] The rich soil of the Weald coupled with close contact with the latest ideas from the Continent had early established a level of household comfort unmatched elsewhere in the country [9, 10], and which, although by then 'old fashioned', was still adequate for the standards if not the fashions of the seventeenth century. In contrast, the

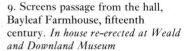

9. Screens passage from the hall, Bayleaf Farmhouse, fifteenth century. *In house re-erected at Weald and Downland Museum*

10. The great hall of the fifteenth-century Bayleaf Farmhouse. This is a typical Wealden hall rising from ground floor to roof timbers with a moulded bressummer at the dais end. The high cills of the windows were necessary before the widespread introduction of glass windows in the late sixteenth century. *In house re-erected at Weald and Downland Museum*

Welsh at this time lived in such primitive conditions that Miss Fiennes ventured no further into the principality than 'Holly Well' (Holywell) where 'they speake Welsh [and] the inhabitants go barefoote and bare leg'd, a nasty sort of people'. Conditions at Aitchison Bank in Scotland were not much better: 'The houses lookes just like the booths at fairs . . . they have no chimneys their smoke comes out all over the house and there are great holes in the side of their houses which lets out the smoake when they have been well smoaked in it; there is no room in their houses but is up to the thatch and in which are 2 or 3 beds even to the parlours and buttery; and not withstanding the cleaning of their parlour for me I was not able to beare the roome; the smell of the hay was a perfume and what I rather chose to stay and see my horses eat their provender in their stable than to stand in that roome, for I could not bring myself to sit down.'[8] If Miss Fiennes had been less 'stand-offish' she would have been below the level of the smoke. In contrast to the surroundings she was offered both salmon and trout to eat and 'some of their wine, which was exceeding good Claret which they stand conveniently for to have from France'.

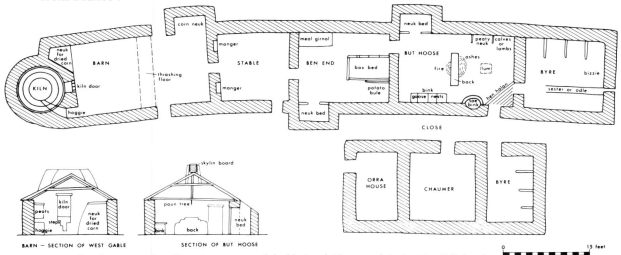

11. ORKNEY farmhouse, *c. 1830. Drawing courtesy of the National Museum of Antiquities, Edinburgh*

Tudor writers, living in a time of great social, religious and aesthetic change, note improvements in comfort. William Harrison wrote that fine possessions extended to 'the lowest sort (in most places of our south countrie)'. '[Possessions had] descended yet lower, even unto the inferiour artificers and manie farmers, who . . . have (for the most part) learned also to garnish their cupboards with plate, their (joined) beds with tapistrie and silke hangings, and their tables with (carpets and) fine naperie, whereby the wealth of our countrie (god be praised therefore and give us grace to imploie it well) dooth infinitelie appeare.'[9]

In Cornwall the situation was very different as Sir Richard Carew's *Survey of Cornwall* of 1602 makes clear. In the duchy, the aristocracy and gentry kept liberal 'but not costly builded or furnished houses'. 'Touching the Yeomanarie . . . Suiteable hereunto was their dwelling, and to their implements of household: walles of earth, low thatched roofes, few partitions, no planchings or glass windows, and scarcely any chimneys other than a hole in the wall to let out the smoke; their bed, straw and a blanket: as for sheets, so much linen cloth had not yet stopped over the narrow channel, betweene them and Brittaine. To conclude, a mazer and a panne or two comprised all their substance: but now most of these fashions are universally banished, and the *Cornish* husbandman conformeth himself with a better supplied civilitie to the Easterne patterne.'[10] Thus even in Cornwall, where Carew compares a hostile attitude to the English with 'the Welsh, their auncient countrimen', the population was beginning to enjoy some of the comforts of their despised neighbours.

By the eighteenth century many of the comforts that we now take for granted such as window glass and fireplace chimneys were all but universal, although carpets and plumbing were very rare. The improvement in living conditions in the second quarter of the eighteenth century was, with some implicit self-praise, well summed up by John Wood in his *A Description of Bath*:

About the Year 1727, the Boards of the Dining Rooms and most other Floors were made of a Brown Colour with Soot and small Beer to hide the Dirt, as well as their own Imperfections; and if the Walls of any of the Rooms were covered with Wainscot, it was with such as was mean and never Painted: The Chimney Pieces, Hearths and Slabbs were all of Free Stone, and these were daily cleaned with a particular White-wash, which, by paying Tribute to every thing that touched it, soon rendered the brown Floors like the Stary Firmament: The Doors were slight and thin, and the best Locks had only Iron Coverings Varnished: The Looking Glasses were small, mean, and few in Number; and the Chimney Furniture consisted of a slight Iron Fender, with Tongs, Poker and Shovel all of no more than three or four Shillings Value.

With *Kidderminster* Stuff, or at best with Cheyne, the Woollen Furniture of the principal Rooms was made; and such as was of Linnen consisted either of Corded Dimaty, or coarse Fustian; the Matrons of the City, their Daughters and their Maids Flowering the latter with Worsted, during the Intervals between the Seasons, to give the Beds a gaudy Look.

*   *   *

As the new Buildings advanced, Carpets were introduced to cover the Floors, though laid with the finest clean Deals, or *Dutch* Oak Boards; the Rooms were all Wainscoted and Painted in a costly and handsome Manner; Marble Slabbs, and even Chimney Pieces, became common; the Doors in general were not only made thick and substantial, but they had the best Sort of Brass Locks put on them; Walnut Tree

Chairs, some with Leather, and some with Damask or Worked Bottoms supplied the Place of such as were Seated with Cane or Rushes; the Oak Tables and Chests of Drawers were exchanged, the former for such as were made of Mahoggony, the latter for such as were made either with the same Wood, or with Wallnut Tree; handsome Glasses were added to the Dressing Tables, nor did the proper Chimneys or Peers of any of the Rooms long remain without well Framed Mirrours of no inconsiderable Size; and the Furniture for every chief Chimney was composed of a Brass Fender, with Tongs, Poker and Shovel agreeable to it.

Beds, Window Curtains and other Chamber Furniture, as well Woollen as Linnen, were, from time to time, renewed with such as was more fit for Gentlemens Capital Seats, than Houses appropriated for common Lodgings; and the Linnen for the Table and Bed grew better and better till it became suitable even for People of the highest Rank.[11]

Later writers, unless straying into those parts of Britain where primitive conditions could still be found, tended either to reflect a rather bourgeois smugness or to react to some extraordinary feature. J. T. Smith, for example, mentions the Italian artist Capitsoldi who 'upon his arrival, took the attic storey of a house in Warwick Street, Golden Square [London] and being short of furniture, painted chairs, pictures and window-curtains, upon the walls of his sitting room, most admirably deceptive'.[12] This account indicates that the furniture in this *trompe-l'œil* must have been ranged round the walls in a regimented fashion, as is known to have been the eighteenth-century practice in grand houses. Judging by Grimm's drawing of the interior of the Saracen's Head, Southwell, Nottinghamshire [12], such was also the custom in smaller rooms where the

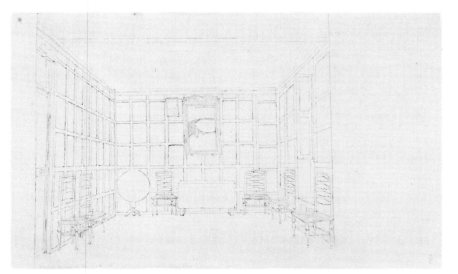

12. *A Part of the Parlour at the Saracen's Head at Southwell, called King Charles' Room, Nott.* Water-colour drawing by S. H. Grimm, late eighteenth century, 13 × 11.5 in (33 × 29.2 cm). The arrangement of the furniture against the walls is typical. *Kaye Collection, British Library, Department of Manuscripts*

resulting spaciousness was the more valuable. The great variety, in terms of quality and size, of tilt-top tables and corner chairs provide still further evidence of the constant ebb and flow of furniture within a room.

Good, bland, middle-class household comfort in cottage surroundings is expressed by Goldsmith through the Reverend Dr Primrose in *The Vicar of Wakefield* (first published in 1766): 'My house consisted of but one storey, and was covered with thatch, which gave it an air of great snugness. The walls on the inside were nicely whitewashed, and my daughters undertook to adorn them with pictures of their own designing. Though the same room served us for parlour and kitchen that only made it warmer. Besides as it was kept with the utmost neatness—the dishes, plates and coppers being well scoured, and all disposed in bright rows on the shelves—the eye was agreeably relieved, and did not want richer furniture. There were three other apartments—one for my wife and me; another for our two daughters within our room; and the third with two beds for the rest of the children.' This description is a remarkably early example of the middle classes returning to the type of house in which their ancestors lived. It was probably on the basis of the need for economy as much as upon French precedent and the Romantic Movement that the *cottage ornée* took root in Britain. As early as the 1730s estate workers had been housed in rows of cottages at Boxworth, Cambridgeshire,[13] and at the same period Ralph Allen built a terrace of houses for his masons at Bath. In general, landowners removed such buildings from the view of the 'big house' but the later desire to combine an ornament to the estate with a home for its workers could also develop into a matter of social conscience.

Blaise Hamlet (1811), by Nash, may have been built to give greater amusement to the rustic scene but it also provided comfortable if improbable housing. Papworth's *Rural Residences* (1818) is mainly preoccupied with the external appearance of such buildings, in contrast to Loudon's *Encyclopaedia of Cottage, Farm and Villa Architecture* which is also concerned with the practical arrangements within them. Loudon's book was avowedly designed to increase 'the comforts of the great mass of society'.[14] Such books must be seen as the precursors of the Prince Consort's attempts to improve the living conditions of the urban masses. Despite the efforts of the establishment and the example of the radical Chartists, these activities and activists had little impact on the housing problems of the nineteenth century. The writings of Richard Jefferies and Flora Thompson show that in the country little changed except for the worse, whilst the indescribable squalor of some areas of the large towns remained to be graphically recorded by Gustave Doré.[15] The 'Necessary House', or as William Halfpenny (and others) described it in the eighteenth century, the 'Bog House', was simply an outside shed providing a degree of privacy which many houses lacked even in the nineteenth century [13]. The water-closet within the house, though invented as early as 1596 by Sir John Harrington, remained a luxury not widely introduced until this century.

Eventually it was not the well-meaning condescension of the rich[16] so much as

13. Privy 'at the decoy Abbotsbury, Devonshire 1790'. Water-colour drawing by S. H. Grimm, 7 × 9.5 in (17.8 × 24.1 cm). The earliest water-closets date as far back as the sixteenth century but their general introduction did not occur until the twentieth century. *Kaye Collection, British Library Department of Manuscripts*

industrialization and transport that was to improve the quality of life for the mass of the population. At first this new-found means of producing objects cheaply tended to result in greater elaboration of the product at the expense of increased production. *The Report to the Juries* regarding the exhibits at the 1851 Exhibition sensibly remarked that, 'It is not necessary that an object be covered with ornament, or extravagant in form, to obtain the element of beauty; articles of furniture are too often crowded with unnecessary embellishment, which besides adding to their cost, interferes with their use.'

It was neither judgements like these nor the increased profits that simplified design would bring to industrialists that ultimately exerted the restraining hand on the excesses of Victorian decoration. It was the attempts of the Arts and Crafts Movement to turn back the clock that succeeded in providing a less cluttered aesthetic though failing to create a new society.

Notes to Chapter 1

1. Anon., *Builder's Dictionary*, A. Bettesworth and C. Hitch, London, 1734. No author given but attributed by contemporaries to James Ralph.
2. Richard Neve, *The City and Country Purchaser*, 1726, p. 122.
3. Including inventories.
4. Ian Bradley, 'The Question Mark over the Future of the Middle Classes', *The Times*, 7 January 1975.
5. In Britain the 'gambrel' is today sometimes used to describe a hipped roof with a pair of 'gablets'.
6. William Cobbett, *Rural Rides*, Penguin edition, pp. 226–9.
7. Christopher Morris (ed.), *The Journeys of Celia Fiennes*, Cresset Press, London, 1947, p. 136.
8. Ibid., p. 204.
9. William Harrison, *Description of England*, London, 1577, F. J. Furnival edition, 1877, II, p. 239.
10. Richard Carew, *The Survey of Cornwall*, London, 1602, 1769 edition, pp. 64, 66–7.
11. John Wood, *A Description of Bath*, London, 1765, pp. 3–5. Significantly, John Wood arrived in Bath in 1727.
12. J. T. Smith, *Nollekens and His Times*, London, 1829, 1919 edition, vol. II, p. 102.
13. M. W. Barley, *The English Farmhouse and Cottage*, Routledge and Kegan Paul, London, 1961, ill. 22b.
14. J. C. Loudon, *Encyclopaedia of Cottage, Farm and Villa Architecture*, London, 1836. From the first sentence of the Introduction.
15. His views of London, 1869–71.
16. For example Prince Albert's designs for model houses which were erected beside the 1851 Exhibition in the grounds of 'Hyde Park Barracks' (see C. H. Gibbs-Smith, *The Great Exhibition of 1851*, HMSO, 1950, p. 139).

2 · Heat and Light

The Fire and the Hearth

The domestication of man probably began when he tamed fire. Even before houses were built fire was central to man's life and in the earliest house it was the *focus* (Latin for hearth) of the room [14]. Indeed so far as the smaller house is concerned the central hearth persisted in England well into the sixteenth century and remained in use on the fringes of the British Isles within living memory [15]. The fire was the heart of the house.

Two of the words most intimately concerned with this fundamental subject, 'fire' and 'hearth' are Germanic in origin. The hearth was practically a synonym for the home, as in the phrase 'hearth and home'. In the north of England the room with the fireplace was once known as the 'fire house'.[1] Because fire was seen as being so crucial to man's survival it was used in England as a yardstick for taxation raised to produce revenue for the Pope. 'Peter's Pence', as it became known, was paid with some regularity until the Reformation.[2] The presence of this '*fumage*' tax discouraged a proliferation of hearths, with profound effects on the planning of houses in England, and probably encouraged the retention of the more efficient if less convenient open central hearth which provided warmth, light and heat for cooking although in summer some cooking would have been done out of doors. In Viking Denmark and Iceland separate kitchens have been found[3] but in Britain they are generally a later innovation and in some areas a recent one. Undoubtedly in most pre-Reformation houses of the smaller kind only one room, known as the 'hall', would have had a fire in it. The parlour, if one existed, would have remained unheated; such grandeur was a cold privilege in winter and for this reason these rooms were not elaborately decorated. Accordingly, the central hearth may be seen as not simply more efficient but, in winter at least, more socially cohesive at a time when a larger house would contain the families of the farmer and the farm servants. The central hearth was the natural theatre in which to gossip and recite traditional stories and songs.

The hearth itself was of earth, clay or stone. Where wood was burnt firedogs were necessary to provide a good circulation of oxygen to assist combustion. At first these took the form of a horizontal bar supported above the hearth by a pair of feet from each end of which sprang vertical members, later known as *staukes*,[4] which prevented the logs from

14. Interior of an ORKNEY croft in *c.* 1900. The central hearth, hanging chain, timber and straw chairs and the cupboard beds are typical. *Photograph: Kirkwall Library*

15. Central hearth in a 'black house'. Smoke-filled rooms necessitated low seating. *In house re-erected at Highland Folk Museum*

16. Early Iron Age firedog from CAPEL GARMON, GWYNEDD. The double-ended firedog was used on the central hearth. This example is typically Celtic. *National Museum of Wales*

falling outwards. Such firedogs have been found over much of Celtic Europe from the British Isles to Czechoslovakia, as have many other examples of early domestic ironwork. Celtic firedogs of the type from Capel Garmon, now in the National Museum of Wales, and another in Colchester Museum are terminated at each end by magnificent ox heads [16]. The alternative name for a firedog, 'andiron' from the French *landier*, may preserve 'through late Latin forms a common Celtic root meaning a bull-calf or a heifer'.[5] The type, though lacking the zoomorphic detail, persisted wherever central hearths were used. A good sixteenth-century example survives on the central hearth of the great hall at Penshurst. With the introduction of fireplaces a pair of firedogs with their *staukes* facing outwards became necessary. This break with tradition encouraged greater variety in form and even name, 'cobiron' being an alternative which may refer to their being knobbed.[6]

The firedog was the perfect means of supporting a roasting spit. At first these were

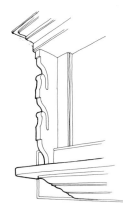

17. Eighteenth-century spit rack (one end) at 21 Grove Terrace, HIGHGATE, LONDON

turned by hand,[7] but various mechanical devices were developed, the most sophisticated of which was a turbine installed in the flue. An example may be seen in the kitchen of the Royal Pavilion, Brighton. Lesser households used the clock spit (operated by clockwork and attached to the chimney bressummer), the 'jack' [18] (also operated by clockwork), and the dogwheel. An aquatint by Rowlandson showing such a wheel occurs in H. Wigstead's *Remarks on a Tour of North and South Wales in the Year 1797* (1800) and a surviving example was located some years ago in the Old Manor House, Mitford, Northumberland—a house of modest size.[8]

18. Wood engraving by Thomas Bewick showing a monkey basting meat. *Museum of English Rural Life, Reading*

Any fire which is exclusively wood-burning needs encouragement. Firedogs helped air to circulate, as we have seen, but there were times when the more vigorous action of bellows was necessary. The word 'bellows' is probably derived from the Anglo-Saxon *blaest balg* or blast bag, so clearly they have a long history. Other items were also necessary to adjust the logs, and references to a 'fire fork' abound in sixteenth-century inventories.

In general the preferred fuel was timber and of these the hardwoods were most favoured being slow burning and producing the greatest heat. One exception was elm which is a poor combustor and once lit produces little heat; for this reason elm was usually selected as the fireplace lintel in houses that were otherwise framed-up of oak. In regions that were not forested and amongst those who did not possess woodland or hold common rights that enabled them to obtain firewood, other kinds of fuel had to be found. The poor in the region of Swanage were exceptionally fortunate in the Kimmeridge shale. Celia Fiennes states that 'they take up stones by the shores that are so oyly as the poor burn it for fire, and it's so light a fire it serves for candle too, but it has a strong offensive smell.'[9]

Another source of fuel was dried dung, the removal of which impoverished the land worked by the crofters, adding to the downward spiral of their poverty. A late eighteenth-century drawing of the New Church at Portland by S. H. Grimm[10] shows a table tomb in the left foreground with cow 'clots' (also known as 'dyths'[11] and in Yorkshire dialect as 'cassons'[12]) left to dry on its top. The indefatigable Celia Fiennes also saw, near Peterborough, 'upon the walls of the ordinary peoples houses the cow dung plaister'd up to drie in cakes which they use for fireing—its a very offensive fewell but the country people use little else in these parts.'[13] Again her acute eye noted the lack of fuel around Penzance where they burnt 'turf and furse and ferne; they have little or noe wood and noe coale. . . . I was surprised to find my supper boyling on a fire always supply'd with a brush of furse and that to be the only fewell to dress a joynt of meat and broth, and told me they could not roast any thing, but they have a little wood for such occasions but it's scarce and dear.'[14] Gorse, twigs and fern were also used as fuel in parts of Wales[15] and in some regions it is likely that fires were lit only when there was cooking to be done.

In Scotland dried horse and cow dung supplemented with seaweed was burnt in houses on the Orkneys and the Hebrides, and in Fife and Angus cow dung was mixed with coal or sawdust dried in the sun and called *dalls* or *daws*.[16]

Peat was a basic fuel not only in much of Scotland but also in Ireland [19], Wales and various parts of England such as Cumbria. In areas where it was scarce or where old-established communities had used up all the nearby peat, turf was sometimes used as a substitute with disastrous long-term effects on agriculture.[17]

When the tax on coal was abolished in 1793 its use became more widespread. In some parts of Scotland, as early as 1795 coal was burnt in the 'front room' but peat continued as the fuel in the kitchen.[18] Coal not only provided a greater heat it also produced a better light. In the parish of Dyke and Moy in Morayshire even the poorer households burnt coal quite early as it provided enough light to continue the domestic industry of spinning after dark.[19]

In the Yorkshire Dales knitting was an activity which could be carried on in the semi-darkness of firelight. William Howitt, in his *Rural Life of England* (1837), gives the following description: 'As soon as it becomes dark . . . they rake or put out the fire; take their cloaks and lanterns, and set out with their knitting to the house of the neighbour where the sitting falls in rotation, for it is a regularly circulating assembly from house to house. . . . The whole troop of neighbours being collected, they sit and knit, sing knitting songs, and tell knitting-stories. . . . All this time their knitting goes on with unremitting speed. They sit rocking to and fro like so many weird wizards. They burn no candle, but knit by the light of the peat fire.'[20]

The utensils of the hearth were always kept to a minimum, metal being expensive and a profusion of gadgets confusing. The 'great dripping pan'[21] was always important for cooking as was the pot-hook and chain, known in the Isle of Man as the 'slouree'. Chains

A. Painted timber screen, 128.75 in (327 cm) × 85 in (215.9 cm), at Cross Farm, WESTHAY, NEAR GLASTONBURY, SOMERSET, *c* 1550–1600 (?). The paint stops 18 in (45.7 cm) above the floor, no doubt to allow for the presence of a bench. The screen itself is probably earlier than the painting which has been applied arbitrarily and without regard for the stud and plank panelling. *Photograph: Delmar Studios. See pages 163–4*

B. Painted plaster fireplace lining, seventeenth century (?), Laurel Cottage, ALHAMPTON, NEAR DITCHEAT, SOMERSET. Such decoration is found in the south-western counties of England and also in Massachusetts. *Photograph: Martyn Brown. See page 43*

C. Mural in an upstairs room at the George Inn, CHESHAM, BUCKINGHAMSHIRE. Judging by the Garter Star the figure on the right is probably intended to represent George I.
Photograph: Hawkley Studios. See page 165

D. Early eighteenth-century mural decoration from another wall in the same room.
Photograph: Hawkley Studios

19. Living-room in a house in CONOGHER (TOWNLAND), NEAR DERVOCK, CO. ANTRIM, ULSTER. This house was the old home of President McKinley's family. *Photograph c. 1910 by R. Welch: The Ulster Museum*

of an early type (their use persisted in the so-called black houses of the Outer Hebrides) are fitted with hooks to facilitate raising and lowering the chain in a loop. Again the introduction of the fireplace brought about a change and although the chain continued in use it usually supported a trammel which provided the necessary adjustable height for the cooking pot. The Scottish 'swee' or 'swey', known in England as the chimney crane, was made of iron and in the south some were devised to adjust the height of the cooking pot. All had the advantage of being capable of swinging the pot away from the fire to inspect the progress of the cooking. These devices were probably first constructed of wood and the Ulster Folk Museum possesses a specimen in wood which nevertheless imitates the iron examples. Another example of wood imitating iron is the trammel hanging over the fire in the 'smoke-room' in the house from Mule, Bord, Faeroe Islands,[22] but wood trammels true to their material were made in Scotland.[23] The Irish example may also relate to the *gjøye* of late mediaeval (if not Viking) Norway. These were great logs which swung out from the wall to provide a point in space over the central hearth from which cooking pots were hung; it served the same function as, and was very similar to, the chimney crane.

Many utensils were of iron including the cooking pots, but posnets and skillets of bronze or bell metal were preferred, according to sixteenth-century inventories in which they are often referred to as 'brass'. In many households until the late sixteenth century such objects represented the most valuable possessions. Most food in mediaeval times was boiled (stews and boiled puddings), ovens other than 'pot-ovens' being a rarity until the introduction of chimneypieces made them possible.

The greatest single disadvantage of the central hearth was the smoke it produced. The reredos [20] was introduced to control the direction of the draught and was in use in the

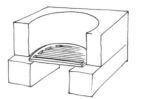

20. Hearth from HADDON HALL, based on a drawing by C. L. Buckler. *British Library, Department of Manuscripts, 37339, p. 122*

Orkneys at the end of the last century [21]. The hearth remained in a central position but the reredos could be enlarged to form a partition wall. In John Phillip's painting of a Highland home it can be seen that this transition has taken place [22]. The migration of the hearth to the wall has begun; the development of the chimney flue is made possible.

An alternative to the central hearth was to build the fire off-centre in a bay or half-bay rising to the full height of the house. This probably developed from the practice of screening over with lath and plaster a pair of adjacent trusses in the roof directly above the fire, a feature that always appears as an afterthought.[24] In cruck-built houses where the hall was a bay-and-a-half or two bays long, a smoke hood could be supported on the tie beam that united the pair of crucks, thus producing a smoke bay, a feature common in Yorkshire [23].

In Westmorland, in the dwellings of 'statesmen' or yeomen and in many smaller houses as well, this 'bay' was loftier than the room and was screened by a 'heck' of stone or timber. The smoke was collected in a funnel of lath and plaster and discharged into a short stone flue at the top of the gable against which the fire was placed.[25]

In most instances the fire was situated against a transverse internal partition wall thus maximizing the heat—but the reredos may be of equal importance in the origin of this arrangement. Later the status symbolized by the chimney led to it being placed more visibly on external walls.

It is impossible to talk with any certainty about the development of the flue in terms of date as documentary evidence is scarce. Central hearths are unrecorded in the southern Pennines,[26] whilst they continued in use in Scotland and Ireland within living memory. It will therefore be necessary to look at various surviving types of fireplace of miscellaneous date which may suggest the likely sequence of their evolution.

21. (*above*) Central hearth with reredos in a croft on BIRSAY, ORKNEY, photographed c. 1900. The bed-cupboard in the background is particularly well 'grained'. *Photograph: Kirkwall Library*

22. (*below*) *The Highland Home* by John Phillip. This painting shows the appearance of the interior of a croft in the second quarter of the nineteenth century. The partition running behind the fireplace reredos is typical. *Aberdeen Museum and Art Gallery*

23. A smoke bay in the cruck house from STANGEND, DANBY, 1704. The witch post on the left is typical of North Yorkshire as are the small built-in salt cupboards at the back of the fire to the right. *Ryedale Folk Museum, Hutton le Hole, Yorkshire*

The earliest type of flue was simply a hood attached to the wall and constructed of lath and plaster [24]. Such an example may be seen in the late nineteenth-century one-roomed house from Meenagarragh, Co. Tyrone, Ulster [25]. In the north of England and Scotland a cowl of overlapping boards was usual. In the highlands of Scotland this feature was known as the *similear crochaidh* or hanging chimney,[27] and in the lowlands as the 'hangin' lum' [27]. When such fireplaces were constructed of stone or brick it became necessary to support them on either corbels or piers and most surviving examples are a combination of both [28–30]. Once a floor is inserted obscuring the flue they assume an appearance compatible with modern ideas of a fireplace [31].

In his *Description of England* (1577) William Harrison remarked that old men in his village had seen great changes in their lifetime, among them 'the multitude of chimneys latelie erected, whereas in their yoong daies there were not above two or three, if so manie, in most uplandish townes of the realme (the religious houses, and manour places of their lords alwaies excepted, and peradventure some great personages), but ech one made his fire against a reredosse in the hall, where he dined and dressed his meat'.[28]

24. Smoke hood in the main room of a cottage from DUNCRUM, MAGILLIGAN. *In house re-erected at Ulster Folk and Transport Museum*

25. Smoke hood in a single-room dwelling from MEENAGARRAGH. The roof lining is confined to the bed outshot. *In house re-erected at Ulster Folk and Transport Museum*

26. The main room of a house in CO. ANTRIM, ULSTER. The fire hood and jamb wall with its screen onto the lobby entrance are typical of areas of Scottish/English settlements. Note the oatcakes or farles shown being cooked. *Photograph c. 1910: Green Collection, Ulster Folk and Transport Museum*

27. Interior of a souter's cottage in TAYSIDE. The timber smoke-hood or 'hangin' lum' is typical. Water-colour drawing. *National Museum of Antiquities, Edinburgh*

28. Fireplace from Don Farm, ST. JOHN, JERSEY, dated 1673. The smoke hood of wattle and daub was inevitably translated into stone and is found as far north as Yorkshire and Scotland as well as in France.
Re-erected at Jersey Museum

29. (*above*) Carved fireplace lintel at HANDOIS, JERSEY, dated 1659. The keyed lintel is typical and is related to certain types of flat arch, the individual voussoirs of which are known in French as *crossettes*. *Photograph: Jersey Museum*

30. (*left*) Fireplace in a house in the Market Place. KENDAL, CUMBRIA. The corbelled lintel derives from the smoke hood but persisted in the Lake District in the eighteenth century thus producing this extraordinary contrast between early forms 'dressed' in eighteenth-century details and including a typical cast-iron hob grate. *Photograph: Royal Commission on Historical Monuments*

31. Fireplace in a cottage from CRUCKACADY. A fireplace with a chimney made possible the insertion of upper floors. The bed outshot was mainly found in the north and west of the province and its position adjacent to the fireplace is characteristic. *In house re-erected at Ulster Folk and Transport Museum*

'The Great Rebuilding'[29] of the sixteenth and seventeenth centuries is characterized by three main features: (a) the insertion of chimneys made possible by (b) the re-introduction of bricks, and (c) the insertion of upper floors resulting from the introduction of chimneys.[30] The latest dated and recorded 'built-in' chimney in the south of England is at Chodd's Farm, Handcross, Sussex, and it bears the inscription 'Bilt 1693'.[31] What is probably the earliest dated floored-in hall is at Hookwood Manor, Surrey, and it is dated 1571.[32] In Ulster all these types of fire from the most primitive onwards were in use in the nineteenth century. It is therefore all the more remarkable that the double flue should have been in use there [32].[33]

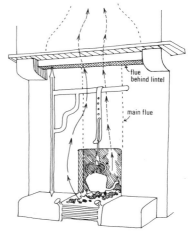

32. Nineteenth-century ULSTER double flue

flue behind lintel

main flue

All early fireplaces with flues have openings which are large in size; they are high and wide. The height of the bressummer or mantel-tree probably has something to do with its origin as a tie beam used to support a chimney hood or smoke bay. Their width was desirable to save labour in sawing wood for fuel. Nevertheless they were and are inclined to smoke, a fact which was of little concern at first as it represented such an improvement on previous methods of extracting smoke. However, it was probably soon discovered that a chimney cloth or fire cloth alleviated this problem. Such a feature may be seen in F. D. Hardy's *Interior of a Sussex Farmhouse* dated '185?' [33]. These chimney cloths were sometimes made of leather and were occasionally stretched on a frame.[34] In lowland Scotland a strip of sheet metal known as a 'smoke board' was used in the nineteenth century.

Wood-burning fireplaces of the type described above are capable of generating

33. *Interior of a Sussex Farmhouse* signed 'FDH 185?' (Frederick Daniel Hardy, 1826–1911). A curtain was often added to the chimney bressummer when fires smoked. The buffet chair and three-legged cricket table are typical examples of English country furniture. *Leicester Museum and Art Gallery*

sufficient heat to cause the bricks at the back of the fire to become friable and collapse. In Norwich it was usual for a panel headed by a four-centred arch in the back of the fireplace to be fitted with a herring-bone arrangement of tiles which, being non-structural, could be easily replaced [34]. In the Weald of Kent and Sussex blast furnaces had been active since about 1540,[35] and iron firebacks became usual, fulfilling the dual role of protecting

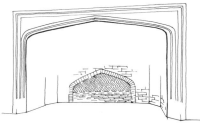

34. Tile 'fireback'. NORWICH

the brickwork of the flue and producing radiant heat. Even in Sussex the presence of cast-iron firebacks may not always be presumed. In the late sixteenth-century Leabridge Cottage, West Burton, a simple panel of projecting brickwork[36] was found in the back of the fireplace, analogous to the use of tiles in Norwich. Early Sussex firebacks are wide and low and carry simple designs impressed into the sand mould—sections of rope being particularly popular [35]. Eventually wood patterns were used to press into the sand and late seventeenth-century examples betray considerable sophistication and some Dutch stylistic influence [36]. They are taller than they are wide so as to be in proportion to the

35. SUSSEX fireback dated 1598 and a pair of firedogs of a type sometimes known as cob-irons. *Photograph: James Ayres*

36. (*left*) Fireback (SUSSEX?), late seventeenth-century, showing Dutch influence. The tall proportion of this fireback is typical. In the sixteenth century firebacks were usually long and low. *Victoria and Albert Museum*

37. (*right*) The Moses Pierce-Hitchborn House (left-hand room), North Square, BOSTON, MASSACHUSETTS. The painted plaster lining of the fireplace is almost identical to similar work found in Plymouth, Devon. *Society for the Preservation of New England Antiquities*

fire surrounds of their day. In Devon and Somerset, as well as in Massachusetts [37],[37] some fireplaces were lined with plaster and painted with geometric designs of apparently seventeenth-century date [B, 38, 39]. The basic colours of the few known examples are or were black and white; the area behind the fire and immediately above it was left either undecorated or painted black.

38. Painted plaster fireplace lining (back only) found beneath the later, more complex decoration illustrated in No. 39 from 21 High Street, PLYMOUTH (now demolished). Early seventeenth century (?). *Drawing: James Ayres, after a drawing by Stanley R. Jones*

39. Seventeenth-century plaster decoration on the back and jambs lining a fireplace in a first-floor room at 21 High Street, PLYMOUTH (demolished in 1960). *Drawing: Stanley R. Jones*

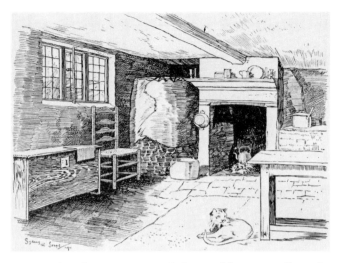

Because these great fireplaces were used for cooking as well as for general heat it became usual for a bread oven and sometimes a smoking flue to be built into them. The bread oven was usually constructed of brick [40] but in the potteries of North Devon around Barnstaple, and in Truro, Cornwall, it became usual for them to be prefabricated in earthenware. These 'cloam' ovens were made until recent years, the last being 'built' at Lake's Chapel Hill Pottery in 1935 [41].[38] They had a wide distribution, being found in much of the West Country as well as South Wales;[39] they were exported to America in the seventeenth century and have been found at Jamestown, Virginia.[40]

40. (*above*) Cottage interior, UPPER BODDINGTON, NORTHAMPTONSHIRE, by S. R. Jones, 1911. The living-room and kitchen are here combined—note the bread oven to the left of the chimney breast. *Bath Public Library*
41. (*below*) Cloam oven of NORTH DEVON type. Such earthenware bread ovens were exported to South Wales and North America. They were made from the seventeenth century until the 1930s. *Castle Museum, Taunton*

42. Fireplace in Hassage Farmhouse, WELLOW, BATH. The wider opening of the seventeenth-century fireplace was reduced in the eighteenth century. *Photograph: Royal Commission on Historical Monuments*

In houses of the North Yorkshire moors salt-boxes hewn out of two great slabs of sandstone were built flush into the back wall and fitted with a small wooden door. The largest recorded example has external measurements of 31 by 21 by 23 in (78.7 by 53.3 by 58.4 cm). The access to these boxes was usually about 6 in (15.2 cm) square, surrounded by an oak frame in which was hung an oak door suspended on leather hinges (which the salt would not corrode). In North Yorkshire the 'great rebuilding' did not begin until the mid-seventeenth century and so most of these salt-boxes date from after this time down to the early eighteenth century.[41] Roughly equivalent to these Yorkshire salt-boxes were the 'keeping holes' found in Ulster, one on each side of the fire.[42]

As fireplace openings became smaller, the general appearance of the chimneypiece was emphasized by the chimney breast, the visible part of the flue [42]. The great size of early fireplaces had stressed the importance accorded to them, both visually and as a source of heat, and made them appropriate centres for embellishment. It was here that the four-centred arch of late mediaeval fashion was used, and it was the chimney breast that bore on its generous proportions the first essays in the Renaissance. The first flush of Italian influence did not appear in smaller houses, but *The Designs of Mr Inigo Jones* were later processed for popular consumption, together with those of *Mr William Kent*, by John Vardy (1744). Before the second coming of Palladianism in England bolection moulding

43. Stone fireplace dated 1707 in the cruck and cob-built Burgh Head Farmhouse (now destroyed), BURGH-BY-SANDS, CUMBRIA. The bolection moulding surrounding this fireplace is typical of its period. *Photograph: Royal Commission on Historical Monuments*

was used around almost everything: windows, pictures and fireplaces [43]. The mantelshelf may well be a late innovation; certainly it seldom occurs in conjunction with the use of bolection moulding. The grand designs of the Renaissance were also scaled down to a size that was large enough to accommodate wood fires but could also house coal-burning grates.

Some types of fireplace popular in the grandest circles did not descend the social order, among them the corner fireplace with its surmounting stepped pyramid on which could be displayed collections of rich and rare porcelain from Cathay, or delft pottery. However, the corner fireplace, with a vertical chimney breast, was a useful device in the design of many small houses, as may be seen in Hogarth's House at Chiswick.

At the vernacular level the fielded panel was popular throughout the eighteenth century and the chimney breast became the main wall surface for its orchestrated use [44]. In most compositions this panelling naturally falls into two main areas, the fireplace itself and, above the horizontal line of the mantelshelf, the overmantel. Overmantel panels have formed an important part of interior decoration from the time of Inigo Jones. Batty Langley's *The Builder's and Workman's Treasury of Designs* (1750) contains no less

44. Overmantel from Wayne's, Queen Street, COGGESHALL, ESSEX, early eighteenth century. The sections of the mouldings are considerably more sophisticated than the carving. *Photograph: Royal Commission on Historical Monuments*

than twenty designs for fireplaces with 'Tabernacle Frames'. In the early seventeenth century mirrors were generally too small to occupy such a position worthily and until the nineteenth they were too expensive to be found in smaller houses. It therefore became usual for this space to be furnished with a panel painting, most often of a landscape. The proportions of these panels, as with the similar 'over door' panels, were conditioned by the height of the room and by the size of the opening. Where possible square overmantel panels were favoured, and among Langley's designs only two were for horizontal panels. Overmantel pictures of a surprisingly primitive sort, although never found in the houses of the nobility, may be seen in the homes of the gentry. Urchfont Manor in Wiltshire contains an almost complete series showing the house and gardens; naive renderings of a splendid Continental formal garden.

Early fireplace surrounds, in the south-east of England, were often of brick, this being the material out of which the flues were constructed. As Isaac Ware pointed out, in *The Complete Body of Architecture* (1756),[43] such brickwork was inclined to crumble and break off and the problem was solved by 'a frame of wood [which was then] carried round it'. This became something of a fire hazard and was soon replaced by stone. In

45. A fireplace in STOBO, BORDERS REGION, showing the typical mottled painting found in Scotland, Ulster and the north of England. *Photograph by Mr G. C. Smith*

nineteenth-century Scotland, Ulster and the north of England the jambs and lintel of the fireplace were often given a coat of tar or paint to which flecks of different colours were added giving a suggestion of marble [45].

In summer the fireplace presented a rather forbidding black hole, relieved in winter by the fire itself. In many households it was a traditional point of honour to maintain the near-sacred fire year in, year out. I remember visiting a farmhouse near Chagford in Devon in the late 1940s and being told that the fire had not been allowed to go out for three hundred years. The truth of the statement is far less important than the sentiment expressed. Undoubtedly, the tradition of the never-to-be-extinguished fire is ancient.[44] Eighteenth-century genre pictures suggest that in less traditional houses it was usual, then as now, to place a vase of flowers or leaves in this otherwise empty space.[45] Wedgwood wrote to his partner Thomas Bentley on 29 July 1772, 'Vases are furniture for a chimney piece, bough pots for a hearth. . . . I think they can never be used one instead of the other.'[46] Judging by the large size of the bough pot in the fireplace which is illustrated in Joseph Highmore's (1692–1780) portrait of Samuel Richardson (1689–1761) this is quite understandable.[47] In 1767, Jones's of 71 Holborn Hill (William

E. Kidderminster carpet, English, c. 1835–40, each piece is 36 in (91.4 cm) wide. The design is arranged as a repeat which may be 'dropped'. Because of their fragile nature carpets of this type and date are very rare. Kidderminster carpets had a very wide social distribution in the second quarter of the nineteenth century. *Judkyn/Pratt Collection. See page 128*

F. Stencilled wall decoration, early nineteenth century, 148 Abbey Foregate, SHREWSBURY. *Photograph: Anthony Herbert. See page 176*

G. (*above*) A 'list' carpet, late eighteenth or early nineteenth century, English or American. *American Museum in Britain. See page 127*

H. Kendal carpet, back (above) and front (below) late eighteenth or early nineteenth century. *Victoria and Albert Museum, on loan from the National Trust. See page 128*

and Thomas Jones—the latter moved in 1774 to 57 Shoe Lane and in 1778 William Jones is recorded at Ray Street, Clerkenwell) supplied a 'Great Variety of Flower Pots and Vases for Chimneys'.

Another method of obscuring the hearth when it was not in use was the chimney board, also known as the fire board. These should not be confused with fire screens which were not designed to cover the fireplace but were to protect a fashionably pale complexion from the effects of the fire when it was in use, as shown in Hogarth's *The Lady's Last Stake* (1758–9). The fire board on the other hand was designed to fit the fireplace opening exactly and was therefore tailor-made. In the eighteenth century it was possible to purchase panels of wallpaper to decorate such boards or to have them painted especially by a decorative painter such as 'Matt⁵ Darly Painter, Engraver, and Paper Stainer at the Acorn facing Hungerford, Strand', whose trade-label is dated 1791 and who provided 'Ceilings, Pannels, Staircases, Chimney Boards etc. Neatly fitted up with Painting, or Stainings in the modern, Gothic or Chinese Tastes for Town or Country'. They could also be commissioned through a retailer such as the 'Upholder', John Potts who provided (circa 1760) 'Ornaments for Halls, Ceilings, Stair-cases and Chimney Boards'.[48]

Fire boards were probably most necessary in large houses, where a fireplace could remain unused for months on end, as well as in garden pavilions which would receive only occasional use. Elegant examples survive at Osterley and at Audley End. When the Earl of Orford's house in Chelsea was sold on his death in 1747 the 'Summer House' contained a lot which consisted of 'Eight Green painted chairs, a walnut table and a chimney board: £0-10-6'. Perhaps the most amusing reference to these boards is to be found in the description of the exhibition that was organized by the fictitious Society of Sign Painters but was in fact put together by William Hogarth together with Bonnell Thornton: 'On entering the Grand Room . . . you find yourself in a large and commodious Apartment, hung round with green Bays, on which this curious collection of Wooden Originals is fixt flat . . . and from whence hang Keys, Bells, Swords, Poles, Sugar-Loaves, Tobacco-Rolls, Candles and other ornamental Furniture, carved in Wood, that commonly dangle from the Penthouses of the different Shops in our Streets. On the Chimney-Board (to imitate the Style of the Catalogue) is a large, blazing Fire, painted in Water-colours.'[49]

In America a great many fire boards dating from the late eighteenth to the mid-nineteenth century survive. A number exist *in situ* and in museums on the Continent. The Stedelijk Museum, Amsterdam, possesses a fine example painted by an unknown artist showing an orange tree growing in a large blue and white pot.[50] In England they are exceedingly rare—why? No doubt the reliable North American summers meant that the fire board could be used confidently in the knowledge that it would remain *in situ* for six months. (In one remarkable and surviving case in Pennsylvania the large fireplace of the Marshall House is enclosed in summer by folding doors with strap hinges.)[51] In Britain, on the other hand, our climate is less predictable. Furthermore, the introduction of coal-burning grates and narrow-throated chimneys in the late eighteenth century made the draught-proofing properties of the fire board less essential. In fact most surviving American examples date from the very time when their use in England, which was probably always less widespread,[52] was declining. Their mobile nature has also encouraged their destruction. One of the few surviving English fire boards is in the Victoria and Albert Museum. It has a distinctly late seventeenth-century Dutch appearance. It is painted on a sheet of pine $\frac{3}{4}$ in (1.9 cm) thick and shows no sign of originally having had battens, though these have been added [46]. As with many of the American examples,[53] it depicts a vase of flowers of the type that was placed in the fireplace as an alternative mode of decoration and, again like a number of the American ones, it is surrounded on three sides by a painted rendering of the delft tiles customarily used in fire surrounds. It probably dates from about the first half of the eighteenth century and its proportions would suggest that it once graced a coal-burning grate.

Coal began to be used in London at the end of the thirteenth century but at first only for manufacturing purposes as it was considered a health hazard. In the early years of the seventeenth century the Port of London handled 11,000 tons, but by the end of the century 500,000 tons arrived annually from Newcastle. Mendip coal from Somerset and 'Cannel' coal from Newcastle-under-Lyme was also important.[54] No wonder that St. Paul's Cathedral was built on the tax levied on this coal and that coal represented one third of all cargoes carried by British shipping at this time.[55] In commenting on the abundant use of coal in Newcastle-upon-Tyne itself Celia Fiennes describes not only the pollution of the air but also the cinder paths. In the course of the eighteenth century the use of coal became general in urban homes, but it was not used in America in any significant quantities until the nineteenth century.

The introduction of coal-burning grates had far-reaching effects upon the design of 'chimney pieces' (as they were called, in preference to 'fireplaces'—a place of fire could be anywhere and did not necessarily demand a flue). The proportions of the rooms in which they were located underwent no less radical changes. The earliest literary reference to a coal grate in *The Oxford Dictionary* is of 1605. By 1658 Sir John Winter had devised a special grate for burning coal. This took the form of an iron box which had a tube for the intake of external air which when opened 'marvelously accelerated the action of the fire'.[56] A similar device was made in 1678 for Prince Rupert by a bricklayer named Bingham.[57] Ham House in Surrey contains some of the earliest coal grates surviving; they are well documented, being mentioned in the inventory of 1679. Meanwhile various improvements were taking place in France, where Nicolas Gauger published his treatise which was translated into English by J. T. Desaguliers and published in 1716. The book contains a useful glossary with information on 'The Mantle-piece' which it describes as 'the ornamental Frame of Timber or Mason's-work', a term which the book compares with the French '*Chambranle* . . . an ornament in Masonry and Joyners-work which

46. Chimney board, first quarter of the eighteenth century, oil on pine, 38.5 × 30.75 in (97.9 × 78.1 cm). Very few such chimney boards have survived in England where narrow-throated chimneys and registers provided the necessary draught-proofing in fireplaces when they were not in use. *Victoria and Albert Museum*

borders the sides of Doors, Windows & Chimneys'.[58] Perhaps the most remarkable recommendation in the book is the proposed adoption of 'The Vent-hole', a tube of between 3 and 4 in (7.6 and 10.2 cm) in diameter designed to draw in air directly from outside the house and deliver it direct to the fire and 'contribute to remedy the inconvenience of Smoak'.[59] The book goes on to state that 'those Persons who have neat Apartments, and valuable Household-Goods ... are very sensible of these inconveniences [of smoke] ... especially on account of their Linen, Lace, Headdresses, Cloaths, &c.'[60]

The provision of such air tubes did much to prevent rooms being draughty and have only recently been adopted with much enthusiasm. However, when Sidney Smith built himself a parsonage at Foston le Clay, Yorkshire, in 1813, he installed such a device.[61]

The more efficient stove of either earthenware or cast iron was always more favoured in those Continental countries where the climate demanded more efficient heating. The same conditions were found in America, but the English tradition there was generally stronger than the influence of the cold winters.[62] Certainly, in German Pennsylvania, cast-iron stoves were in use in the early eighteenth century and they were probably the inspiration behind the ingenious Dr Franklin's stove. He describes his invention in his autobiography: 'Having, in 1742, invented an open stove for the better warming of rooms, and at the same time saving fuel, as the fresh air admitted was warmed in entering, I made a present of the model to Mr Robert Grace, one of my early friends who, having an iron furnace, found the casting of the plates for these stoves a profitable thing, as they were growing in demand. To promote the demand, I wrote and published a pamphlet, intitled *An Account of the new-invented Pennsylvania Fire-places &c.*'[63] Franklin's stove incorporated many European ideas derived from Bingham of England and Gauger of France. Nevertheless, Franklin obtained a patent for his device from George Thomas (circa 1693–1774), the Royal Governor of Pennsylvania and the Lower Colonies (now Delaware). Despite the patent the autobiography goes on to say that 'An ironmonger in London, however, assuming a great deal of my pamphlet ... got a patent for it there, and made, as I was told a little fortune by it.' The offending 'ironmonger in London' may have been J. Durno of Jermyn Street, Piccadilly, who published a pamphlet in 1753 describing a stove much of which was constructed of brick. Some of his 'Machine Grates' were adapted to burn coal. In his pamphlet Durno makes no reference to Franklin but does say that he (Durno) ignored the fireplaces devised by Gauger 'on account of their expense'.[64] As Franklin's unfinished autobiography ends with the year 1757, Durno is the likely culprit, but there was at least one other possible culprit active in England before Franklin's death in 1790. James Sharp of Leadenhall Street published in about 1781 an '*Account of the Principle and Effects of the Pennsylvania Stove-Grates* (which warm Rooms &c. by a continual Introduction and Exchange of dry fresh air) commonly known by the name American Stoves' [47]. Sharp claimed to have made 'Additions and Improvements' to these stoves 'For which his Majesty's Patent is

AMERICAN STOVES, ON THE IMPROVED CONSTRUCTION.

by James Sharp, Leadenhall Street.

47. 'American stoves' from James Sharp's *Account of the Principle and Effects of the Pennsylvania Stove-Grates*, London *c.* 1781. *British Library*

obtained'. His factory was at 133 Tooley Street, Southwark. In the pamphlet he gives full credit for 'the Invention [to] the celebrated and ingenious Dr Benjamin Franklin', an acknowledgement that doubtless did little to dampen his opportunism. How successful this side of Sharp's business was however, is doubtful; he only cites two examples of his stoves in use (in the Drapers' Hall and in St. John's Church, Southwark).

These stoves were undoubtedly efficient; they were in fact more efficient than the Continental stoves which produced heat exclusively by radiation. The Franklin stove transmitted heat by radiation and by the circulation of warm air. Despite their effectiveness they were little used in Britain, perhaps because at the turn of the century the designs of another American, Sir Benjamin Thompson (Count Rumford), were adopted more energetically. In London one hundred and fifty homes were fitted with fireplaces to his design which reduced the throat of the chimney to 5 in (12.7 cm) or less, set the cheeks of the fireplace at 135 degrees to its back and brought forward the fire itself. Unlike Franklin he believed, erroneously, in avoiding the use of iron (except for the actual grate) as a wasteful absorber of heat.[65]

In describing the Franklin stove, Loudon refers to the 'great benefits [that] have been experienced from the introduction of the American stove into some farm houses in Kent' [48].[66] A drawing by Arthur Vine Hall (circa 1840) of a room in a house near Maidstone, Kent, remarkably enough illustrates this type of stove, and the one in Loudon's book is identical to it [49]. In Britain the real importance of the stove was to be as a cooking 'range'.

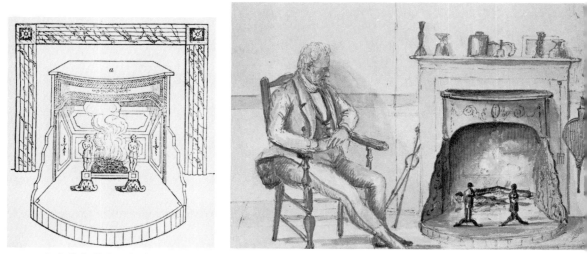

48. (*left*) J. C. Loudon's illustration of a Franklin stove. Benjamin Franklin invented his stove in 1742. *Bath Public Library*

49. (*right*) 'John Vine Hall Snr—Maidstone or district, in a small room he called his office' by Arthur Vine Hall (1824–1919), water-colour on paper, *c.* 1840, 9 × 5.5 in (22.9 × 14 cm). The Franklin stove is seldom seen in English interiors but the one illustrated here is of a type identical with that described by Loudon in the 1830s as being introduced in farmhouses in Kent. *Collection of Mrs Polly Rogers*

In the middle of the eighteenth century the coal-burning hob grate was devised and these were manufactured in great numbers, principally by the Carron Company of Falkirk in Scotland (who had the advantage of having both Robert and James Adam as directors) and the Dale Company of Coalbrookdale in Shropshire. When it became necessary to reduce the width of a wood-burning fireplace to accommodate coal this was done by filling up the unwanted space to left and right. In cast iron this arrangement resulted in a fireplace constructed of three elements, two cheek pieces linked by a central basket. In time the two cheek pieces were united forming an hour-glass shape, the top part of which held the coal whilst the lower half held the ashes [50].[67] A variant on this type of hob grate was the 'duck's nest' or 'Sussex grate' [51].[68]

Although such grates are often of extreme sophistication they were cheap to produce and were therefore used at many social levels.

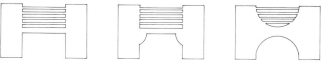

50. The evolution of the hob grate

52. (*right*) Kitchen range with circular oven typical of the colliery villages in north-east England. *Photograph c. 1900. Beamish Open Air Museum*

51. Farmhouse interior, EAST HENDRED, BERKSHIRE, by S. R. Jones, 1911. The 'Duck's Nest' or 'Sussex grate' and the settle with an additional draught-proofing curtain are important details. *Bath Public Library*

Towards the end of the eighteenth century it was found possible to adapt the hobs of these grates to provide an oven and side boiler for kitchen use. In this way the cooking range developed. Early examples often carry the name of the iron foundry that made them; later specimens are likely to bear the name of the company that sold and installed them. There were many such foundries in England and Wales. In the Yorkshire Dales such ranges carry the names of Spence of Richmond, Iveson of Hawes, Manby of Skipton, and Todd Bros. of Summerbridge, Nidderdale, though the latter two once had their own foundries as well.[69] Such objects may appeal to today's catholic tastes, but

53. Kitchen range in a Minffordd cottage, CLWYD. The brass stand was manufactured in the Brymbo Foundry. *Photograph: Welsh Folk Museum*

they were not always designed for elegance: by this date the kitchen/living-room was declining in middle-class houses although it remained in farmhouses and cottages, where the kitchen range expressed the handsome rather than pretty qualities of the engineering enjoyed by the Age of Steam [53].

Light

Before the introduction of electricity and certainly before the appearance of gaslight the darkness which descended at night was every bit as terrible and total as is described in Genesis. At night rooms were much darker, a moving candle ascending a stair more frightening than we like to recall until confronted by an immobilizing power cut. As we have seen, many houses were lit by little more than the fire on the hearth. In parts of Scotland where peat was burned this source of light was so feeble that in areas with textile 'out-workers' the introduction of coal could be paid for by the extra hours of work that it illuminated. In the north of England Howitt tells us that knitting, a craft that may be performed in almost total darkness, was done communally in one house which was both more friendly and more economical.[70]

The provision of artificial light was expensive, wax candles especially so. The cheapest candles were made of tallow and Sir Hugh Platt in *Delights for Ladies* (1605? edition) gives a recipe for *A delicate Candle for a Ladies Table*: 'Cause your Dutch candles to bee dipped in Virgin waxe . . .' thus giving them a veneer of elegance. Until the end of the eighteenth century wax candles cost 30s a pound and with the development of whaling, spermaceti candles were an expensive but better form of illumination. In 1758 one dozen spermaceti candles cost £1 7s 0d.[71] This sort of expenditure was beyond the means of cottagers and the yeoman class severely rationed their use.

As we have seen, Kimmeridge shale was used to provide fires and lighting for those living on the Dorset coast. The early and often multiple cressets of stone[72] later gave way to the more general type of oil lamp, common in coastal areas where fish oil was available, which was the wrought-iron 'cruisie', sometimes equipped with a secondary container to catch the drips. On the Gower peninsula[73] and on the Aran Islands[74] the simplest type of lamp was a twisted rag in an oyster- or scallop-shell containing either fat or oil. In central Scotland and in Co. Antrim, where fish oil was not available, splinters of resinous fir wood, or for preference fir knots, were used as 'fir candles' which were sometimes held aloft by a child or old person rather than by means of a candlestick [54]. As recently as

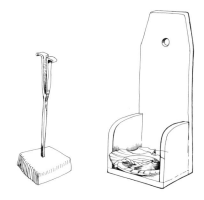

54. Examples of early lighting utensils. A fir 'candle' holder from CO. ANTRIM, and a scallop-shell lamp on a wood sconce from the ARAN ISLANDS

1951 it was estimated that only one in every six crofts in Scotland had electric light.[75]

Rushlights may have produced a meagre light but they were all that most cottagers could generally afford although rushlight holders usually incorporate candle holders for use on special occasions. The rushes were collected in late summer or autumn. 'You peels away the rind from the peth, leavin' only a little strip of rind, and when the rushes is dry you dips 'em in grease, keepin' 'em well under; and my mother she always laid hers to dry in a bit of hollow bark. Mutton fat's the best, it dries hardest.'[76]

In 1673 John Aubrey recorded that 'the people of Ockley in Surrey draw peeled rushes through melted grease, which yields a sufficient light for ordinary use, is very cheap and useful and burns long.'[77] Gilbert White in his *Natural History of Selborne* calculated that a good rush, 28 in (71 cm) long, would burn for fifty-seven minutes and that rushes costing 3s per pound went 1,600 to the pound. The grease for the rushlight was melted in a special elliptical pan (with a handle running at right angles to the axis of the ellipse) known as a 'grisset'.

In stone-built houses candle niches will sometimes be found as in the flint-built basements in the early Tudor houses excavated at Pottergate, Norwich, in 1963. Such niches had to be reasonably large so as to avoid the development of an unsightly stain of candle soot. Amongst the peasantry in Ireland tables were rare and where they existed at all did not usurp the pre-eminence of the fireplace as a focus of living. For this reason the hob lamp rather than the table lamp evolved there.[78] In all parts of the British Isles various types of standard and pendant devices [56, 57] were in use to hold rushlights, fir 'candles', tallow, wax and spermaceti candles, as well as oil lamps.

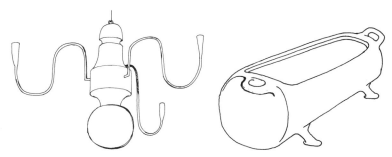

56. (*left*) Eighteenth-century candelabrum of turned wood and wrought iron from STANTON HARCOURT, OXFORDSHIRE. *Oxford City and County Museum*
57. (*right*) Earthenware candle-trough, sixteenth or seventeenth century. *Ashmolean Museum, Oxford*

For certain crafts a candle was used and when even this expensive light was insufficient the candle would be magnified by means of a water-filled, clear glass globe known in England as a 'flash'.[79] The earliest reference that I have found to this device appears in Sir Hugh Platt's *The Jewel House of Art and Nature* (1594): 'one candle [magnified by a

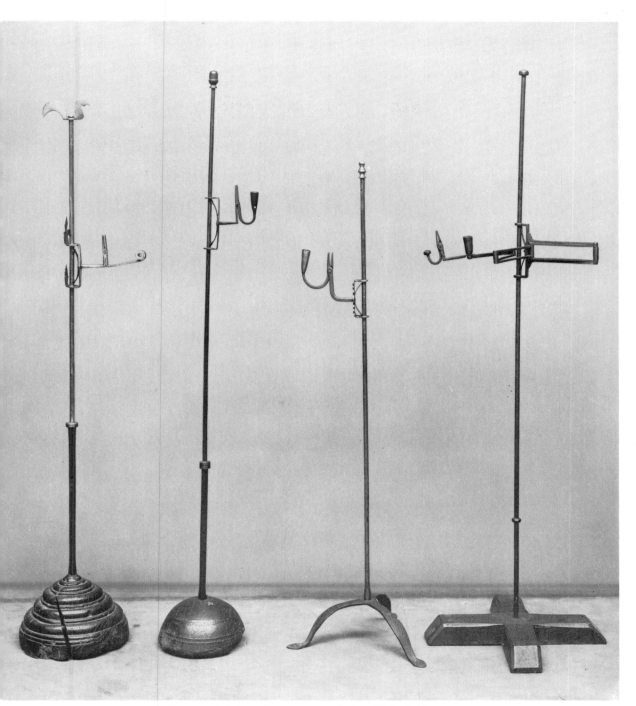

55. A group of eighteenth-century standard rushlight holders.
The tallest measures 56 in (142.2 cm). *Victoria and Albert Museum*

"flash"] will give a great and wonderfull light, somewhat resembling the Sun beames.'[80]
He ascribes the invention to the Venetians and mentions that it was particularly useful to
a jeweller in Blackfriars. John White's description of this gadget in *A Rich Cabinet with a
Variety of Inventions* (1651) clearly derives from Platt. 'How to make a glorious light with
a Candle like the Sun-Shine.' White also recommends this source of light for 'Jewellers,
Ingravers, or the like', a tradition that continued until the nineteenth century,[81] but they
were also adopted by lace makers in England, as in Denmark by cobblers who used them
in conjunction with daylight.[82]

The limitations of artificial light conditioned the crafts that people did in the evening
and tended to confine the working day to the hours between sunrise and sunset, except
when the harvest moon permitted longer working.

Notes to Chapter 2

1. Mercer, *English Vernacular Houses*, p. 23.
2. *Encyclopaedia Britannica*, 11th edition.
3. Barley, *The English Farmhouse and Cottage*, p. 13.
4. Alison Kelly, *English Fireplaces*, Country Life, London, 1968, p. 11.
5. Stuart Piggott, *Ancient Europe from the Beginnings of Agriculture to Classical Antiquity*, Edinburgh
   University Press, 1965, 1973 edition, p. 247.
6. F. G. Emmison, *Elizabethan Life*, Essex County Council, Chelmsford, 1976, p. 25.
7. A tailpiece vignette in Bewick's *British Birds* (1797–1804), 1826 edition, p. 243, shows a monkey
   wearing dark goggles turning a spit by hand.
8. Photograph, Beamish Open Air Museum, neg. no. 9840.
9. Morris (ed.), *The Journeys of Celia Fiennes*, p. 11. Celia Fiennes writing c. 1685.
10. British Library, Department of Manuscripts, Add 15537, Folio 170.
11. Barley, *The English Farmhouse and Cottage*, p. 94.
12. Ibid., p. 171.
13. Morris (ed.), *The Journeys of Celia Fiennes*, p. 161.
14. Ibid., p. 262.
15. Iorwerth C. Peate, *Tradition and Folk Life, a Welsh View*, Faber and Faber, London, 1972, p. 42.
16. Alexander Fenton, *Scottish Country Life*, John Donald, Edinburgh, 1976, p. 193.
17. Ibid., p. 193.
18. Ibid., p. 198.
19. Ibid.
20. Howitt, p. 238.
21. Emmison, p. 25.
22. Now in the Frilandsmuseet, Copenhagen.
23. I. F. Grant, *Highland Folk Ways*, Routledge and Kegan Paul, London, 1961, fig. 35c and p. 164.
24. R. T. Mason, *Framed Buildings of the Weald*, Coach Publishing House, Horsham, 1964, 1969 edition,
    pp. 76–7. See also Eric Mercer, *English Vernacular Houses*, p. 62.
25. Royal Commission on Historical Monuments, *Westmorland*, London, 1936, Preface, p. lxi.
26. Mercer, *English Vernacular Houses*, p. 21.
27. Grant, p. 163.
28. Harrison, II, pp. 239, 240.
29. W. G. Hoskins, 'The Rebuilding of Rural England 1570–1640', *History Today*, 1955, pp. 104–11,
    republished as chapter VII in *Provincial England*, 1963.

30. Mason, p. 44. Mason argues that W. G. Hoskins's thesis for 'The Great Rebuilding' should be termed 'The Second Rebuilding', the first and more radical being in the fifteenth century. Although this is true of the Weald, Hoskins's thesis is generally accepted for most other parts of England.

31. Ibid., p. 77.

32. Mercer, *English Vernacular Houses*, p. 5.

33. An example may be seen in the hill farmhouse from Coscib, near Cushendall, now in the Ulster Folk Museum.

34. Frederick Edwards, *Our Domestic Fireplaces*, London, 1870, pp. 15, 219.

35. Mason, p. 55.

36. Now destroyed.

37. Nina Fletcher Little, *American Decorative Wall Painting 1700–1850* (Sturbridge, Massachusetts, 1952), Dutton, New York, 1972, pp. 72, 76.

38. Barley, *The English Farmhouse and Cottage*, p. 168.

39. Peate, *Tradition and Folk Life*, p. 41.

40. C. Malcolm Watkins, 'North Devon Pottery and Its Export to North America in the 17th century', *US National Museum Bulletin No. 225*, Smithsonian Institution, Washington DC, 1960.

41. Bertram Frank, 'Salt Boxes of the North Yorkshire Moors', *The Dalesman*, December, 1970.

42. Emyr Estyn Evans, *Irish Folk Ways*, Routledge and Kegan Paul, London, 1957, p. 65.

43. Isaac Ware, *The Complete Body of Architecture*, T. Osborne and J. Shipton, London, 1756, p. 554.

44. Peate, *Tradition and Folk Life*, p. 39.

45. e.g. Mezzotint by J. Boydell after Zoffany, *Mr Foote in the Character of Major Sturgeon*, 1765.

46. Quoted by Nina Fletcher Little, *Country Arts in Early American Homes*, Dutton, New York, 1975, p. 112.

47. The National Portrait Gallery, London.

48. Ambrose Heal Collection, British Museum. Quoted by Ambrose Heal in his *The London Furniture Makers*, Batsford, London, 1953, p. 143.

49. Larwood and Hotten, *History of Signboards*, London, 1866, p. 521, quoting 'a monthly sheet entitled *The London Register* for April [1762?] . . . under the title of "Particular Account of the Great Exhibition in Bow Street . . ." '.

50. Illustrated by Peter Thornton, *17th Century Interior Decoration in England, France and Holland*, Yale University Press, 1978. See also his footnote that refers to a similar one in a private collection in London in 1950.

51. Little, *Country Arts in Early American Homes*, p. 13.

52. Very few trade-labels in the Heal Collection mention fire boards.

53. Some of the American examples illustrated by Nina Fletcher Little have painted flowers arranged in a vase strikingly similar to Plate 14 in Stalker and Parker's *A Treatise of Japaning and Varnishing*, Oxford, 1688, Tiranti reprint, London, 1971.

54. Morris (ed.), *The Journeys of Celia Fiennes*, pp. 8, 176–7.

55. Ibid., Introduction, p. xli.

56. Edwards, p. 25 (see note 34, above).

57. L. A. Shuffrey, *The English Fireplace*, Batsford, London, 1912, p. 175 and Appendix.

58. Nicolas Gauger, *Méchanique du Feu* (The Mechanism of Fire), translated by the Reverend J. T. Desaguliers, England, 1716, pp. XI, XV.

59. Ibid., II, part I, p. 48.

60. Ibid., II, part III, p. 64.

61. B. Anthony Bax, *The English Parsonage*, John Murray, London, 1964, p. 124.

62. Even in New England there were occasional exceptions to this generalization. See Josephine H. Peirce, *Fire on the Hearth*, Pond-Ekberg, Springfield, Massachusetts, 1951, p. 33.

63. Ibid., p. 39.

64. Shuffrey, p. 224 (see note 57, above).

65. Raymond Lister, *Decorative Cast Ironwork in Great Britain*, Bell and Sons, London, 1960, p. 106. See also *Who's Who in American History*, Marquis, Chicago, 1963.
66. Loudon, p. 656.
67. Michael Owen, *Antique Cast Iron*, Blandford Press, Poole, Dorset, 1977, p. 74.
68. Lister, pp. 108–9 (see note 65, above).
69. Marie Hartley and Joan Ingilby, *Life and Tradition in the Yorkshire Dales*, Dent, London, 1968, pp. 3, 4.
70. Howitt, p. 238.
71. Quoted by E. H. Pinto, *Treen and Other Wooden Bygones*, Bell and Sons, London, 1969, p. 114.
72. Christopher Howkins, 'Lights for Mediaeval Worshippers', *Country Life*, December 1974.
73. Examples in the Welsh Folk Museum at St. Fagans.
74. Evans, *Irish Folk Ways*, fig. 27.
75. Grant, p. 184.
76. Old village woman recorded by Gertrude Jekyll. Gertrude Jekyll and Sidney R. Jones, *Old English Household Life*, Batsford, London, 1925 (new edition 1975), p. 19.
77. Therle Hughes, *Cottage Antiques*, Lutterworth Press, London, 1967, p. 163.
78. Evans, *Irish Folk Ways*, p. 89.
79. Pinto, p. 118.
80. Sir Hugh Platt, *The Jewel House of Art and Nature*, London, 1594, pp. 31–2.
81. See the engraving by Robert William Buss (1804–75) showing a wood engraver working in his studio at night. Victoria and Albert Museum, E3100–1931.
82. P. V. Glob, *De Næsten Ukendte*, Dansk Kulturhistorisk Museumsforenig, 1971, p. 61.

3 · Walls

Walls may be divided into two main categories: load-bearing and non-load-bearing, both external and internal. Where crucks were employed in the construction of houses [58] the external walls were not load-bearing but were necessarily more substantial than internal partitions. For example, wattle hurdles would provide adequate partitions within a house, at a time when privacy had not elevated itself to the status of a human right, but would do little to help keep the wind out if used on external walls. In a mud cottage at Llithfaen, Pwllheli, Gwynedd, recorded at the end of the nineteenth century, the partition was 'made of cloth' and in 1847 in a cottage at Tal-y-llyn, Gwynedd, the sleeping end was 'separated from the rest of the hut by wisps of straw forming an imperfect screen'.[1] In 1798 John Evans saw a one-room house near Barmouth, Gwynedd, 'divided by a partition of lath and reeds'[2] and in this century similar partitions were used as party walls between cottages at Rumney, Gwent.

For external non-load-bearing walls the wattle hurdle was often considered adequate for farm buildings, but for domestic purposes received its due portion of daub or mud. The wattle consisted of vertical rods with horizontal split rods of ash or hazel interwoven.[3] Various names were given to such hurdles including 'freeth' or 'vreath', and perhaps 'wreath' in the west of England and parts of Wales. Before the Reformation, hurdles used as platforms or windbrakes by builders on wooden scaffolding were known as 'flakes'. All these words may be associated with the Danish verb *flette*, to plait.[4] In the late nineteenth century a carpenter from Caernarvonshire recalled that in the Llyn district interior partitions were once made of ropes of twisted rushes or straw woven in and out of upright poles in the same manner as wattle work.[5] The more usual wattle screen is known to have been widely used in this way.[6] The daubed surface was often plastered both inside and out, and became on both sides a surface to decorate with scribed lines and with paint. Decoration incised in plaster imitating masonry may be seen in the thirteenth-century internal plastered walls of Hinton Priory, Avon. Plaster used externally afforded some protection from the weather, and in the case of cob walls or those of 'clay lump' (clay bricks), a plinth of stone and strongly projecting eaves of thatch were essential.

Structural walls of square panels of timber frame or of stud and mud[7] were important long before the 'Great Rebuilding'.[8] C. F. Innocent quite firmly states that there were 'probably few locations where the use of stone as a principal material for the walls of minor buildings is of any antiquity'. The tradition for the use of timber is therefore of considerable age and importance in the study of vernacular architecture.

One of the most remarkable early walls in England is the Saxon period 'stave'-built wall of Greensted Church, Essex [59]. It consists of a series of vertical split oak logs

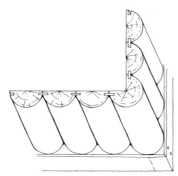

59. Log wall of Saxon period.
GREENSTED CHURCH, ESSEX

joined by means of splines (tongues) of oak let into grooves worked down their sides, each half log providing a flat surface on the inside face, the corners being of three-quarter logs. This one wall proves that Scandinavian methods of building in timber were once used in parts of England.[9] Such lavish use of timber produces a formidably powerful and magnificent effect which makes the use of stud and plank partitions seem almost delicate! Certainly panelling and partitions of stud and plank construction relate to the Greensted work.

Panelling was used in mediaeval England for one of two reasons. It was either used to line a wall as an alternative to tapestry or to provide a partition 'spur' or 'spere',[10] and these could be made in a variety of ways and materials. A 'spur' or screen of one slab of slate separating the sitting area from the draught of the door may be seen in the one-room cottage dated 1762 from Llainfadyn, Rhostryfan, Gwynedd [60]. In South Yorkshire thin slates were sometimes slotted between grooved studs. Slates for this purpose were known as 'grey slates' and were plastered over between the studs.[11] The same technique is also recorded at Stamford, Lincolnshire.[12]

The evolution of the screen is difficult to assess as there are very few in domestic settings that survive from before 1500. However, by looking at mediaeval rood screens in churches and at the surviving examples in Tudor houses it is possible to draw a few tentative conclusions. The use of edge-to-edge horizontal plank partitions was rare, but examples have been found at Milton Regis Court Hall, Kent.[13] Vertical matchboarding has had a long and continuous history. By means of the tongue and groove it was possible

58. Cruck-built barn from STRYTLYDAN. The cruck is found throughout the north and west of England and in Wales and may be of Celtic origin. *Re-erected at Welsh Folk Museum*

60. Interior of a single-roomed cottage built in 1762 at RHOSTRYFAN, GWYNEDD. The spur, spere or screen is a single slab of slate and provides a draught-proof sitting area by the fire. A hanging timber food-tray is visible at the top of the photograph. *In house re-erected at Welsh Folk Museum*

to present a flat face on one or both sides of the work. The most usual and one of the simplest, and therefore earliest, methods of lining a room with timber was by means of a series of vertical boards set into a cill and a lintel [61, 62a, b]. This produces an effect analogous to the timber wall of Greensted Church described above. In high-class stud

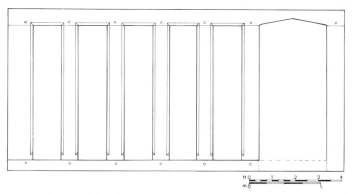

61. Stud and plank partition, Cross Farm, WESTHAY, NEAR MELLS, SOMERSET. Although the painted decoration on this partition illustrated in Colour Plate A probably dates from the mid-sixteenth century the partition itself could be up to one hundred years earlier. *Drawing: James Ayres*

62a, b. Abernodwydd Farmhouse from LLANGADFAN, POWYS, built in the sixteenth century and floored-in in the seventeenth century. The stud and plank partition resting on a high ground-cill is typical. The chimney bay is an insertion creating on the left a 'baffle entry' and on the right space for a ladder providing access to two bedrooms above. *In house re-erected at Welsh Folk Museum*

and plank work the posts were elaborately worked with mouldings, but in many instances they were scarcely thicker and certainly almost as wide as the 'panel' and a simple chamfer was considered adequate. This chamfer was often 'stopped' some feet from the floor implying the presence of a fixed bench.[14]

To reduce the amount of grooving in the stud or heavier plank it became usual to bevel the plank that formed the panel. This process probably suggested the ribbing that is such a feature on some surviving examples [63]. Indeed the so-called 'parchemin panels' (a

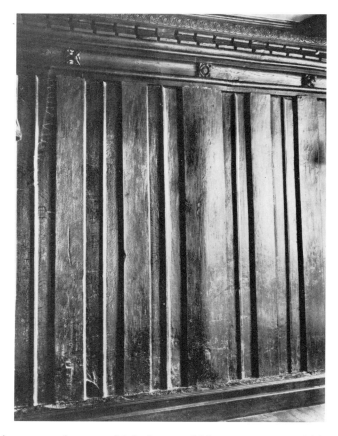

63. Late fifteenth-century stud and plank panelling in Wilsley House, CRANBROOK, KENT. The chamfering of the planks suggests the origin of the so-called 'parchemin' or 'linen-fold' panelling. *Photograph: Royal Commission on Historical Monuments*

nineteenth-century term referring to parchment which they could be seen to resemble) may almost be arrived at by bevelling a rectangular panel on four sides and when the panel is moulded on one axis the 'stop' of ogival curves is inevitable. From these humble beginnings the rich effects of the high Tudor linenfold developed. Early examples such as may be seen at Compton Wynyates, Warwickshire, or Paycockes at Coggeshall, Essex, are worked in panels which are noticeably taller and narrower than later examples, perhaps a silent acknowledgement to their origin in plank panelling. Certainly 'linenfold' is another nineteenth-century term; although Tudor documents sometimes describe it as 'drapery pannell'[15] the more usual term was *lignum undulatum*, wavy woodwork. Linenfold panels are often found in association with early Renaissance carving (known as 'Romayne work') but in themselves they may be regarded as neither Italianate in origin nor mediaeval in spirit. Such work was expensive and is generally outside the scope of this book.

As we have seen, plank panelling stressed the vertical, and the horizontal only existed at the lintel and the cill, equivalent in some ways to the dado and cornice of classical architecture. With the addition of more horizontal members or rails the vertical axes declined. Even in the simplest schemes the stiles (as the vertical members are known) and rails are chamfered. Because of the nature of such construction the 'stops' of the chamfering could only be completed once the work was 'made up' and it was here that the mason's mitre was employed [64]. This method of construction and finish was expensive,

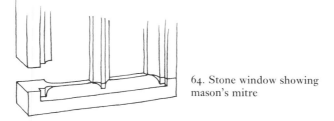

64. Stone window showing mason's mitre

and later (i.e. early seventeenth-century) panelling used the cheaper 'run out' stop. As with parchemin panels such features of design evolved as a natural function of craftsmanship. As design moved from the bench to the drawing board such substantial qualities were doomed, but they lingered longest at the vernacular level.

In his *Description of England* William Harrison describes the internal treatment of walls in Tudor England: 'The wals of our houses on the inner sides in like sort be either hanged with tapistrie, arras worke, or painted cloths, wherein either diverse histories, or herbs, beasts, knots, and suchlike are stained, or else they are seeled with oke.'[16] It is clear from this that neither panelling nor hangings were general until the Tudor period. Woven tapestry was exceptional until the sixteenth century and so it remained, being in later times only found in grand houses—a mediaeval practice of comfort and social prestige which not even the Renaissance could displace. John Milton uses a reference to tapestry as emblematic of luxury in *Comus, a Mask*:

> . . . honest-offer'd courtesie
> Which oft is sooner found in lowly sheds
> With smoky rafters, than in tap'stry Halls
> And Courts of Princes.

By the end of the sixteenth century stained cloth hangings are referred to quite often in houses of many social levels.[17] In yeoman houses in Sussex the dais reredos was either panelled or hung with tapestry under the coved reredos bressummer.[18] That feature also occurs in Halifax and Huddersfield on a much larger scale to become a canopy so that the hanging on the dais reredos may be regarded as a 'cloth of estate'.[19]

By the seventeenth century panelling had become quite usual in farmhouses but was constructed of less substantial timber [65]. The influence of classicism was often felt

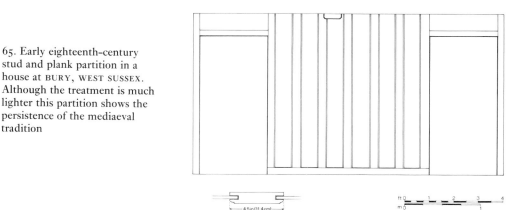

65. Early eighteenth-century stud and plank partition in a house at BURY, WEST SUSSEX. Although the treatment is much lighter this partition shows the persistence of the mediaeval tradition

rather than seen. It became usual to terminate panelling with a top row of horizontal panels, two panels wide. These panels were often carved in a vaguely classical way and greater emphasis was achieved by 'punching' the ground. Until about the middle of the seventeenth century it was usual to 'offer up' sections of panelling about six panels wide. These were then fixed with no attempt being made to mask the joins. Later it was possible for these joins to be hidden by pilasters. Because panelling was fixed so simply it could easily be removed and testators had to make it clear when panelling should be regarded as a fixture. In 1581 John Manninge of Maldon, a shoemaker, left 'to my wife Elizabeth my tenement in the parish of All Saints called by the sign of the Spread Eagle during her life, provided she shall not remove any of the wainscot nor the glass'.[20] Originally much of this panelling must have been painted, and nearly all the examples that I have seen reveal, when cleaned, if not actual areas of pigment, grains of paint or gesso in the interstices.

At the vernacular level, the half-knowledge of Classicism usually associated with the period of Elizabeth I and James I survived into the early eighteenth century in areas distant from London such as Westmorland. This is especially true of interiors [66], perhaps because most early books on architecture were concerned primarily with the basic structure and planning of buildings and their external elevations. In the panelling of rooms, as in the panels of furniture, this is particularly noticeable, not only in the

66. Panelling in the main reception room of Silver Street House, BRADFORD-ON-AVON, WILTSHIRE, mid-eighteenth century. The garbled knowledge of classical architecture would often produce charmingly ridiculous details such as the triglyphs in this room.
Photograph by Derek Balmer

detailed carving but also in the overall size of the panels. Despite the use of glue, size and gesso by mediaeval craftsmen they did not rely on such substances. The mortice and tenon was not only glued (as was considered adequate for furniture in the eighteenth century) but it was dowelled as well. Similarly, panels were not made that were larger than the tree was capable of producing. Planks were originally always quarter sawn, not because this produced the finest 'figure' in the medullary rays of oak, but because such boards seasoned best and warped least. By the time the centre of the log had been removed (the boxed heart being very strong but very temperamental) the maximum width of such boards was usually about 18 in (45.7 cm). This conditioned the width of panels although, as with plank panelling, their length (i.e. height) could be considerable. The importance of quarter sawing survived the demise of master-carpenter-designers but has succumbed in our century to commercial interests.

In the first half of the seventeenth century, perhaps coinciding with the emergence of the architect-theoretician rather than the craftsman-architect, the once proud master-joiner succumbed to the whim of a master not himself. It was at this time that the decadent mitre was introduced, to become general in the second half of the century. It had probably first come into England in the late sixteenth century as the 'frenche panell'.[21] At this time large panels were made up by means of glueing. In other words, the proportions ordained by classicism and drawn on paper by the interpreting architect had to be obtained by the craftsman without respect for his craft but out of obedience to the new orders.

It is just possible that the late seventeenth- and early eighteenth-century fashion for large panels emerged from their use for the 'hanging' of silk, leather or paper. In such a circumstance the wood of the panels could split or the joints 'give' without being a visible disaster. Panelling of this type, not designed to be seen, may be found in some of the houses in Grove Terrace, Highgate (begun 1769) [67a, b]. Here the walls separating entrance hall from parlour, or bedroom from staircase, are pine partitions of this kind. Being designed to take hangings, neither the panels nor the 'framing up' are embellished in any way with mouldings, etc.[22] This feature in houses as small as these is rare.

In mediaeval and Tudor England oak was the favoured timber but some softwood was also used, although very little has survived. The large panels preferred in the second half of the seventeenth and into the eighteenth century were customarily of fir, but in high quality work of pine. They were generally painted. When the panelling was left unpainted oak remained in favour. According to Celia Fiennes, Irish oak was sometimes selected as in 'this wood no spider will weave on or endure'.[23] At the top of the social scale various exotic woods brought in at great cost by trade with distant lands, such as cedar and olive, were in use by the late seventeenth century and these woods were simulated by painted graining and marbling (see chapter on Paint and Painting).

In the *Complete Body of Architecture* (1756) Isaac Ware states that in 'general, the stucco rooms . . . are cold; those wainscoted are naturally warmer; and those which are hung warmest. The stucco room, when heated becomes hottest of all . . . a wainscoted room, painted in the usual way is the lightest of all; the stucco is the next in this condition, and the hung [with paper, silk, tapestry, etc.] room the darkest of all.'[24]

After planing (and even carving), the final smoothing of wood was sometimes done by means of 'a skin called hundys fishskyn [dogfish skin] for the carpenters'.[25] I have myself used shark-skin for this purpose. Unlike glass- or sandpaper, shark-skin does not leave a gritty deposit which could blunt edged tools or disrupt gilding. With carved work the proportion of time spent sharpening tools is so high (particularly when 'working' softwoods) that glasspaper should be avoided at all costs despite the difficulty of obtaining dried shark-skin. Another natural abrasive available to craftsmen and used within living memory is the so-called 'Dutch rushes'. These were used by gilders in establishing a particularly smooth surface on gesso or by painters when smoothing their final coat of paint before the application of varnish.[26] The Dutch rush is known by non-craftsmen as the 'horse's tail', *equisetum hiemale*, and it contains a certain amount of silica.

So unimportant was the mitre considered for structural purposes that Joseph Moxon in his *Mechanick Exercises or the Doctrine of Handy-Works* (1677), alludes to the use of a

67a, b. Entrance passage and detail of pilaster capital in 23 Grove Terrace, HIGHGATE, LONDON, third quarter of the eighteenth century. The scale of such details is beautifully adjusted to the small size of these houses, the entrance hall being a bare 3 ft (91.4 cm) wide. *Photograph by the author*

'Mitre Square' only for 'Picture Frames and Looking Glass-frames'.[27] Although much of Moxon's writing refers back to earlier standards of craftsmanship he is quite clearly of his time when describing the wainscoting of rooms:

> In Wainscoting of Rooms there is, for the most part, but two heights of Pannels used; unless the Room to be wainscoted be above ten foot high. . . . Heights of Pannels are used: As . . . The *Lying Pannel* above the *Base*, . . . The *Large Pannel* above the *Middle Rail*, And . . . The *Friese Pannel* above the *Friese Rail*.
>
> The *Friese Rail* is to have the same bredth the *Margent* of the *Stile* hath; the *Middle Rail* hath commonly two bredths of the *Margent* of the *Stile* viz. one breadth above the *Sur-base*. And the *Upper and Lower Rails* have each the same breadth with the Margent of the stile.
>
> Sometimes (and especially in Low Rooms) there is no *Base* or *Sur-base* used, and then the *Middle* and *Lower-Rail* need not be so broad. . . .
>
> You may if you wish adorn the outer edges of the *Stiles* and *Rails* with a small Moulding: And you may (if you will) Bevil away the outer edges of the *Pannels* and leave a Table in the middle of the Pannel.[28]

Most of the terms used by Moxon are recognizable except for the word 'margent'. Fortunately he includes a glossary and defines this word as 'the flat breadth of the stiles besides the mouldings'.[29] Moxon's proportions for the panelling of rooms is very much a 'rule of thumb' method. By the mid-eighteenth century various publications had

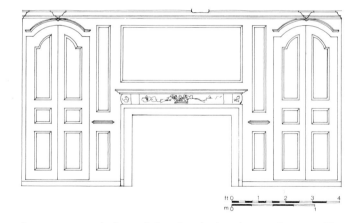

68. Early eighteenth-century chimneypiece wall from a pine-panelled room in a house at BURY, WEST SUSSEX. Such exquisite and small-scale rooms as this are reminiscent of American work

given architects and joiners a deeper appreciation of the classical orders — the panelling of a room was after all nothing less than the proportions of a classical building turned inside out from plinth to cornice, from skirting to ceiling. This awareness went further than the élite publications of Colin Campbell and others. In Batty Langley's *Builder's Jewel* (1754) may be found 'Rules . . . To find the breadth of the dado of the Tuscan

69. Early eighteenth-century scheme of panelling in Holland House, BARNSTAPLE, DEVON. The fielded panelling, the 'tabernacle frame' no doubt designed for an overmantel picture, and the dado which marked the extent of the plinth in this classically conceived interior give a solemn dignity to this relatively small room. *Photograph: Royal Commission on Historical Monuments*

order', and similar 'Rules' for 'Dorick', 'Ionick', 'Corinthian' and 'Composite'. These rules extend to such details as 'The division of the mouldings'.[30] The 'sur-base' is defined in Peter Nicholson's *New Practical Builder* (1823–5) as 'The upper base of a room, or rather the cornice of the pedestal of the room, which serves to finish the dado, and to secure the plaster against accidents from the backs of chairs and other furniture on the same level.'[31]

The bevelling of the panels in Moxon's description is a clear and early reference to the 'fielded panel'. It was and is usual in the assembling of panelling to glue and dowel the mortices and tenons of stiles and rails firmly together leaving the panel loose so that it may expand and shrink without splitting. William Salmon makes this very clear when describing the timberwork panels for painted sundials:

> . . . let the edges [of the panel] be shot true, and all of a thickness, that they may fit into the Rabets of the Mouldings, put round it just as a panel of Wainscot doth in its Frame.
>
> This will give the board liberty to shrink and swell without rending, whereas mouldings nailed round the edges, as the vulgar way is, doth so restrain the motion of the wood, that it cannot shrink without tearing.[32]

It should be added that panels when congested with generations of paint often split because such movement is restricted. It was found at an early date that if the panels were

70. Fireplace wall in 57 Upper Brook Street, WINCHESTER, HAMPSHIRE, *c*. 1800. Provincial joiners were quite capable of adapting the more frivolous aspects of the Classical Revival to a scale appropriate to their clients. The projection in the ceiling is caused by the hearthstone of the fireplace in the room above. *Photograph: Royal Commission on Historical Monuments*

bevelled it not only made the work cheaper but guaranteed that they had 'liberty to shrink'. This necessary feature was often used for decorative effect on the front of the panel which became known as the 'fielded panel' [69].

As the use of panelling declined in the eighteenth century (quite when is related to status and geographical location), the skirting and dado, or chair rail, persisted not so much as vestigal remains of panelling but as fundamental elements of the architecture of a classical room. Here again the techniques employed in this woodwork persist down to the present day. The simplest method of fitting a skirting board round a room is by means of the despised mitre and in poor quality work this is what is done. However, the dictates of good craftsmanship demand that such junctions be butted, the mouldings being accommodated by sawing its section around a scribed line [71]. Wood only shrinks

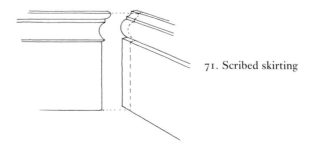

71. Scribed skirting

in its width and a mitred skirting board tends to shrink away from the joint, a hazard to which a 'scribed skirting' would not be subject. In the nineteenth century this problem was sometimes overcome by 'running' the skirting in plaster by means of a zinc template.

Strictly speaking, the making up of panelling was the province of the joiner, an 'art and mystery' that has been distinguished from carpentry by the former's use of the plane,[33] but the demarcation between the two crafts was by no means clear. A more satisfactory distinction would be that the joiner works at a bench (generally in a workshop) in contrast to the carpenter who works on buildings *in situ*.

In the nineteenth century the use of wood panelling in smaller houses declined. Loudon recommended that 'For the plainest description of cottage the walls may be completely finished with one coating of plaster.' In larger rooms the walls might be 'thrown into compartments' by means of applied mouldings or could be plastered in imitation of panelling. Loudon states quite categorically that 'walls and ceilings of "Plain Cottages" are seldom panelled on account of expence other than by painted lines or coloured papers'.[34]

Elaborate plasterwork is rare in small domestic buildings either on walls or ceilings. On early daubed walls a design was often simply scratched onto the surface. With more elaborate 'pargetting' the first layer of daub was applied to the laths of beech or oak (sometimes identified in accounts as 'sap and heart' suggesting the use of branches)[35] and the relief decoration was achieved in the final coat of plaster. In the seventeenth century, ornamental plasterwork appeared in smaller houses, the focal point of the chimney breast forming one favourite surface and the frieze between the top of the panelling and the ceiling another. An example of the latter is in The Old Croft, Washford, near Minehead, Somerset, and a somewhat earlier frieze survives in a house at Six Wells, Llandow, Glamorgan [72]. Examples of plasterwork overmantel decorations, which are such a feature in seventeenth-century houses in Cumbria,[36] are also to be found elsewhere in Britain as, for example, at the Old Manse, Beckington [73], and a house at Penwrlod Chapel, Llanigon, Powys, both dating from the seventeenth century.

72. (*left*) Seventeenth-century plaster frieze in a house at Six Wells, LLANDOW, GLAMORGAN
73. (*right*) Plaster overmantel decoration, The Old Manse, BECKINGTON, SOMERSET

John White's *A Rich Cabinet With A Variety of Inventions* (1651) contains an extraordinary conglomeration of facts which the author excuses on the following grounds: 'For the laborious Bee gathereth her cordiall Honey, and the venemous Spider her corroding poysen many times from one Flower.' Among White's 'Variety of Inventions' is: 'Receit LX *A dainty strong and glistering Mortar or Plaistering for Seelings, or for Walles*. It is said, that in *Italy* they much use this Conceit for the Plaistering of ther Seelings, Floors or Walls, which is by mixing and well tempering together Oxen and Carves blood with fine Loame or Clay, and it will be very strong and binding substance, and being well smoothed it will glister, and become very hard.'[37] This may be the so-called 'black plaster' quoted in the 1340 accounts at Westminster.[38] Plaster of Paris or 'French plaster' must have come into use in Britain in the middle of the thirteenth century possibly as a result of Henry III's many building projects. Nevertheless, a couple of centuries later many substitutes were used as William Horman (1519) makes clear. 'Some men will have thyr wallys plastered, some pergetted, and whytlymed, some roughe caste, some pricked, some wrought with playster of Paris.'[39]

Whitewash was widely used both inside and out, hence the name of the White Tower of the Tower of London. Evidently whitewashing was considered as much a responsibility of the plasterer as the painter. *The Practical Plasterer* by Wilfred Kemp, first published in London in 1893 (and as recently as 1926), states that, 'Whitewashing and the application of coloured washes to walls, technically known as "distempering", fall usually within the province of the plasterer, although often done by painters and decorators.'[40] Kemp's book also clarifies the terms 'pargetting', 'pergetting' or 'parge-work' which 'were and are applied somewhat loosely, and are used in several distinct senses, sometimes for plain plastering on walls, but usually for that of an ornamental character'. However, later in the same chapter he adds: 'The word "pargetting" although now but little used, except by bricklayers for the coarse plastering of the inside of chimney flues, often occurs as applied to ornamental work in ancient records', examples of which he goes on to cite.[41]

At York the plasterers joined with the bricklayers and tilers to form a united guild thus establishing officially their long-standing association.[42] It is possible that these relatively new (in terms of post-Roman Britain) trades kept together for mutual support.

Plaster of Paris being white was often left as the final finish. This was something of a convenience for it was generally agreed that 'Walls should not be painted until finished one year.'[43] Nevertheless, when Sidney Smith was building his parsonage at Foston le Clay, Yorkshire, this process was speeded up by keeping fires burning in each room for two months before the family moved in on 20 March 1814.[44]

Tapestries were once hung on bare walls not only for purposes of decoration but also to absorb the condensation which would otherwise have appeared on the hard stone surface. Plastered walls provided an alternative solution to this problem, a principle which present-day manufacturers of plaster seem to have forgotten. In the restoration of old property it is advisable to retain as much of the original absorbent plaster as possible, particularly in small kitchens and bathrooms, which despite the presence of good ventilation and central heating will be greatly at risk from the effects of condensation.

Notes to Chapter 3

1. Iorwerth C. Peate, *The Welsh House*, Hugh Evans and Sons, Liverpool, 1946, p. 91, quoting respectively *The Royal Commission on Land in Wales, Minutes of Evidence*, and the *Report* of the Commissioners on Education (1847).
2. Ibid., p. 91.
3. C. F. Innocent, *The Development of English Building Construction* (Cambridge University Press, 1916), David and Charles, Newton Abbot, 1971, p. 129.
4. Ibid., p. 125.
5. Ibid., p. 132.
6. S. O. Addy, *The Evolution of the English House*, George Allen and Unwin, London, 1898, 1933 edition, pp. 48, 49, 128.
7. As it is known in Lincolnshire and the south, or 'daub and stower' in the north, or 'raddle and daub' in Cheshire and Lancashire. Innocent, op. cit., p. 133.
8. Hoskins, pp. 104–11.
9. This remarkable survival is described in many books, among them Nathaniel Lloyd's *History of the English House* (1931), The Architectural Press, London, 1975, pp. 6, 7.
10. Margaret Wood, *The English Mediaeval House*, Phoenix House, London, 1965, ch. 9, 'Development of the Screen; Internal Partitions'. See also Evans, *Irish Folk Ways*, p. 64, which mentions the 'sconce' of Cumberland and the 'jamb wall' or 'hollan-wall' of Ulster and southern Scotland.
11. Innocent, pp. 139–40, fig. 30.
12. 'No. 10 High Street', *Stamford*, Royal Commission on Historical Monuments, 1977.
13. Wood, p. 146.
14. Barley, *The English Farmhouse and Cottage*, p. 122.
15. L. F. Salzman, *Building in England down to 1540*, Clarendon Press, Oxford, 1952, p. 258, quoting John Ripley who provided such panelling for Westminster Palace in 1532 for the sum of 21d.
16. Harrison, II, p. 235.
17. Emmison, pp. 9, 22.
18. Mason, 1969 edition, p. 83.
19. Mercer, *English Vernacular Houses*, pp. 14–15.
20. Emmison, p. 9.
21. Lloyd, p. 78.
22. John Fowler and John Cornforth illustrate one of the rooms at Clandon stripped of its hangings to reveal similar wood lining. *English Decoration in the 18th Century*, Barrie and Jenkins, London, 1974, 1978 edition.
23. Morris (ed.), *The Journeys of Celia Fiennes*, p. 66. The entry, in the journal for 1697, concerns the panelling of Hinchingbrooke Hall, Huntingdonshire.
24. Ware, p. 469.
25. Salzman, p. 346. Such fish skin was bought in 1355 for 9d for use at Westminster.
26. Stalker and Parker, p. 2.
27. Joseph Moxon, *Mechanick Exercises or the Doctrine of Handy-Works*, London, 1677, p. 85.
28. Ibid., p. 106.
29. Ibid., p. 100.

30. Batty Langley, *The Builder's Jewel*, London, 1754, pp. 4, 5. See also plate 76 'To proportion cornices to Rooms of any height'; plate 77 'Mouldings for Pannels'; plate 78 'Mouldings for tabernacle Frames'; plate 79 'A Cove ¼ of the entire Height', which also shows the chimney-breast end of a room with tabernacle frame.

31. Peter Nicholson, *New Practical Builder*, London, 1823–5, p. 230.

32. William Salmon, *Polygraphice Or the Arts of Drawing, Engraving, Etching, Limning, Painting, Vernishing, Japanning and Gilding &c*, London, 1672, 1701 edition, III, ch. 17.

33. John Harvey, *Mediaeval Craftsmen*, Batsford, London, 1975, p. 155.

34. Loudon, p. 274.

35. Innocent, p. 138, quoting Professor Thorold Rogers.

36. Barley, *The English Farmhouse and Cottage*, p. 237.

37. This recipe is very similar to one given by Sir Hugh Platt, p. 76 (see page 62, note 80).

38. Harvey, p. 146.

39. Salzman, p. 155.

40. Wilfred Kemp, *The Practical Plasterer* (London, 1893), Crosby Lockwood and Son, London, 1926, p. 145.

41. Ibid., pp. 67, 70.

42. Harvey, p. 145.

43. Loudon, p. 274.

44. Bax, p. 124.

4 · Doors and Doorways

As with walls, doors are either designed for internal partitions or to face the elements for external use. The primitive one-room house only required the latter type. Some of the earliest types of door were not side-hung on hinges but were simply placed in the doorway when required. The earliest side-hung doors swung on 'harrs' an ancient species of pin hinge that lingered in primitive houses on the northern and western fringes of the British Isles until the end of the nineteenth century [74]. There are exceptions where such hinges are found in the context of an elegant house; some of the magnificent mahogany doors of the state rooms in the majestic Hagley Hall, Worcestershire (built between 1754 and 1760 at a cost of £34,000) are unaccountably of this type.

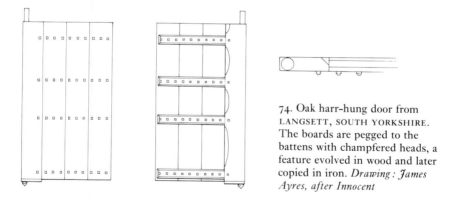

74. Oak harr-hung door from LANGSETT, SOUTH YORKSHIRE. The boards are pegged to the battens with champfered heads, a feature evolved in wood and later copied in iron. *Drawing: James Ayres, after Innocent*

Houses constructed of wattle hurdles plastered with mud were lived in by much of the population until the sixteenth century. Such houses had wattle-hurdle doors and these persisted in use until the end of the nineteenth century. In Ireland they are still used on farm buildings where the most rudimentary 'door' consists of nothing more substantial than a bundle of brushwood [75].[1]

75. Nineteenth-century Irish hurdle and brushwood doors. *Drawing courtesy of the National Museum of Ireland, Dublin*

In the late nineteenth century a derelict cottage at Great Hatfield, Mappleton, East Yorkshire, was recorded as having 'doors' and indeed 'windows' of 'harden', a kind of coarse sackcloth which 'could be lifted up like a curtain'.[2] At about the same period on the Isle of Lewis in the Outer Hebrides 'a straw mat or a cow's hide on a frame might be used as a door', and as recently as the 1960s wickerwork doors are reported as being in use in Wester Ross.[3] In Wales, where the door-hurdle was known as the *dorglwyd*, an example was recorded in use in a ruined farmhouse at Strata Florida, Dyfed.[4] J. Evans, in his *Letters . . . in North Wales in 1798* says of the cottages in Caernarvonshire: 'Door there is none: but this deficiency is supplied by a hurdle, formed of a few wattlings and rushes, which in bad weather is raised perpendicular to stop the gap.'[5] The whole question of hurdle doors has been most thoroughly studied in Ireland by A. T. Lucas. They seem to have been more usual in the northern and western parts of the country. The Irish examples were either made of woven wattle or wicker and sometimes of brushwood, the latter being generally reserved for outbuildings. What was probably the last brushwood door to be made in Ireland was constructed for a cow shed in 1955 by Sean Fitzgerald of Kilcrohane Parish. It was of birch branches held between two pairs of split halves of 3 in (7.6 cm) diameter ash, tied with bog-fir rope. In Irish cabins with the typical cross passage one wattle door (or half door) and one wood-batten door was quite common. The wood door was hung on strap hinges and it was usual to place it in the doorway facing the prevailing wind—if the wind changed the door was simply lifted off its pintles and hung in the other doorway. This custom probably represents a transitional stage in modernization. To wind-proof the wattle door it became usual to hang a straw mat on the inside [76]. A description of such a door was recorded in 1942 from an informant aged seventy-four:

The door consisted of four [superimposed] hurdles. The innermost was made of rods: it had ribs and the rods were woven as in a basket and it was square in shape like the

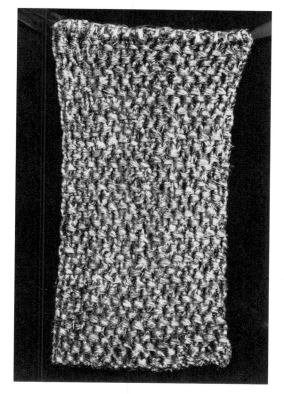

76. Woven straw door-lining
from PORTACLOY, CO. MAYO,
IRELAND. The hurdle doors of
Ireland were often wind-proofed
on the inside by means of such
straw-mat hangings. *Photograph:
National Museum of Antiquities,
Dublin*

frame [of the door]. There were three others outside that with three sticks tied [transversely] with withies on them. They [the hurdles] were fixed to each other . . . and the four were fixed so tightly together that a person would find it very difficult to pull them apart. . . . The innermost one, which was made like a basket, was plastered with yellow clay, and no wind could penetrate it then. There was a [separate] cross bar to put across the middle of the door [when it was in position in the doorway] and two holes in the wall into which the ends [of the bar] were entered.[6]

Sometimes such doors were hung on hinges of plaited straw but these wattle or straw 'shields' (*sciathógaí*) were more often simply placed in the doorway, although the straw lining mats were sometimes hung by means of hooks from the inside wall. For this reason the doorway required no framed surround of wood onto which hinges could be fixed. Indeed the same held good when the ancient harr was used. The harr could be achieved by extending either one outer stile in a framed-up door or one plank in a ledge door to provide a pair of 'horns' on which the door could swing.[7]

In the traviated form of a timber-frame building the jamb existed as a necessary part of the structure, but in stone houses the door frame of wood had to be introduced as it had not been necessary with either the wattle or the harr-hung door. The use of the wooden architrave made possible the introduction of various types of metal hinge. The square-headed door is usual for timber-frame buildings as a natural consequence of their structure. In fine yeoman's houses in the Weald door-heads are sometimes given a two-centred arch by means of naturally curved jambs.[8] As timber was customarily used with the natural growth inverted such boards were easily obtained from the trunk and the point near the ground where the girth of the tree widens. The use of the two-centred arch in vernacular houses of the Weald contrasts with the four-centred arch favoured for grander buildings of the Perpendicular period. However, the 'four-centred arch' was used in vernacular houses and could easily be cut out of the solid lintel. In a screens passage such as that at Hines Farm, Earl Stonham [77], the shaped door-head was housed in the jambs below the lintel. The door-head illustrated in Plate 78 is of this type and the simple carved feather design would probably have been visible from the screens passage while the elaborate tracery would have enriched the hall. It is rare to find such pure tracery combined with such a pure Renaissance detail as the guilloche, two features which point to a date between about 1530 and 1550.

Batten doors for internal and external use are constructed of a series of vertical boards held together by means of horizontal boards or 'ledges', usually four in number. The best external doors of this type are composed of two layers of boards (which are sometimes lapped) with the vertical boards on the outside, so as to shed water, and the horizontal boards on the inside [79]. The two layers are united by nails driven through from the

79. Oak door at Newhouse Farm, LLANFAPLEY, GWENT, first half of the seventeenth century. Doors constructed of two layers of boards set at right angles to each other were held together by numerous nails cleated over on the inside. The resulting decorative arrangement of these nails was often emphasized by scribed lines. *Photograph: Welsh Folk Museum*

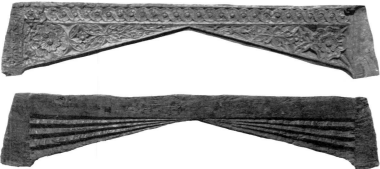

77. The north/south cross-passage of Hines Farm, EARL STONHAM, SUFFOLK, sixteenth century. *Photograph: Royal Commission on Historical Monuments*

78a, b. Front and back of a door-head, oak, mid-sixteenth century. Such a feature probably occurred over the door or doors in the screens passage as at Hines Farm. The simpler side probably faced onto the passage. The purity of the Perpendicular tracery combined with the classical guilloche is rare. *Ayres's Collection*

front of the door and cleated over on the inside. Many nails were needed for this purpose and it was customary to arrange them in patterns which were emphasized by scribed lines in the wood. 'Batten' doors were similar in construction to plank panelling and, on occasion, were also worked with mouldings such as a 'bead and quirk'. In Ulster, despite the historic deforestation of the country by the English, doors made up from generously wide boards in the nineteenth century were sometimes grooved in imitation of narrow boards.[9] The half-door in Ireland sometimes consisted of two doors, one full length, the other half its height providing in effect an extra window which was high enough to keep farm animals out of the house. In various parts of the British Isles another type of half-door may occasionally be found where the door is divided vertically and hinged in the middle [80a, b, c].[10]

The 'strap and pintle' and the 'cross garnet' (as Moxon describes it)[11] had the advantage of providing a door with additional strengthening. Strap hinges of wood, which dispensed with the luxury of iron, were made and in use on the Isle of Lewis within recent years.[12] But throughout much of the seventeenth and eighteenth centuries the 'H' and 'HL' hinge of iron became usual. The well-known 'cockshead' hinge used on furniture and internal doors is an elaboration of the 'H' hinge. Such hinges were replaced by the 'butt' hinge which was in turn superseded by the 'rising butt' made necessary by the widespread use of carpets in the nineteenth century. Moxon describes various types of hinges and their use: Joiners should 'consider what sort of Hindges are properest for the Door they are to *Hang*. When they have a *Street door* (which commonly is to take off and lift on) they use *Hooks and Hindges*. In a Battend-door, Back-door or other Battend-door, or Shop windows, they use *Cross-Garnets*. If a *Frame'd Door, Side Hinges*; and for *Cup-board Doors* and such like Duf-tails [butterfly hinges].'[13]

One of the earliest methods of locking a door was by means of a horizontal beam sliding in large iron staples fastened to the internal wall. Sometimes this beam slid into holes cut in the thickness of a stone wall. An example of the latter has been found in a stone house in Dalkeith, Scotland, where the hole is lined with timber, presumably to make the beam slide more easily and last longer.[14] Wooden latches and bolts have a wide distribution in the British Isles. In the Scottish Islands as well as in Devon and Cornwall the simple wood 'pin lock', as old as Ancient Egypt, was in use in the nineteenth century,

81. Seventeenth-century wooden bolt on a door in an attic room, Green Farm, BUSHLEY, NEAR TEWKESBURY. Overall measurements 8 × 12 in (20.3 × 30.4 cm)

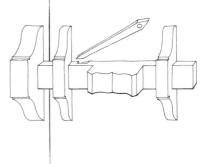

80a, b, c. The front door of
Cross Street Farmhouse, WEST
BURTON, WEST SUSSEX, divides
vertically and is dated 1634.
Photographs by the author

a possible legacy of the Phoenicians. Moxon[15] refers to '*Locks* for several purposes, as *Street-door Locks*, called *Stock-locks, Chamber-door Locks*, called *Spring-locks*', a distinction which survives to this day except that 'Stock-locks' have generally been replaced by 'rim locks'. Stock locks tended to use less metal and were therefore cheaper than rim locks as the 'stock' could be of wood [82].

82. Mid-nineteenth-century stock lock with iron mounts

Locks were once items of great value and in mediaeval and Tudor times were decorated in accordance with their status. It is thought that the Beddington lock (now in the Victoria and Albert Museum) was carried from palace to palace when Henry VIII, whose arms it bears, was on a 'progress'.[16] In nineteenth-century Scotland, locks were still considered as tenant's property and the numerous keyholes in many old doors bear witness to this. George Hope, recalling the dwellings at Fenton Barns, Scotland, in the year 1861 spoke of 'a door covered with key holes, made to suit the size of the lock of each successive occupant'.[17]

The framed door, as we have seen, is probably older than the use of 'framed-up' panelling but its use increased as framed panelling became more common. The two-panelled door of the early seventeenth century, embellished with applied mouldings, became simpler towards the end of the century in keeping with the restraint of Classicism. The door surround too, often felt the impact of the Renaissance as interpreted by Palladio: '*Doors* within the House, in the least Building, ought not to have less than two Foot and a half in breadth, and five Foot and a half in height: Those from three to four Foot broad must have in height twice their breadth; and to great Buildings you may allow ev'n to five or six Foot in breadth and the height double.'[18] Externally the doorway could be simply framed by a bolection moulding in stone. The pediment was also widely used externally at the vernacular level where it was favoured virtually throughout the eighteenth century. Internally, however, the pediment must have been found to be too powerful and 'architectural' and it was often reduced by being 'broken' or eliminated, the door-head being simply terminated by a cornice. In about 1700 the transome light over the door provided light in the entrance hall where it was particularly valuable in the terraces of the fast expanding towns. The lunette, fanlight or transome light of cast iron became widespread as a decorative feature in the late eighteenth century when they could be cheaply produced with delicate astrigal mouldings by factories in Coalbrookdale and elsewhere.

Throughout the eighteenth and for much of the nineteenth century the standard door was framed up to produce six panels. On external doors the top four panels were fielded, but the lower two panels were often finished flush with the stiles and rails and marked out with a bead in light relief. This simple treatment of the lower panels helped to repel rain at the most vulnerable part of the door. In small houses the ceiling height was insufficient to accommodate six panels and four-panel doors were quite usual. The fielded panel persisted at the vernacular level throughout the eighteenth and even into the nineteenth century. With the Classical Revival the panel was given emphasis by the use of an astrigal moulding marking its margin. This fashion was all but universal by the early nineteenth century, at which time the edge of the panel was sometimes given 'colour' by carved flutes running at right angles to the astrigal and with paterae in the corners.

Many woods were used in the making of doors and doorways. Early examples are mostly of oak and in the eighteenth century grand houses favoured mahogany. By the early nineteenth century Loudon considered only one wood appropriate for smaller houses and cottages: '*Specification of Joyners Work* All inside framing, and all the outside work, to be of sound, well seasoned, dry yellow deal. . . . To put proper door-cases (door cases are called proper when wrought, i.e. planed, framed and beaded) of fir (fir is generally applied by builders to Baltic timber; what they call pine generally comes from America . . .'.[19]

The architrave served the functional purpose of covering the junction between a wood door or window frame and its surrounding masonry so that the timber could shrink without producing a visible and unsightly crack. These architraves, from the simplest bolection moulding of the late seventeenth century to the austere reeded forms of the early nineteenth century, reflect not just the architectural styles of their time but also, by their precocious adoption or persistent use, their social background and geographical location.

Notes to Chapter 4

1. A. T. Lucas, 'Wattle and Straw Mat Doors in Ireland', *Arctica, Studia Ethnographica Upsaliensia*, XI, pp. 16–35, fig. 7.
2. Addy, p. 64.
3. Grant, p. 165.
4. Peate, *The Welsh House*, 1946 edition, p. 123.
5. J. Evans, *Letters . . . in North Wales in 1798*, 1804, p. 161.
6. Translated from the Irish. Lucas, p. 24 (see note 1, above).
7. Although for small cupboard doors one slab of wood can be cut with projecting horns to create harr hinges this would not be possible in a larger scale. The direct successor to the harr hinge is the pin hinge but again it is only suitable for lightweight small cupboard doors.
8. Mason, pp. 73–6.
9. An example may be seen in the front door of the Coscib Farmhouse at the Ulster Folk Museum.

10. Another door of this type is illustrated in the *Journal of the Cork Historical and Archaeological Society*, vol. 76, 1971. A. T. Lucas, 'A Straw Roof Lining at Stradbally, Co. Waterford'.

11. Moxon, p. 17.

12. Grant, pp. 165–6.

13. Moxon, p. 160.

14. This architectural detail is now in the National Museum of Antiquities, Edinburgh.

15. Moxon, p. 21.

16. Bernard Hughes, 'English Domestic Locks', *The Connoisseur Year Book*, London, 1957, pp. 100–8.

17. Fenton, p. 188, quoting the *Memoir of George Hope* by his daughter, 1881, p. 231.

18. '*The First Book of Architecture by Andrea Palladio* translated out of the Italian w[th]: diverse other designs necessary to the art of well building by Godfrey Richards', first published in Italy in 1570, p. 145.

19. Loudon, pp. 39, 49.

83. (*right*) A conjectural reconstruction of a Saxon hut before the addition of daub and thatch. *Weald and Downland Museum*

5 · Windows

No feature is of such importance to the interior and exterior of a house as is the judicious arrangement and proportion of its windows. Many eighteenth-century houses have such plain external elevations that their quality and distinction is entirely dependent upon their fenestration. The opening sentence of Walter Gedde's *Sundry Draughts Principaly Serving for Glaziers and not Impertinant for Plasterers and Gardiners* (London, 1615–16) added that this work is primarily concerned with the arrangement of lead cames and the pattern that they create: 'As the principal beautie, and countenaunce of Architecture, consists in outward ornament of lights, so inward partes are ever opposite to the eies of the beholder, taking more delight in the beauty thereof, being cuningly wrought, then in any other garnishing within the same.'

Primitive houses were both lit and ventilated by their doorways. The type is well represented by the so-called 'black houses' of Scotland, the stone-built, beehive huts of the Isle of Lewis and the somewhat similarly constructed pigsties of Wales which are also of stone. The tepe-like, conical shelters of turves laid on a timber framework made by charcoal burners also lack windows, as do the Saxon houses excavated at Erringham-above-Shoreham in Sussex [83] which are similar in type to those still in use in Athelney,

Somerset until the middle of the nineteenth century [84].[1] The Athelney example, being late in date, included a short funnel to take away the smoke from the fire and this 'smoke-hole' served as an auxiliary window. Another method of admitting light and air, as we have seen, was by means of the half-door, the lower half of which when closed served to keep farm animals out of the house. In Ireland double doors were used, one full height and one half height. An informant aged over eighty in 1937 and recorded in Cloganeely, Co. Donegal, remembered that 'The large door was always open except in a storm; and the little door was always kept shut. It [the latter] kept out the hens and ducks and let in enough air and light.'[2]

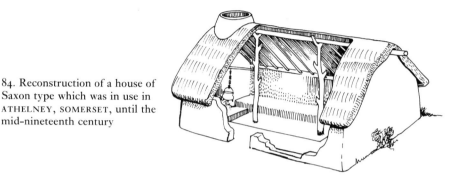

84. Reconstruction of a house of Saxon type which was in use in ATHELNEY, SOMERSET, until the mid-nineteenth century

Small wonder that when windows were introduced such unglazed orifices were known as the 'wind eye', the origin of our window. The insertion of windows also caused problems of security, and Richard Carew in his *Survey of Cornwall* states that the 'ancient' houses of the country had windows that were 'arched and little, and their lights inwards to the court'.[3] In timber-frame buildings there was no structural necessity for the insertion of mullions but clearly such bars would serve to keep out intruders. In stone buildings the mullions reduced the stress on the lintel which in turn was often assisted by a 'relieving arch', and the presence of mullions did away with the need for a monolithic lintel.

The insertion of such mullions divided a single window into a number of 'lights' or 'days'.[4] The top-floor windows in timber-frame houses in Norwich are often very long and low and divided into numerous lights. These are weavers' windows, as is confirmed by the presence of shuttles found under floor boards in these rooms. In large vertical windows it was necessary to divide the space still further by the introduction of horizontal members known as transomes. In grander houses of either timber or stone the upper portion of the window was often reserved for tracery which is usually referred to in mediaeval documents as 'forms', 'form-pieces' and occasionally 'moulds'.[5]

Mullions, transomes and tracery were masoned, with sections of varying complexity, with their intersections being worked in wood as in stone with the mason's mitre so

85. Ground-floor mullioned window in a deserted house at LLWYNAU MAWR, LLANFIHANGEL CWM DU, POWYS. Simple wood mullion windows were common throughout England and Wales in the sixteenth century. Note the survival of early, if not original, shutters. *Photograph: Welsh Folk Museum*

characteristic of the mediaeval tradition. In the simplest windows of wood the mullions are square in section but set diamond-wise in the cill and lintel [85]. In either wood or stone the simple rectangular opening is common, whilst the elaboration of 'plate tracery' or the 'fretted slab'[6] in either wood or stone employs the rudimentary technique of simply piercing a slab. Such openings were often used to provide 'borrowed light' within a house by piercing a screen or partition wall [86].

86. 'Borrowed light' was often an important feature inside houses. This example of pierced plank-panelling comes from EYARTH, RUTHIN, CLWYD. *Welsh Folk Museum*

Having made such apertures it was necessary to find some means of reducing or suppressing the draught so created. Despite the presence of window glass in Roman Britain, its use in windows was exceptional until the late sixteenth century and in remote parts of the country until the nineteenth century. In the west of Ireland many peasants in the last century had to make do without glass in their windows. In 1939 an informant aged eighty in Feakle, Co. Clare, remembered 'scores of old houses that had neither glass nor doors. A sop o' hay took the place of glass and the doors were made of woven rods.'[7]

The draughts from unglazed windows were more usually excluded by means of shutters which also eclipsed the light. In contrast to continental Europe these shutters were usually hung on the inside walls in post-mediaeval England. Fourteenth-century accounts use the word *fenestrae* to describe shutters and the translation of this word as 'window' is generally considered incorrect or at least imprecise.[8] In halls where windows occur on both sides of the room the shutters were closed to shut out the prevailing wind, leaving the leeward side open to admit light and permit smoke to escape from the central hearth. Various methods were used to hang shutters, by means of sliding (horizontally or vertically) or by hinges. Numerous types of hinge were used including the primitive pin hinge or its successors the strap, butterfly and H hinges. In houses with large windows with transomes it was usual for the shutters to seal off the lower lights leaving the upper ones open at a height where the light would be advantageous but the draught would be least inconvenient [87]. This feature may be seen in many early paintings such as the

87. Detail of *The Annunciation* (c. 1425) by Robert Campin. The window is typical of a wealthy house of the fifteenth century and shows two types of folding shutter and a fenestral. The small amount of glazing is confined to the two 'lights' above the transome.
Metropolitan Museum of Art (Cloisters Collection), New York

89. (*right*) A first-floor room in the mediaeval Lodging at BURWELL, CAMBRIDGESHIRE, late fifteenth century. In general, early stone walls were thick enough to accommodate shutters in the reveals of windows. In this example the shutters were opened flat into the flanking recesses. *Photograph: Royal Commission on Historical Monuments*

central panel of the altarpiece in St. Pierre, Louvain, showing *The Last Supper* (1464–7) by Dieric Bouts. The slightly earlier *Marriage of Arnolfini* (1434) by Van Eyck shows that in some instances the upper lights were glazed. In America this tradition persisted in the courthouses of Tidewater, Maryland, where the Oxford Courthouse of 1808 had 'wooden shutters for the lower part of the windows and glass for the upper'.[9] In thick-walled, stone or cob houses, shutters could simply be folded back within the splayed reveal of the window [88]. Where however the width of the window and the thickness of

88. *Interior, Sherborne, Dorset* by S. R. Jones, 1911, showing a window seat created in the thickness of a wall. The high cill resulted in a stone back to such seats thus protecting the fragile and valuable leaded windows from damage. *Bath Public Library*

the wall made this impossible the shutters were housed flat on the inside walls [89]. In the Perley Parlor from an eighteenth-century timber-frame house from Boxford, Massachusetts, USA, to be seen at the American Museum in Britain, the shutters slide back into the thickness of the wall. This simple expedient permits pictures to be hung on

90. (*left*) Reconstruction of a vertical sliding shutter, Bayleaf
Farmhouse. *In house re-erected at Weald and Downland Museum, Sussex.*
91. (*right*) Sash shutter of deal in the old kitchen at Castle Bank, APPLEBY-IN-
WESTMORLAND, CUMBRIA, mid-nineteenth century. These shutters are double
hung like the windows which they serve. *Photograph by the author*

the piers between the windows. Sash shutters [90] such as the early nineteenth-century
examples in the old kitchen at Castle Bank, Appleby-in-Westmorland [91], similarly
leave the intervening wall visible. Shutters provide greater warmth and additional
security. However, Charles Kingsley found conventional wooden shutters insufficiently
secure in the parsonage at Eversley, Hampshire, and had steel ones fitted following the
murder of a neighbour.[10]

The introduction of glazing combined with the use of sashes encouraged the
development of larger windows, despite which shutters remained in use. These larger
windows demanded larger shutters which had to be housed when not in use. The
problem was usually met by dividing the shutter vertically one or more times, enabling it
either to fold into the reveal of the window or to open out across it. Such shutters were
designed to fill the entire window but in some instances oval apertures were cut in the
upper panels to admit light and air. Throughout history shutters have been constructed
with the design and constructional elements found in the doors and panelling of their
period.

We have seen that glazed windows were an unheard of luxury in post-Roman Britain
before the late sixteenth century, and William Harrison, writing shortly before 1587,

describes the alternatives that were used: 'Of old time, our countrie houses, instead of glasse, did use much lattise, and that made either of wicker or fine rifts of oke in chekerwise. I read also that some of the better sort, in and before the times of the Saxons . . . did make panels of horne in steed of glasse, and fix them in woodden calmes. But as horne . . . is . . . quite laid downe in everie place, so our lattises are also growne into less use, bicause glasse is come to be so plentifull.'[11] The diaper of wooden laths that Harrison refers to was a feature that persisted much later in remote parts of the British Isles. Francis Stevens in *Views of Cottages and Farm Houses in England and Wales* (Ackerman, 1815) includes a lithograph of a farmhouse at Seaton in Devonshire with lattice windows on the ground floor. J. Evans in his *Letters . . . in North Wales in 1798* describes[12] 'lattices for the admission of light, formed of interwoven sticks'[13] which provided the ideal basis for carrying paper or linen, waxed to admit light. Windows were treated in this way from a very early date. In 1217 the town of Witney spent 9d on 'linen cloth for the windows of the church'.[14] Such a feature was described by William Horman in his *Vulgaria*, published in 1519.[15] 'Paper, or lyn clothe, straked a crosse with losynges, [to] make fenestrals in stede of glasen wyndowes [92].' Thomas More apparently

92. Simple mullioned window of oak in the gable end of a farmhouse at WEST BURTON, WEST SUSSEX. This window was designed to carry sliding fenestrals

considered such windows more than adequate as he approved them for the houses in *Utopia* (1516). Sir Hugh Platt in *The Jewel House of Art and Nature*, published in 1594, describes how to make parchment opaque for this purpose:

> . . . then straine . . . [the finest, thinnest parchment] upon a frame . . . and when it is drie oile it all over with a pensill [brush], with oile of sweet Amonds, oile of turpentine, or oile of spike, some content themselves with linseed oile, and when it is thorow dry, it wil shew very cleere, and serve in windowes in stead of Glasse, especially in such roomes as are subject to overseers. You may draw anie personage, beast, tree, flower, or coate armour upon the parchment before it be oyled, and then cutting your parchment into square panes, and making slight frames for them, they will make a prettie show in your windowes, and keep the room verie warm. This I commend before oyled Paper, because it is more lasting, and will endure the blustring and stormie weather much better then paper.[16]

As recently as 1937 a person aged eighty in Glencolmcille, Co. Donegal, remembered that 'The houses in those days were not half the size they are now. . . . There was a strip of sheepskin in the window instead of glass.'[17] In East Yorkshire, mud houses surviving to the end of the nineteenth century included windows and also doors of 'harden', a kind of coarse sack-cloth.[18] On the Merionethshire/Denbighshire border in the last century many houses had but one window which the occupants had contrived to fill with a fixed sheet of glass which helps to explain why windows were broken on the death of the occupant to permit the soul to escape.[19]

In Tudor England glazed windows were found only in richer houses and being fitted into easily detachable casements were not regarded as fixtures.[20] Even in the seventeenth century glass windows were only to be found in the houses of the well-to-do. Aubrey states that, 'Glass windows, except in churches and gentlemen's houses were rare before the time of Henry VIII. In my own remembrance before the Civil Wars, copyholders and poor people had none in Herefordshire, Monmouthshire, and Salop: it is still so.'[21]

The Roman method of making window glass in large sheets was apparently not known in mediaeval times when it was only possible to make up a large sheet of glass by assembling many small pieces of blown glass within lead cames. The word 'pane' describes such an assemblage of small pieces to form one unit and was often applied to textiles as in 'counterpane'.[22] A sketchbook in the C. A. Buckler Collection in the British Library[23] shows that the designs used were almost as numerous as those for patchwork quilts. Walter Gedde's *Sundry Draughtes Principaly Serving for Glaziers* (London, 1615–16) illustrates no less than one hundred and eighty designs for leaded windows. In general, the diaper pattern was most commonly adopted [93, 94] and continued the traditional arrangement of 'fenestrals' of split oak, where the diagonal arrangement shed rain-water more effectively.

93. (*left*) Seventeenth-century pierced-lead ventilation quarel from WITHAM, ESSEX. *Colchester and Essex Museum*
94. (*right*) Seventeenth-century pierced-lead ventilator quarrel from a window at DEDHAM, ESSEX

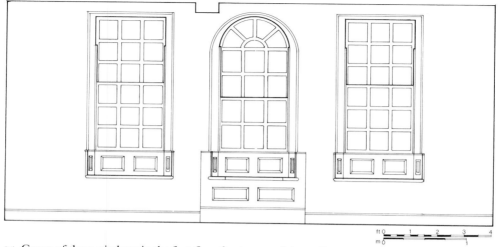

95. Group of three windows in the first-floor front room of Ames Cottage, FRESHFORD, early eighteenth century. Note the wide glazing bars. Only the lower halves of these sash windows are movable

Sir Hugh Platt, writing in the late sixteenth century, refers to Sussex window glass of adequate quality,[24] but much of the glass made in England then was produced by craftsmen from the Low Countries. In the late seventeenth century, when Dutch influence was at its height, great improvements were made in glass production in England. Some authorities have suggested that sliding sash windows also came from the Low Countries, but their widespread use in houses of high quality in the late seventeenth century may be coincidental with the Dutch fashions of the Restoration court. Innocent has drawn attention to William Horman's reference (as early as 1519) to 'many prety wyndowes shette with louys goynge up and downe',[25] which may refer to a sliding sash window. Be that as it may, they certainly appeared at Chatsworth between 1676 and 1680, at the Banqueting Hall, Whitehall in 1685, followed by Windsor Castle, Kensington Palace and Hampton Court[26] a little later. Celia Fiennes, in her journals (which were written between about 1685 and 1703), makes constant reference to this new fashion. Writing in 1697 about Blyth Abbey, which was rebuilt in 1684, she says that it was 'a very sweete House and Gardens and Grounds, it was of brick work coyn'd with stone and the Windows with stone all sashes'.[27]

In early sash windows the glazing bars are notable for their bulk—indeed they often measure $1\frac{1}{2}$ by $1\frac{3}{4}$ in (3.8 by 4.4 cm) [95]. Towards the close of the eighteenth century and particularly in the early nineteenth century this measurement had changed to $\frac{5}{8}$ by $1\frac{3}{4}$ in (1.59 by 4.45 cm). In early examples the weights are hung in grooves in the solid wood frame of the window which itself is all but flush with the face of the building, but later examples are hung in boxed-up frames. To prevent the spread of fire from room to room, and in terraces from house to house, legislation was introduced in 1709 which stipulated that window frames should be set at least 6 in (15.2 cm) back from the external face of the wall.[28] Internally this had the effect of reducing the apparent thickness of walls. In Moxon's book of 1677 two further advantages are given. He recommends that the frame of the window project 'an Inch and a half beyond the [in] side of the Building, and to plaster against its sides for the better securing of the rest of the Carcase from the weather'.

When Celia Fiennes visited Ashtead Park, Surrey, she noted the 'double sashes to make the house warmer for it stands pretty bleake'.[29] This almost sounds like a reference to double glazing but she is more likely referring to the double sash which is composed of two window frames of equal or approximately equal size, both hung and counterbalanced by means of pulleys and weights. Simple sash windows dispensed with weights and relied solely on pegs or some similar device to hold the window open or closed. Sometimes upper windows are not divided into two equal parts. In Holland this unequal horizontal division was usual and the upper section was generally immovable (a 'chassis dormant').[30] Many surviving late seventeenth- or early eighteenth-century English sash windows also have this feature. Sliding sashes where one half of the window slides horizontally across the other half are found throughout the country but seem to be especially favoured in Yorkshire where they are known as 'Yorkshire lights'. M. W. Barley suggests that this may be a native version of the sash window and states that it is found all over the Midlands and the north where one of the earliest examples is at Moss Farm, near Doncaster, which was built in 1705. I have seen late eighteenth-century examples set in seventeenth-century timber-framed houses as far south as Leominster, Herefordshire. In my opinion both the horizontal and the vertical sash may well derive from the earlier use of sliding shutters, the remains of which are quite common in timber-frame houses in the south-east. The Metropolitan Museum possesses an interesting window with a 'guillotine' shutter [96] which, being American, is late in date but I believe its early character confirms this hypothesis.[31] These examples serve to explain Horman's remarkably early reference to sash windows cited above. That sash windows evolved in timber-frame buildings remains a matter for debate. Barley suggests that they 'must have originated in a region of brick building with wooden window frames'.[32]

In eighteenth- and even nineteenth-century houses sash windows are often only found on the principal floors and elevations of the house, attics and other less evident parts retaining casement windows. Indeed the casement window was never utterly outmoded and its use was generally retained for cottages. In a few instances it appears as a significant motif in a scheme of sash windows as in the central pediment of the terrace of houses known as Prior Park Buildings, Bath [97], which were built in 1821 almost certainly to the designs of John Pinch.

The familiar bull's-eye window of bottle glass now so popular in some suburban

96. (*left*) Late seventeenth-century window which may be from PLYMOUTH COLONY, MASSACHUSETTS. Its string operated 'guillotine' shutter (not visible) may cover either the lower louvred portion of the upper leaded light. Such sliding shutters point to the possible origin of the sash window. *Metropolitan Museum of Art, New York*
97. (*right*) Casement window in the central pediment of Prior Park Buildings, BATH, c. 1821. Despite the very general use of the sash window in the eighteenth century the casement window was never completely displaced. *Photograph by the author*

developments was once 'the coarsest kind in common use'.[33] The persistence of the casement window made up of small pieces of blown glass held together by means of lead cames may be entirely attributed to cheapness. Loudon makes this very clear: 'We do not like latticed windows because they are generally cold and gloomy; but as they are much cheaper than sashes hung with cords and pulleys, where economy is the main object, recourse must be had to them, or to iron windows. Windows cast of iron very fit for cottages are now made of different forms, and very cheap.'[34] Such cast-iron windows were made by William Strutt for his cotton mills and for the cottages of his workers.[35]

No doubt because windows were few in poorer houses that could not afford glass, the window tax was seen as a method of taxing the rich, but in fact it fell most heavily on the middle classes. The Reverend John William, curate of Lincoln, paid 13s in window tax in 1751 on a house which he rented for £7 11s 4d per annum.[36] It was first levied in England in 1697 in an attempt to defray the cost of making up the deficiency caused to the Exchequer by the clipping of silver coinage. The tax was assessed according to the number of windows on houses worth more than £5 per annum and with more than six windows, the maximum dimensions of each taxed window being 11 ft (3.35 m) in height and 4 ft 9 in (1.45 m) in width.[37] Windows in dairies were exempt. The tax was increased six times between 1747 and 1808 but was reduced in 1823. It was abolished, appropriately, in 1851, the year of the Crystal Palace. Many windows were blocked in response to this tax. However, not all 'blind' windows are examples of this. The classical concern with symmetry often necessitated the use of bogus windows to give balance to the façade or even to reduce the weight of the masonry over doors, etc, and in parts of a house where windows were not required. One way of distinguishing between blocked windows and intended blind windows is that in the latter the stonework or brickwork is 'bonded in'.

Nathaniel Whittock in *The Decorative Painters' and Glaziers' Guide* (1827) [98] gives instructions for the making of painted window blinds [K] which may be seen as the successors to the 'fenestrals' of waxed and painted linen. In the nineteenth century Scotch cambric was favoured for such blinds. Manufacturers of window blinds in

98. Designs for transparent window blinds from Nathaniel Whittock's *The Decorative Painters' and Glaziers' Guide. British Library*

London are mentioned in Ambrose Heal's *The London Furniture Makers* and I have found others in the Heal Collection in the British Museum. The following list is not comprehensive but serves to indicate how widespread the use of window blinds was in eighteenth-century London:

Thomas Atkinson, 1755
John Brown, 1730. Took over the business of William Rodwell who advertised in 1727
Henry Buck, 1741–50
James Cox, 1753–62
William Darby, 1760 and 1770
Richard Elliot, c. 1780
William Gwinnell, 1741
John Hatt, 1759–79 (successor to John Arrowsmith)
William Kirk, 1749
Landall and Gordon, c. 1750
Charles Legg, c. 1750
John Newman, 1755
Francis Pyner, 1765–92
Benjamin Rackstrow, 1738
William Rodwell, advertised 1727
Nathaniel Skinner, 1730
John Whitcomb, c. 1760
John White, c. 1750

Manufacturers of window blinds were numerous in the nineteenth century and they were often made or at least provided by jobbing builders and undertakers such as W. Thompson of Chenies Street, Tottenham Court Road, London (c. 1860) or I. O'Brien who made 'Venetian, Parlour, Spring, Roller and Outside Blinds in Cases' (c. 1820).

John White's label listed above reads: 'Pictures Painted, Mended, Cleaned, and Framed, Blinds for Windows Painted on Canvas or Wire . . . At the Golden Head, Shoe Lane, Fleet Street, London.' Quite what form such wire window-blinds took in the eighteenth century is uncertain but at all events reference to them is rare and often confined to one important room in an imposing house.[38] When the Earl of Orford's home in Chelsea was sold following his death in 1745, 'his Lordship's dressing Room, on the Ground floor' included a lot containing 'A walnut tree corner cuboard, a frame of a cabinet and 2 brass wire window blinds'. This was apparently the only room in the house to have such blinds and the lot fetched the not inconsiderable sum of 15s, a figure which may be attributed to the blinds rather than the other items in the lot because, like textiles, all metalwork was expensive until after the Industrial Revolution. Evidently, these wire-gauze blinds were often painted decoratively, a feature that would not be visible by day. Only in rich households where candles were used in abundance would this decoration be seen clearly at night. John Brown in the 1730s made and sold all sorts of chairs and cabinet work and also stocked 'Blinds for Windows made and Curiously Painted on Canvas, Silk or Wire'.[39] The application of paint to brass wire must have presented numerous problems as the paint would tend to peel off such a surface in a position as exposed as a window. This problem is implicit in the following description that occurs in another label dated 1729 in the Heal Collection: '. . . made and sold Window Blinds of all sorts, painted in Wier, Canvas, Cloth, and Sassenet, after the best and most lasting manner ever yet done so that if ever so dull an dirty they will clean with sope and sand and be like new; where may be seen great choice of the same being always about them. Likewise at the same place is made the new fashion Walnut Tree Window seat cases to slip off and on.'

Despite the prevalence of painted linen or cotton blinds in the nineteenth century few seem to have survived.[40] Certainly Nathaniel Whittock gives elaborate instructions on how to apply decorative painting to blinds of 'Scotch cambric or lawn'. Small blinds were apparently painted with pigments held in a medium of isinglass dissolved in boiling water, 'but for large blinds the dimensions of a common sash window parchment size' was used. Blinds of this type are illustrated in Whittock's book, one splendid example showing a classical landscape with architectural fragments. Another illustration shows a 'blind properly strained on a framework resembling a quilting frame'. Whittock states that such work was well within the abilities of the house painter who, when he has 'succeeded in painting landscapes in distemper on walls or in water colour on paper, will find he has acquired the power of painting transparent blinds'.[41]

The abundant use of metalwork and textiles for interiors before the industrialization of Britain was evidence of wealth. The use of billowing drapery in seventeenth- and eighteenth-century portraits may thus be seen as more than a device used by painters to assist their compositions but as early examples of 'conspicuous consumption'. For these reasons, as Fowler and Cornforth have pointed out, the upholsterer as the main specialist in one of the most expensive household commodities generally became the principal contractor in the furnishing of a grand house: he was the interior decorator. In small houses no such specialist would be summoned or required for curtains were used there either sparingly or not at all. The use of textiles even in grand houses was limited until as late as the Restoration.

It was probably the frugal use of textiles that made window blinds so widely popular — a simple width of cloth with nothing lost in folds. The draw curtain was used sparingly in the seventeenth century and before as it was inclined to use cloth lavishly. 'Festoon' curtains where drawstrings pull the curtain up vertically, and 'drapery' curtains where the drawstrings pull the curtain up diagonally and apart into a pair of swags were economical in the use of material [99a, b]. This meant that although they were sumptuous in appearance and relatively complicated to make, householders could afford to fit them to more windows. This speculation is confirmed by Loudon who describes a

99a, b. 'Drapery' (left) and 'festoon' (right) curtains produced a rich effect with a most frugal use of cloth. The dotted lines indicate the points along which the cords would travel through rings between the curtain and its lining

type of Venetian curtain consisting of 'a piece of dimity, or other material . . . [nailed] to a flat piece of wood, in one end of which are inserted two pulleys; while two others are let into it, one in the middle and the other at the opposite extremity. Three pieces of tape are sewed down the curtain, one on each side, and one in the middle, to which are affixed small rings, at regular intervals.'[42] Cords passing through these rings and up and over the pulleys raised the curtains when pulled. Once the mechanization of the textile industry was accomplished textiles could be used more lavishly and the draw curtain became general in the mid-nineteenth century as the 'French curtain'. In general the smaller, simpler and earlier the house the fewer textiles would have been used.

Notes to Chapter 5

1. Henry Laver, 'Ancient Types of Huts at Athelney', *Somerset Archaeological and Natural History Society*, vol. LV, 1909, pp. 175–80.
2. The informant was speaking in Irish. Lucas, p. 16 (see page 89, note 1).
3. Richard Carew, *The Survey of Cornwall*, London, 1602, also 1769 edition. See also Addy, pp. 146, 147, 151.
4. Salzman, p. 93.
5. Ibid. Today masons use the word 'mould' in reference to their zinc templates.
6. Ibid., p. 174.
7. Lucas, p. 22 (see page 89, note 1).
8. Salzman, p. 256.
9. H. Chandlee Forman, *Old Buildings, Gardens and Furniture in Tidewater, Maryland*, Cambridge, Maryland, 1967, p. 21.
10. Bax, p. 153.
11. Harrison, II, p. 236.
12. p. 160.
13. Peate, *The Welsh House*, 1946 edition, p. 185.
14. Salzman, p. 173.
15. Quoted by Salzman, p. 173.
16. Platt, pp. 76–7 (see page 62, note 80).
17. Lucas, p. 17 (see page 89, note 1).

18. Addy, p. 64.
19. Peate, *The Welsh House*, p. 186.
20. Salzman, p. 185.
21. Quoted by Addy, p. 132.
22. *Encyclopaedia Britannica*, 11th edition, 1910–11, see 'pane'.
23. Department of Manuscripts, no. 37.339.
24. Platt, pp. 38–9 (see page 62, note 80), which concerns tracing drawings through glass.
25. Quoted by Innocent, p. 261.
26. John Woodforde, *Georgian Houses for All*, Routledge and Kegan Paul, London, 1978, p. 113.
27. Morris (ed.), *The Journeys of Celia Fiennes*, p. 74.
28. J. H. Peel, *An Englishman's Home*, Cassell, London, 1972, p. 151.
29. Morris (ed.), *The Journeys of Celia Fiennes*, p. 339.
30. Woodforde, *Georgian Houses for All*, p. 113.
31. Blair Gift, Metropolitan Museum of Art, New York, 45.144.
32. Barley, *The English Farmhouse and Cottage*, pp. 263–4.
33. *Chambers's Encyclopaedia*, 1862, see 'glass'.
34. Loudon, p. 154.
35. Barley, *The English Farmhouse and Cottage*, pp. 267–8.
36. Bax, p. 143.
37. Ibid.
38. By the nineteenth century Loudon (p. 342) alludes to 'short inside wire blinds, [which] are not unsuitable for the better description of cottages'.
39. Heal, *The London Furniture Makers*, p. 15 (see page 61, n. 48).
40. The 1853 watercolour drawings of Renishaw Hall, Derbyshire, by Mrs Campbell Swinton show venetian blinds in use in the Oak Parlour and transparent blinds painted in imitation of stained glass. Both water-colours are reproduced in John Cornforth's *English Interiors 1790–1848*, Barrie and Jenkins, London, 1978, pl. 71, pl. 73.
41. Nathaniel Whittock, *The Decorative Painters' and Glaziers' Guide*, London, 1827, ch. V, p. 188. Another source of information is the unpublished thesis by William J. Jedlick, 'Landscape Window Shades of the nineteenth century in New York State and New England', New York State Historical Society, Cooperstown. The Abby Aldrich Rockefeller Folk Art Collection at Williamsburg, Virginia, holds a photostat copy of this thesis.
42. Loudon, p. 341.

6 · Floors

Beaten earth floors are so basic as to be timeless and universal. In some parts of Britain they have been found in houses within living memory and doubtless are still in use. They were the rule rather than the exception in much of Ireland, Wales and Scotland until this century, despite the use of tiled floors at a high social level in thirteenth-century England.[1]

The farmer Henry Best of Elmswell in the East Riding of Yorkshire, writing in the second quarter of the seventeenth century, gives instructions on making such floors.[2] The earth was first dug and raked and then mixed with prodigious quantities of water, the resulting mixture being as soft as mortar. After about two weeks the mixture was sufficiently 'leather hard' to be beaten smooth with broad, flat pieces of wood, and blemishes were mended with clay or 'clottes from the faugh field'. Local knowledge played its part in the selection of the type of clay and Best remarks that 'wee use to digge and leade clay for our barne from John Bonwickes hill'. In Armagh, Ulster, the floor was sometimes simply dug up and trampled down again and according to J. Binns in *The Miseries and Beauties of Ireland* (1837), 'They sometimes have a dance for that purpose.'[3] The experience of the Weald and Downland Museum in Sussex has shown that such floors would have to be remade fairly regularly. In an attempt to prevent them breaking up, bones were either mixed with the mud or driven into the floor to form a pattern, as is described by Dean Aldrich (a contemporary of Wren) in his *Elements of Architecture*.[4] An example of this type of floor used as external paving in Broad Street, Oxford, consisted of 'trotter bones laid in a pattern of squares arranged angle-wise within a border. The pattern was defined by bones about 2 in. square, rubbed or sawn to an even surface, and filled in with small bones of sheep's legs, the knuckles uppermost, closely packed and driven into the ground to a depth of from 3 in. to 4 in.'[5] This interesting pavement was destroyed in 1869 but I have seen similar floors in eighteenth-century grottoes. So long as this type of floor remained undamaged it had a long life but (as with parquet) the removal of one bone resulted in the successive and rapid collapse of its neighbours. In these floors the mud was not so much the floor as the matrix which held the floor together. True mud floors generated much unwelcome dust. The rushes that were laid over the floor also produced much pollen and dust which the regular use of earthenware watering 'cans' served to mitigate [100]. The use of rushes on floors remained traditional in Caernarvonshire where, within living memory, 'rushes and fern would be strewn on the floor'.[6] In 'Norwegian farmhouses where so many of our ancient customs still [1862]

100. Earthenware water pot used in the garden and to lay the dust of rush-covered floors

exist'[7] juniper twigs were spread on the floor. Sir Hugh Platt's *The Jewel House of Art and Nature* was published in 1594 and in it he recommends that floors should be made of a composition of fine clay tempered with ox blood.[8] Such a composition would also serve for rendering an internal wall and, so Platt claimed, produced a smooth, glistening and hard surface. In some parts of Caernarvonshire earth floors were washed with water containing soot which produced a hard, shiny surface.[9]

Erasmus, in his well-known description of houses in England, was obsessed with the filth that he found underfoot in English houses: 'Again almost all the floors are of clay and rushes from the marshes so carelessly renewed that the foundation sometimes remains for twenty years, harbouring there below spittle and vomit and urine of dogs and men, beer that hath been cast forth and remnants of fishes and other filth unmentionable. Hence, with the changes of weather, a vapour exhales which in my judgement is far from wholesome for the human body.'[10] Not for nothing was the area below the dais in larger houses sometimes known as the 'marsh'.[11] In fact, the interesting conglomerate of matter which such floors absorbed was of great importance to the 'saltpetre man'. In the search for nitre much inconvenience and friction was caused by this official whose officers pulled up the floors of cottages and even churches looking for this important ingredient in the manufacture of gunpowder.[12]

The so-called 'grip floor' (composed of a mixture of lime and ash) was a great improvement on mud or clay. Thomas Rudge describes this in a cottage in Gloucestershire in 1807. A moist mixture of lime and ash was laid to a depth of between 4 and 5 in (10 and 12.7 cm) and worked and rammed with a heavy slab of wood; and to this, Isaac Ware recommends the addition of 'smith's dust'.[13] William Marshall describes similar floors in his *Rural Economy of Yorkshire*, published in 1787. In Derbyshire such 'plastered' floors were laid in upper rooms on laths and further south on straw. 'In Leicestershire and other districts, where good lime is to be had, many of the old floors were formed altogether of plaster. In place of floor boards laid on the layer of reeds 2 ins.

101. (*right*) The living-room of the Lismacloskey House from TOOME BRIDGE, CO. ANTRIM, ULSTER, late eighteenth century. This two-storey farmhouse is typical of the 'planters' houses', as are the 'English' tiles on the floor which are alternate grey-blue and buff. The hanging cup-hooks and the folding table are typical of Ulster. *In house re-erected at Ulster Folk and Transport Museum*

or 3 ins. well-tempered plaster is spread and thoroughly floated over and brought to a smooth surface. This gets almost as hard as cement concrete, and the under surface of the reeds is plastered to form the ceiling.'[14] A good example of a plaster floor in an upper room is to be found in the attic of the fifteenth-century George Inn at Norton St. Philip, Somerset. Isaac Ware suggests that at least some floors of this type were for 'elegant houses' and that by adding other ingredients to plaster of Paris they 'may be coloured to any hue . . . some of it looking like porphiry'.[15]

It could be supposed that the use of tiles for flooring was most widespread in the eastern counties where, thanks to influence from the Low Countries, bricks first made their reappearance in post-Roman Britain (discounting the re-use of Roman bricks in such structures as St. Alban's Cathedral). However, in Norwich beaten clay floors remained usual in domestic buildings throughout the sixteenth century when clay 'pamments', fired to a yellow or orange colour and measuring 12 by 12 in (30.5 cm) or 9 by 9 in (22.9 cm) and between $1\frac{1}{2}$ and 2 in (3.8 and 5 cm) thick, became usual.[16] Very similar tiles were used in Ulster in the nineteenth century, but examples in Northern Ireland had a series of parallel holes drilled through their thickness which served to insulate the floor from the cold ground in winter. An example of a floor with these 'English' tiles may be seen in the 1717 Lismacloskey House from Co. Antrim now at the Ulster Folk and Transport Museum [101].

The use of the word 'pamment' in East Anglia for clay tiles is paralleled by the word 'pennant' (a blue, stone paving slab used in the Bristol area and South Wales) and is presumably related to the now universal 'flag' stone.

In the eighteenth century and onwards paving bricks for both internal and external use became general in those districts that did not have access to suitable, which is to say hard-wearing, stone. The colour of these bricks was conditioned by the nature of the available clay but red was the most common. In and around Norwich they were of an orange or yellow hue and measured about 8 by 4 in (20 by 10 cm) and about $1\frac{1}{2}$ to 2 in (3.8 to 5 cm) thick. Such bricks lacked a 'frog'.

The use of stone for flooring seems to have been less widespread than its use in the construction of houses. Undoubtedly the reason for this must be that much of the stone of these islands is soft freestone which, once masoned, is case-hardened by the silica or 'quarry sap' which comes to the surface to form a protective skin. In flooring this skin would soon be worn through and the extra expense of the pavier's work could not be justified unless the resulting floor was long lasting. Bath stone has been used for flooring often with disastrous undulating results. However, in some instances such floors have lasted reasonably well, a tribute to the local knowledge of the hard 'beds'. Today insufficient quantities of stone are quarried (in the skilled meaning of the word) for selection to be possible or the knowledge acquired.

Roach bed Portland stone was used, the abundant fossils providing a hard-wearing aggregate through the stone, and floors in the larger houses with which we are concerned were sometimes composed of slabs measuring about 18 in (45.7 cm) square set diamond-wise in the floor. Their corners were cut leaving a space for small squares of Tournai marble (also known as Belgian Black) or even slate. The hall floor at Chippenham Park, Cambridgeshire, was of this type and described by Celia Fiennes as 'paved with freestone a squaire of black marble at each corner of the freestone'.[17] Whilst in Cornwall in 1698 she made the following notes in her journal: 'Bastaple [Barnstaple] and the north sea [sea to the north of Cornwall] which conveys the stone or rather marble [in fact slate] which they take from hence a Bole [Delabole Quarries] . . . remarkable Quarrys for a black stone exceeding hard and glossy like marble very dureable for pavements; this they send to all parts in tyme of peace and London takes off much of it.'[18]

In Sussex a hard white stone was often used in the eighteenth century for floors and occasionally the Sussex 'winkle stone' may be found. This material resembles Purbeck marble (in fact a hard limestone which will bear a friction polish and was made popular in the late twelfth century for internal architectural use by William of Sens).[19]

In her journals Celia Fiennes gives particular credit to those towns which are well paved. In Dorchester, Dorset, for example, 'the streets are very neatly pitch'd and of good breadth'.[20] Such paving was composed of wedge-shaped pieces of stone rammed edgewise into the ground by means of a beetle. The stone was in fact 'pitched', which is to say it was 'pitched off' a block of stone with a 'pitcher' and a 'pitching hammer'. Paving of

102. 'Pitched' stone floor in a house at PENRHYIW, TREFEGLWYS, POWYS. *Photograph: Welsh Folk Museum*

this kind was used inside houses, and examples have been recorded in Wales (Powys [102] and Dyfed),[21] and in England (Lancashire, Cheshire, Derbyshire, Northampton-shire, Herefordshire, Hampshire and the Isle of Wight, Wiltshire, Somerset and Devon).[22] Pitched stone paving was often arranged in patterns and sometimes incorporated white pebbles with the initials of the pavier.[23]

The great problem with stone floors was that they were not only hard underfoot but they were also cold and often damp. Modern damp-proof membranes (polythene sheeting) can be laid under paving to solve this problem. Some materials, such as slate and granite, are themselves supreme damp-proofing materials by comparison with which most contemporary products are mere substitutes. A traditional slate floor is a dry floor except for condensation and at the joints. Transport was always a problem, especially with heavy materials unless they were 'water-borne', but in slate-producing districts the size of flooring slabs could be truly gigantic, as at the Penparcau Tollhouse (now at St. Fagans) where a number of the slates are about 5 ft (1.5 m) square [103].

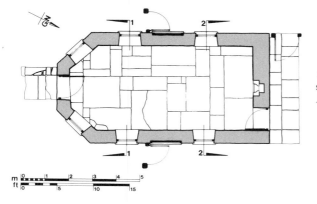

103. Plan of the PENPARCAU Tollhouse showing the scale of the slate paving. *Re-erected at Welsh Folk Museum*

In most humble houses mud long remained in use for floors, except for the hearthstone and the threshold. Stone was reserved for these two features which retained a semi-mystical significance and survived the brutalizing impact of repetitive rows of back-to-back houses in the industrial heart of England where, against all the odds, housewives continued to whiten or redden their doorsteps every day. For this purpose street traders provided the lump whitening or the yellow material known as 'Flanders brick'[24] which was often bartered in exchange for empty bottles.

> As through the streets I takes my way
> With my bag at my back so gay,
> Crying out 'hearthstones' all day,
> 'Hearthstones!' and 'Flanders brick!'
> A penny a lump, a penny a lump!
> Who'll buy, buy-y-y-y-!?[25]

The tradition of decorating doorsteps and hearthstones with designs of a calligraphic character is known in Scotland where it is recorded in Strathclyde, Lothian, Dumfries and Galloway, Central Region, Fife and Grampian [105].[26] This type of decoration was also applied to floors in the north of England, and in Yorkshire milk was used to darken the stone floors on which curlicues were drawn around the border of the room 'with a piece of light coloured sandstone after each week's cleaning'.[27] The designs being fugitive it was customary for them to be renewed every Saturday in anticipation of 'Sunday best'. In Wales, white clay was dug in the Holyhead district and in Llyn, and sold in dry balls for the decoration of floors and hearthstones. The patterns were mainly confined to the perimeter of the room and particular emphasis accorded to the dresser and long-case clock.[28] In his seminal book *The Evolution of the English House*, first published in 1898, Sidney Addy gives a good description of such work in Derbyshire where ' "pot moul" and "rubbing stones" are used for the decoration of floors. Some women make spots on the hearth. This is done by dipping a piece of rag into a basin of "pot moul", or pipe-clay, moistened with water. Either the whole or part of the stone floor is covered by squares drawn by means of a sharpened piece of pipe clay used like a crayon, and sometimes a small flower is drawn in the middle of each square.'[29]

Sand was another material that is sometimes referred to as having been swept into patterns, but information on this is rather vague, and there is even doubt as to whether sand or sandstone was used. In Lancashire, stone doorsteps, both tread and riser, were dampened, 'and to the damp surface . . . [was] applied dry sand or sandstone'.[30] According to some accounts the red, yellow or white sand was strewn around the perimeter of kitchen floors and passages in patterns which were very similar to those employed for floors, doorsteps and hearthstones.[31] In scullerys the wash tub was often surrounded by such decoration as evidence that the week's washing was finished and the 'copper' would not be used for another week—an embellishment as a mark of triumph.

104. Farmstead interior from OSTENFELD, SCHLESWIG-HOLSTEIN, showing the approach to the 'house part' across the threshing floor or threshold. *Re-erected at Frilandsmuseet, Copenhagen*

105. Scottish designs for decorating doorsteps. *Drawing after Mrs Lyons by James Ayres*

Addy describes the use of sand in this way in Derbyshire as follows: 'The threshold is usually sanded, and a serpentine line or letter S made in the sand. This decoration is done by a brush, and women rarely omit it. They are very particular about keeping patterns clean from one Saturday to another, on which day they are renewed.'[32] In regions far from the sea this sand became an article of trade commemorated in the old 'round' song:

> White sand and grey sand!
> Who'll buy my white sand?
> Who'll buy my grey sand?

Certainly in the north of England (and in America) it was customary for the floor of farmhouse kitchens and the public bar of public houses to be strewn with sand just as in the south of England such places favoured sawdust. The last such floor known to the author was in an eel and pie shop in Greenwich in the late 1950s. Today many butchers continue to spread sawdust on their floors to absorb blood from the carcases, and damp sawdust has of course long been used to suppress rising dust when sweeping floors.

The decoration of floors with sand or whitening was exceedingly temporary and paint was often used on timber floors with more permanent results. It is known that in grand houses floors were decorated in this way and examples survive at Belton House, Lincolnshire, Crowcombe Court, Somerset,[33] and The Lindens, Washington DC (removed from Danvers, Massachusetts, in the 1930s by the late Judge and Mrs George Morris). Louisa Goldsmid's water-colour drawing (circa 1818) of the White Room at Aubrey House, London, shows a floor painted or stained with a series of pale octagons arranged at intervals (not touching) on a darker ground. Each octagon occupies three, 6 in (15.2 cm) boards [106].[34] In settings of grandeur such floors may have been

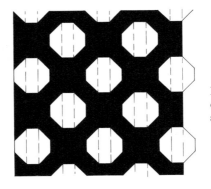

106. Stained wood floor after Louisa Goldsmith's 1818 drawing of the White Room at Aubrey House, LONDON

conceived as fleeting pleasures as were those decorated with whitening in humble households. Such a possibility is indicated by Wordsworth's lines:

> These all wear out of me, like Forms with chalk
> Painted on rich men's floors for one feast-night.[35]

Despite the widespread use of painted and decorated floor boards in small domestic interiors in America I have not succeeded in locating surviving examples in small houses in this country. However, I have found early nineteenth-century floors painted with one colour. Loudon refers to this as follows: 'When a parlour carpet does not cover the whole of the floor, there are various ways of disposing of the margin between it and the wall. Some recommend oil-cloth, others baize, drugget, coarse broadcloth, or brown linen; for our part, we greatly prefer to any of these, painting that part of the boards of the floor which is not covered with the carpet, of the same colour as the woodwork of the room.'[36] Sometimes the whole of the floor was painted and in one early nineteenth-century example (at Tollhouse, Freshford, Bath) the floors of the upper rooms were painted with a yellow ochre glazed over with a red ochre. Time and wear gave these floors a beautiful variation in colour. In America, yellow or red ochre were the colours favoured by the Shakers for their painted floors. It is tempting to see in these colours the influence of the earth floors treated with ox blood.

Ground-floor rooms were boarded in quite early times and there is even evidence for the use of split-timber floors in the Iron Age lake villages of Glastonbury.[37] Such early examples however scarcely established a trend. A writ of Henry III orders a room on the ground floor of Windsor Castle to be 'boarded like a ship',[38] which implies the exceptional use of this feature. Even Richard Carew's *The Survey of Cornwall* of 1602 states categorically that the houses of the 'Yeomanrie of Cornwall' had 'no planchings [plankings]'.[39]

In general the central hearth made the space above it unusable for anything but storage. With the introduction of the chimney flue it became useful to floor-in the attic for human occupation. As has been seen, plaster floors were sometimes used for upper rooms; doubtless they were cheaper. In the *General View of the Agriculture of Ayr* of 1811 'the generality of farmhouses' in the late eighteenth century had attic floors of brushwood covered with divots of moss or grass.[40] Floor boards of timber were clearly more suitable for upper rooms, but oak or elm were expensive and for this reason they were often not fixed, neither were they regarded as 'fixtures', as is confirmed by surviving wills. Testators like Gilbert Isaac of Rayleigh, Essex, found it necessary to state that he regarded various items as fixtures that are today accepted as such: '. . . all the glass in the windows of my house, the windows, doors, locks, bolts, benches, shelves, all the boards and planks in the garrets and upper chambers and floors beneath, nailed and unnailed, the gates and pales of my yard and iron work, as they now stand, to remain to the house' (1597).[41] By 1677, when Joseph Moxon published his *Mechanick Exercises*, it was usual for boards to be nailed 'an Inch or an Inch and a half within the edge of the Board'.[42] In contrast to modern practice, he recommends that alternate boards should first be fixed and the intervening boards pushed into position by two or three men jumping on them assisted by 'Forcing Pins and Wedges'. The oak boards to which Moxon implicitly refers were used in substantial widths and thicknesses, 12 by 1 in (30.5 by 2.5 cm) being usual though in Norwich boards measuring as much as 16 in (40.6 cm) wide have been encountered.[43] Hand-sawn boards often differed in width and thickness, a problem for carpenters on which Moxon gives advice: 'If the second Board prove thicker than the first, then with the adz (as aforesaid) they hew away the under side of that Board (most commonly cross the Grain, lest with the Grain the edge of the Adz should slip too deep into the Board) in every part of it that shall bare upon a Joyst, and so sink it to a flat superficies to comply with the first Board. If the Board be too thin, they underlay that Board upon every Joyst, with a Chip.'[44]

The use of parquet floors was confined to grand establishments, but Celia Fiennes describes 'Mr Ruths' (Rooth's) house in New Inn Lane, Epsom, a substantial home befitting Lady Donegal's husband. This house was seen by Miss Fiennes between 1701 and 1703 and she states that instead of parquet 'the half paces [landings] are strip'd, the wood put with the graine, the next slip against the graine, which makes it looke pretty as if inlaid'.[45] This device was a cheap way of achieving a rich effect in hardwood and may well have been employed in smaller houses.

Because of the natural strengths and weaknesses of timber it was at first usual and is now general for floor boards to be arranged so that they run at right angles to the joists that support them. This is true even where the use of a dragon beam in a house jettied on two adjacent faces, results in the joists meeting the dragon beam at an acute angle; in such instances the floor boards above meet in a mitre. However, what was usual and logical was not at first universal and some sixteenth-century examples of floor boards placed on the same axis as their supporting joists are known. In such examples the boards have generally and inevitably split down the middle. A stronger and therefore probably earlier example of this type, once in Dove Hill Houses, Endcliffe, Sheffield (now destroyed), is recorded where alternate boards were sufficiently stout to be themselves the joists [107].[46] Floor boards were often lapped and also tongued and grooved. From the eighteenth century onwards softwood floors became more common, but oak was

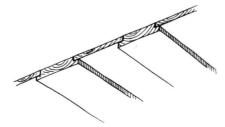

107. Floor made from alternate thick and thin boards. The thick boards effectively doubled as joists. *Drawing: James Ayres, after Innocent*

always preferred with elm (oddly) as a less good alternative to softwood. Henry Best refers to the purchase of 'firre-deales' in Hull as early as 1641. He states that they were 'brought from Norway' and recommends 'reade-deale which is allmost as durable as oake, and will not worme-eate so soon as white deale; besides they are handsomer and better, both for smell and colour; and (for the most parte) better flowred'. The word 'deal', now used as a vague term for second-rate softwood, once referred to the dimensions of softwood planks which Best defines as 'full twelve foote longe, full twelve ynches in breadth, somewhat more than ynch thicke'.[47] By the middle of the nineteenth century deal floor-boards were commonly about 1 in (2.5 cm) thick and from 7 to 9 in (17.8 to 22.9 cm) wide, 'but for better floors a width of only 3 inches to 5 inches [7.6 to 12.7 cm] is used. The advantage of the narrow boards is that the shrinkage and warping have not so much effect on the spaces between.'[48]

To some extent it was possible by the late eighteenth century to gauge not only the importance of a house but also the status of individual rooms according to their type of flooring. In 1787 John March, carpenter of Stoney Middleton, Derbyshire, submitted an estimate for demolishing and rebuilding the parsonage at Godington. The parlour was to have an oak floor, the bedrooms white deal and the garrets elm, whilst the dairy was to be floored with stone or brick.[49]

In France, where parquet floors achieved astonishing elaboration, all wood floors in large houses were polished in the eighteenth century by a specialist servant known as a *frotteur*.[50] Caroline Halsted writing in 1837 states that 'even in the present day in France . . . parquets . . . [are] kept constantly rubbed with wax, by men who have brushes affixed to their shoes for the purpose'. She also mentions 'highly-polished oak, as is still visible in many an ancient picture gallery, and in staircases, libraries, and best apartments of old manor houses'.[51]

Eighteenth-century genre paintings by artists such as Arthur Devis show that the inhabitants of even quite grand interiors were content with bare floor boards. In mediaeval and Tudor England carpets imported from the east as well as from Brussels were reserved for use as 'table carpets'. There are a few exceptions to this rule as in Isaac Oliver's portrait of Richard Sackville, third Earl of Dorset (1589–1624), in which a rich oriental carpet is shown ostentatiously on the floor.[52] However, even at this social level it is carefully placed upon a woven straw mat and indeed such mats were the more usual way of furnishing floors at this date [108]. Matthew Paris graphically describes the indignation of mediaeval Londoners at the sight of the youthful Archbishop Elect of Toledo and his entourage. 'They remarked that the manners [of the Spanish] were utterly at variance with English customs and habits; that while the walls of their lodgings in the Temple were hung with silk and tapestry, and the very floors covered with costly carpets, their retinue was vulgar and disorderly; that they had few horses and many mules.'[53] This 'extraordinary' custom of placing carpets on floors was noted when Eleanor of Castille arrived at Westminster where she found her apartments adorned

108. The parlour of Kennixton Farmhouse from LLANGENNYDD on the Gower Peninsula, c. 1630. The mat on the floor is modern but of a type once common before the introduction of carpets. The tridarn on the right is dated 1702. *In house re-erected at Welsh Folk Museum*

(through the care of the ambassador) with rich hangings 'like a church and carpeted after the Spanish fashion'.[54]

Inventories, wills and sale catalogues re-affirm what the eighteenth-century pictures suggest—floor coverings were rare. When the contents of the Earl of Orford's house in Chelsea were auctioned in April 1747 not one carpet was included, but there were a number of references to mats which may well have been of a type described by Carew in *The Survey of Cornwall* of 1602: 'The women and children in the West of *Cornwall*, doe use to make Mats of a small and fine kinde of bents there growing, which for their warme and well wearing, are carried by sea to *London* and other parts of the Realme, and serve to cover floores and wals. These bents grow in sandy fields, and are knit froom over the head in narrow bredths after a strange fashion.'[55]

Floor cloths or oil cloths like mats probably had a wide social distribution before the introduction of linoleum in 1860. In Britain the earliest reference to floor cloths so far discovered is the 1736 inventory of Denham Hall which includes a 'large floor cloth'.[56] Of the seventy-five American inventories of 1758 cited by Rodris Roth only three mention floor coverings of any kind and by 1777 the proportion had increased to only nine out of seventy-five, of which four included floor cloths.[57] When William Burnet (Governor first of New York and New Jersey and later of Massachusetts) died in 1729 he left 'two old chequered canvases to lay under a table' and 'a large painted canvas square as the room'.[58] Since many of the floor cloths in use in the colonies were imported from the mother country it is likely that such floor coverings were in use in Britain at a date prior to 1729. By 1739 John Carwithen had published his *Floor-Decorations of Various Kinds . . . Adapted to the Ornamenting of Halls, Rooms, Summer-houses &c . . . .* In some editions of this work, which was published in London, the author, who was an engraver by trade, explains that the designs are suitable 'wither in Pavements of Stone, or Marble, or wth. Painted Floor Cloths'.[59] Another source was Batty Langley's *The Builder's and Workman's Treasury of Designs* of 1750. The plates, mostly bearing the date 1739, are of 'Decorations for Pavements &c . . . Irregular Octogons & Geometrical Squares . . . Trapezoids [and] Parallopipedons and Cubes Erect'. Carwithen illustrates twenty-four designs in his book showing each on plan and in perspective demonstrating its effect *in situ* in a room. All his designs are geometric in character with the strong tonal contrasts found in marble floors of the period.

The utilitarian nature of floor cloths would make the survival of early examples unlikely although the sample books of Nairns (now at Kirkcaldy Museum, Fife) go back to the 1840s.[60] A potential source of eighteenth-century examples has been discovered by Coventry City Art Gallery and Museum [109].[61] Recent conservation work on a number

109. Floor cloth printed in yellow, blue, green, white and black. This well-preserved example is on the back of the funerary hatchment for Sir John Eardley Eardley-Wilmot, painted by David Gee in 1847 and now in St. John the Baptist's Church, BERKSWELL, WEST MIDLANDS. *Photograph: Coventry Museum and Art Gallery*

110. (*above*) Floor cloth, oil on canvas, probably late eighteenth century. *Henry Francis du Pont Museum, Delaware, USA*

111. (*right*) The trade-label of Alexander Wetherstone, 1763, 'at ye Painted Floor Cloth & Brush'. *Ambrose Heal Collection, British Museum, Department of Prints and Drawings*

of funerary hatchments or escutcheons in churches in the Midlands has shown them to be painted on the back of floor cloths. The earliest of these was a design which consisted of a series 'of discs of brown and cream in simple diagonal patterns' found on the back of the 1833 hatchment for Francis Gregory in St. James's Church, Styvechale, Coventry. Two further, but later, examples (one of which I illustrate) have been found on the back of hatchments, and no doubt others will be found. The eighteenth-century association between the painting of hatchments and floor cloths is known through the trade-label of B. Philpott of Great Carter Lane near St. Paul's, London. The label which dates from the third quarter of the eighteenth century states that Philpott painted 'Escutcheons, Trophies & all Requisites for Funerals . . . Coach, House, Sign & Floor Cloth Painting at the Lowest Rates'. The Henry Francis du Pont Museum in America possesses what is probably the earliest floor cloth to have come to light so far [110]. It is composed of dark and light lozenges which though now dark brown and yellow may once have been black and white. A very similar design occurs on the trade-label of Alexander Wetherstone (c. 1760) 'at ye Painted Floor Cloth & Brush in Portugal Street', London [111]. In this example the design is centred by a 'compass rose' in which the initials of the cardinal points are omitted. As houses in the eighteenth century were often planned on the north/south or east/west axis, with the rooms inevitably following this plan, it is likely that floor cloths with such a feature were aligned with the compass when in use. Undoubtedly the nautical connection with oil cloth was long established. John Smith mentions oil cloth in 1676, not for use on floors but for water-proof clothing.[62] 'An Experiment relating to Oyl Colours of great use to Travellers of Some kinds: To the chief Officers of Camps and Armies, to Seamen and such like.' Smith's book went through a number of editions in the eighteenth century and in 1821 was re-issued with additions by W. Butcher who simply states that oil cloth is 'now used for umbrellas, hat-cases, and many other uses' without specific reference to floor or table covers. Whilst geometric designs were favoured it is clear from contemporary descriptions that plain colours were also common. The use of plain colours was probably inspired by John Smith's description of how to make water-proof cloth for clothing—the probable origin of floor cloths. The following is taken from Butcher's edition of 1821: 'Take drying or burnt linseed oil, set it on the fire, and dissolve in it some good rosin or gum-lac. . . . you may either work it by itself, or add to it some colour; as verdigris for green, or umber for a hair colour, white-lead and lamp-black for gray or indigo and white for light blue.'[63] Floral patterns were employed in addition to geometric designs, and many illustrations that appear on trade-cards show floor cloths with the favourite design of lozenges surrounded by a 'fluid' border. A characteristic range is listed on a mid-eighteenth-century label: 'At Biggerstaff's & Walsh's, Floor-Cloth Warehouse Behind the three Wheatsheaves at Islington, Are Made and Sold all Sorts of Painted Floor Cloths, Such as Plain, Ornamented, Check, Matt and Carpet Patterns, Entirely New. The Cloth Prepared so as not to Crack or Peel. Old Cloths new Painted and Repair'd [112].'[64]

Cracking and peeling was something of a problem when floor cloths were exported and it was recommended that they should be dispatched when the paint was thoroughly dry with 'some slight woolen Rolled up with the floor Cloths to Prevent their Rubbing so as to be Defaced by Getting the Paint off'.[65] The importance of this was recognized by Messrs. Crompton and Spinnages (in about 1769) whose warehouse was at Cockspur Street but who also 'Painted Floor Cloths of all Sorts and Sizes, Painted in Summer at their Manufactory at Knightsbridge dry and fit for immediate use'.[66] A number of floor-cloth manufacturers were located in this part of London and it is possible that Crompton and Spinnages simply 'bought in' their stock.

Floor cloths are known to have been fitted to rooms in the eighteenth century and to have been placed under dining tables to facilitate cleaning. They were tough enough to be mopped over with water.[67] In Britain their use was probably less exclusively élitist in the eighteenth century, but early in the next century Loudon, whilst conceding that floor cloths are among 'the kinds of carpets most suitable for cottages', gives some cautionary advice concerning their use: '*Painted Floorcloths* may sometimes be used in the lobbies

112. The mid-eighteenth-century trade-label of Biggerstaff's and Walsh's showing the various activities involved in house decoration. Note the floor cloths and craftsman on the right using a muller to grind pigment. *Ambrose Heal Collection, British Museum, Department of Prints and Drawings*

and passages of cottages; but they are not economical articles, where there is much going out and coming in of persons generally employed in the open air, and of course wearing strong shoes, probably with nails in the soles. When they are used in cottages, the most appropriate patterns are imitations of some materials usually employed for floors, such as tessellated pavement, different-coloured stones, wainscot, &c.; but, for the better description of dwellings, where oilcloths are considered chiefly as ornamental coverings, there seems to be no reason why their patterns should not be as various as those of carpets.'[68]

Charles Eastlake in his *Hints on Household Taste* quotes a ridiculous example of a floor cloth 'intended to represent the spots on a leopard's skin'.[69] He strongly believed that 'a floor-cloth, like every other article of manufacture . . . should seem to be what it really is, and not affect the appearance of a richer material. There are endless varieties of geometrical diaper which could be used for floor-cloth without resorting to the foolish expedient of copying the knots and veins of wood and marble.' He stresses that the design should not 'attempt to indicate relief or raised ornament in the pattern.'

Along with the more widespread use of carpets in wealthier houses in the opening years of the nineteenth century, floor cloths remained in use. An advertisement in the *Salisbury and Winchester Journal* of Monday 1 January 1827 lists items to be sold at auction, including 'Brussels and Turkey carpets, bed round and stair-case ditto, hearth rugs, painted floor cloth'. By Loudon's day, floor cloths had moved downwards in social importance and were only found in the utilitarian areas of grand houses, and as a result manufacturers found that their business was mainly confined to 'Exportation, & Country Dealers', or the making of 'Prepared Cloths for Verandah's &c.'[70] Nevertheless, the deck of Queen Victoria's royal yacht was covered with oil cloth painted to simulate planking.[71]

These floor coverings were variously described as floor cloths, oil cloths, painted canvas, canvas and various combinations of the above. They were made or at least sold according to eighteenth- and early nineteenth-century trade-cards by a variety of shops, most important of which were: those who did ornamental painting; oil and colourmen; turners and strangely enough, Leghorn hat sellers. An example of the latter was 'James Cox at ye Hat & Star near St. Martins Lee Grand in Newgate Street, London', whose card for 'The Hats & Floor Cloth Warehouse' dates from the third quarter of the eighteenth century.[72] He is listed in the London directories for 1760 and 1762 at Blow-bladder Street, as the east end of Newgate Street was then known. It is possible that the sale of straw hats and floor cloths may have originated in the sale of straw mats [113]. Certainly Cox was no exception, as Gatfield and Co., listed in the directories in 1777 and 1784, also made and sold 'Painted Floor Cloths, Leghorn and Straw-hats'.[73] Others included Thomas Iliffe and 'John Shepherd at the Straw Hat and Floor Cloth Warehouse opposite St. Clement's Church in the Strand, London' (c. 1751). By the early nineteenth century many floor cloths were sold by those who specialized in 'Awnings and

The HATT and FLOOR-CLOTH WARE-HOUSE by Thomas Iliffe at ye Hatt, & Bonnett, opposite the Hospital Gate, in Newgate Street. LONDON. As Sold all sorts of Leghorne, Bermuda and English Straw-Hatts, and Bands, with Bermuda, Straw and Chip platts, Likewise all sorts and sizes of the best painted Floor Cloths, and fine Matts for Rooms, with Turnery and Tunbridge Wares, at Reasonable Rates.

113. The trade-label of Thomas Iliffe, mid-eighteenth century. Floor cloths or oil cloths were often sold by leghorn-hat merchants. This card illustrates the two principal types of oil-cloth design, the chequered and the painted carpet. *Ambrose Heal Collection, British Museum, Department of Prints and Drawings*

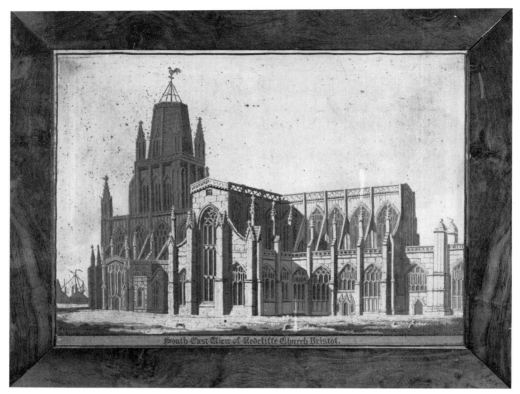

114. *South East View of Redcliffe Church, Bristol,* a picture printed in oil on canvas by Hare's of Bristol, 28 × 20.5 in (71.1 × 52.1 cm) (sight), mid-nineteenth century. Hare's no doubt realized that if they could print patterns on floor cloths they could print editions of oil pictures to hang on the wall. At least three 'pulls' from this woodblock are known. *Ian McCallum Collection*

Portable Rooms', such as Hare and Co. of Newington Causeway, and John Samuel Hayward of the same address.[74] There may be a connection between Hare of Newington Causeway and Messrs. John Hare and Co. of Bristol, the manufacturers who exhibited at the International Exhibition of 1862 a remarkable copy in floor cloth of a Roman mosaic from Cirencester.[75] The Bristol company employed the technique of printing in oil on canvas to produce 'prints' of *The South East View of Redcliffe Church, Bristol.* Unlike some floor cloths these pictures had paint applied on only one side of the coarse canvas [114]. The earliest reference to Hare of Bristol occurs in a Bristol directory of 1787. He is also mentioned in *The National Commercial Directory* for Gloucestershire in 1830 (published by Pigot and Co.). It is the only company listed under 'Floor Cloth Manufacturers' and the address is given as Temple Gate, Bristol.[76] The Heal Collection includes a number of receipts which mention floor cloths, among them one to Mr John Wallis from James Cox, dated 1753, which refers to '16 yds of Check painted floor cloth . . . a pole and packing Mat . . . a pair of Window Blinds' for a total of £1 15s 0d.[77]

Another receipt, dated 1818, records that Frederick Booth of Spring Gardens paid H. Buckley £2 17s 6d for 'floor cloth No. 129'.[78]

By consulting the hundreds of labels in the British Museum I have drawn up a list, which I include, of at least some of the shops, warehouses and manufacturers who were active in London in the second half of the eighteenth and the first quarter of the nineteenth century. Allowing for the fact that many publicly stated that they were involved in 'exportation'[79] or supplying 'country dealers' it is clear that in London at least such floor covering was widely used.

The great problem for the manufacture of floor cloths was that the basic fabric should be seamless because any ridge would produce uneven wear. The introduction of John Kay's fly shuttle, patented in 1733, made it possible for canvas to be woven in reasonable widths. In the early nineteenth century the floor-cloth manufacturers Buckley and Son congratulated themselves on making 'Canvas 7 yds wide without a Seam'.[80] By the middle of the century these problems had been overcome. *Chambers's Encyclopaedia* of 1862 speaks of the canvas basis which was manufactured in Dundee (also well known for its sailcloths) where it was woven from 18 to 24 ft (5.5 to 7.3 m) in width, and in lengths of from 100 to 113 yds (91.4 to 103.3 m). The canvas was stretched on frames some of which measured 100 by 24 ft (30.5 by 7.3 m). The back was primed with size and pumiced to keep it smooth. The object of this was to prevent the paint penetrating the canvas and making it brittle. The paint itself was mixed with linseed oil, with little or no turpentine, making it thicker than ordinary oil paint. It was first applied with a brush and then smoothed with a steel trowel and allowed to dry for twelve to fourteen days, after which a second coat was added completing the back. The process was repeated for the front but the first coat of paint was smoothed with pumice and the final coat of paint carefully applied with a brush. This was the surface upon which the pattern was printed by means of wood blocks cut in pear tree backed by two layers of deal [115], the three layers

115. Woodblock for printing floor cloths, 10 × 9.5 in (25.4 × 24.1 cm), late eighteenth century (?). *Kirkcaldy Museum and Art Gallery*

having the axis of their grain opposed for strength (as in plywood). Stencils were also used to paint decorations onto floor cloths.[81] The best quality floor cloths were allowed to dry for several months in a drying-room and to be really durable it was important that a floor cloth should remain with the manufacturer for three or four years.

'Narrow floor-cloth, 18 ins, 24 ins and 36 ins [45.7, 60.9 and 91.4 cm] wide, for stair-carpeting, passages &c.' was made in the same way but was cut in strips before being decorated. The designs usually had 'a large pattern in the middle and a border of a smaller design'.[82] The basic commodity in the manufacture of floor cloths was canvas, and it is probably for this reason that in the second half of the nineteenth century the two great centres for their manufacture were ports where sailcloth was important. As we have seen, Bristol where John Hare was in business was one of these centres but the other was Kirkcaldy, Fife, where the still-prospering firm of Michael Nairn and Co. was established in 1847 [116]. As 'American cloths', oil cloths to cover kitchen tables

116. Mid-nineteenth-century floor cloth from Nairn's sample book. This sample is printed in green on a yellow ground. *Kirkcaldy Museum and Art Gallery*

remained in use until recent years, but their use on floors rapidly declined in the late nineteenth century as a result of industrialized methods of producing linoleum (their direct successor), ceramic tiles and carpets. 'The laying of lobbies and passages with encaustic tiles has lately led to the superseding of floor cloth in such situations, while . . . [for the] covering of floors in churches, reading-rooms, and waiting-rooms at railway-stations it is superseded by the newly invented material called kamptulicon, or vulcanised India-rubber cloth. . . . This new material is made plain or figured to resemble painted floor-cloth.'[83] Kamptulicon was patented in 1844 by E. Galloway[84] and linoleum, as we would now call it, was patented in 1860 and 1863 by F. Walton. It is very similar in composition to floor cloth except that the oxidized linseed oil is mixed with ground cork as well as pigment. A related material was Lincrusta-Walton which was embossed and used as wallpaper.

As has been seen, floor covering of any kind was rare in the eighteenth century. The alternatives after floor cloths were 'list' carpeting, 'hair' cloths and straw mats. In the 1760s Alexander Wetherstone sold at his shop near Lincoln's Inn 'floor Cloths, Hair Cloths, List Carpets, Royal and other Matting'.

English-made straw, rush and grass matting was supplemented in the late seventeenth century, probably through the Dutch East India Company (the source of split cane for chair seats and backs), with grass mats from the Far East. Their popularity was greatest, however, in those countries which suffer temperatures of greater extremes than are found in Britain. Some rather grand households in England are known to have changed their floor coverings for winter and summer but it does not appear to have become a general practice here as it did in France.[85] In America, from Baltimore south, the arrival of summer is marked by replacing curtains of silk or wool with linen or cotton, and wool carpets are displaced in favour of grass mats. It is known that this household custom dates back in America to the eighteenth century but it was not usual even there at that time. Jacques Pierre Brissot de Warville wrote of his *Travels in The United States* in 1788 that, 'A carpet in summer is an absurdity; yet they spread them in this season [summer], and from vanity: this vanity excuses itself by saying that the carpet is an ornament; that is to say, they sacrifice reason and utility to show.'[86] Caroline Halsted's *Investigations or Travels in the Boudoir* of 1837 takes the form of an educational dialogue between mother and daughter and describes 'The floor covering in your papa's study . . . composed of split portions of rattan, or cane, manufactured into a fine matting by the inhabitants of Sunda and other islands east of China.'[87]

'List' carpets were probably the great alternative to the ubiquitous floor cloth in the eighteenth century, one reason being that they were cheap and they could be made at home [G]. In architecture a 'list' is a synonym for a 'fillet', a flat, narrow band or ribbon running along the axis of a moulding.[88] List carpets were constructed of a warp of woollen yarn into which a weft of strips of rag tied together was woven. This strongly textured and indeed rather knobbly carpeting of humble appearance was probably once found in all walks of life before industrialized methods of production brought the cost of textiles down to a level which would increase their use. By the nineteenth century, list carpets were generally replaced by the so-called 'Venetian' carpets but hair carpets remained in use from the mid-eighteenth century almost to the present day. Hard-wearing hair carpets were, as their name implies, made of a shiny hair or fibre. Although dangerously slippery they were used on stairs as well as in passages as runners. Stair carpets were something of a luxury well into the nineteenth century. Archdeacon Julius Hare (1795–1855) in *The Story of My Life* describes the rectory at Stoke-on-Tern in which 'the stair carpet was taken up unless there were visitors and the drawing-room furniture draped in wrappings'.[89] According to Thomas Sheraton in his *Cabinet Dictionary*, 'Venetian' carpets derive their name from their place of manufacture and were 'generally striped', the pattern being all in the warp. 'Dutch' carpet was a coarser and cheaper version which sometimes contained cow hair.

Perhaps the most decorative of all these simple floor coverings were the 'Kidderminster' [E] and the 'Scotch ingrain'. These carpets, such as the Kendal carpet illustrated in Colour Plate H, did not have a pile but being 'ingrain' retained their patterns even when worn. The introduction of looms with Jacquard attachments in the early nineteenth century resulted in quite elaborate designs. Sheraton's *Cabinet Dictionary* (1803) describes 'Scots carpet . . . [as] one of the most inferior kind'. In Caroline Halsted's book *Investigations or Travels in the Boudoir* (1837) a very clear pecking order is given to the different types of floor covering available at that time: 'The carpets usually styled Kidderminster, are an improvement on the Scotch, which are the cheapest and commonest kinds manufactured . . . being within reach of persons of limited incomes, and . . . used also for sleeping-rooms, and offices in larger establishments.'[90] *Travels in the Boudoir* provides much useful detailed information on Kidderminster carpets, in which 'each distinct part of the pattern is hollow like a bag' whereas the Scotch carpet is 'not separate in this way'.[91] '[Pile] carpets, such as we are now accustomed to see were only uncommonly used in England in the early part of the last [eighteenth] century; as we read of a Mr Moore having received a premium from the Society of Arts in 1757 for establishing a manufacture in London in imitation of those of Turkey and Persia.'[92]

'Brussels carpets' were made at Wilton in Wiltshire as early as about 1740, and 'Wilton' carpets were made there by 1754. In Devon, Axminster carpets began production in the 1750s. Despite the splendour of these carpets their width remained restricted to about 3 ft (91.4 cm) which meant that large carpets had to be made up of strips sewn together. Motifs could be organized so that the designs could be 'dropped', thus camouflaging the joins. By 1755 Thomas Whitty of Axminster succeeded in weaving a carpet 36 by 21 ft (11 by 6.4 m). The Royal Society of Arts thought it worthwhile to institute premiums for the best pile carpets measuring not less than 15 by 12 ft (4.5 by 3.6 m). Not unnaturally Whitty won the prize in both years that it was awarded but had to share it in 1757 with Thomas Moore of Moorfields, and in 1758 with Claude Passavant of Exeter. For the most part, however, at this date English-made pile carpets were too grand for the vernacular interiors with which we are concerned.

By 1837, when Loudon published his *Encyclopaedia of Cottage, Farm and Villa Architecture*, carpets were more general. Even so, 'for neither the parlour nor the bedroom would we recommend the carpet to be fitted to the room' in cottages. Instead, Loudon suggests for the parlour a 'square of carpet [which] may be changed eight times so as to be worn equally in every part of both sides. For a cottage's bed-room, we would chiefly recommend one piece of carpeting placed by the dressing-table, and pieces neatly fitted to each other to go round the foot and sides of the bed. Stair carpets give an air of great comfort and finish to a house; and a cottage should never be without one.'⁹³ In the previous century the use of strips of carpet round three sides of a bed was quite usual in more pretentious surroundings. In 1752 Mrs Delany mentions, in one of her illuminating letters, that her 'candlelight work, is finishing a carpet in double-cross-stitch, on very coarse canvas to round . . . [her] bed'.⁹⁴ As carpet became more available such mitring round of carpet strips tended to be confined to smaller houses and the edges of a room where the carpet border was fitted. Sheraton's *Cabinet Dictionary* (1803) states that 'to most of the best kind of carpets there are suitable borders in narrow widths'. He describes the method of laying such carpets, starting at the most conspicuous part of the room—the focal point occasioned by the fireplace hearth.

Loudon makes it clear that home-made carpets and rugs were the answer for many houses and describes how to make '*Paper Carpets*' which were made by 'cutting out and sewing together pieces of linen, cotton, Scotch gauze, canvas, or any similar material &c.', sizing it as necessary 'and carefully pasting it round the margins so as to keep it strained tight. . . . When the cloth thus fixed is dry, lay on it two or more coats of strong paper, breaking joint, and finish with coloured or hanging paper, according to fancy.'⁹⁵ These appear to have been a type of home-made oil cloth. Clearly a great deal of work was put into making various floor coverings but unfortunately few if any paper carpets survive. Among the *Substitutes for Carpets* mentioned in the *Encyclopaedia of Cottage, Farm and Villa Architecture* are green baize and drugget, but Loudon also describes a 'kind of patchwork' carpet, surviving examples of which I have been unable to locate. 'Remnants of cloth bought from the woollen-draper, or taylor, and cut into any kind of geometrical shapes, may be sewn together, so as to form circles, stars, or any other regular figures that may be desired; and, when arranged with taste, produce a very handsome and durable carpet at a very trifling expense.'⁹⁶ Caroline Halsted's book, which is roughly contemporary with Loudon's, refers to the home-made carpets of the eighteenth century: '. . . the coverings of ordinary apartments were merely square pieces of painted canvas, or woollen stuffs, baize, and coarse cloth; the latter ornamented with curious devices figured in the middle, or bouquets of flowers in the corners.'⁹⁷

Just as the carpet was first presumed to be a textile covering for a table, so the rug (derived from the Swedish *rugg*, rough hair) was assumed to be a bed cover rather than as now a small textile floor-covering. Despite the fact that bed rugs are known to have been used in seventeenth- and eighteenth-century England, no examples have come to light, although a number have been found in America. Hooked rugs employ a different technique from bed rugs [117]. They are popular in the north of England and may be of

117. Hooked rug, early twentieth century. *Museum of Lakeland Life*

Norse origin.[98] Most date from the late nineteenth century or later and are made of strips of rag looped through a coarse canvas backing. In parts of Scotland they are known as 'clootie' rugs and in the north of England as 'hookies and proddies', a clear reference to the process by which they are made. 'Stobbies' or 'stobbie rugs' were made in Cumberland 'with the ends sticking out'.[99] In the richer south of England 'Berlin' woolwork rugs were usual by the mid-nineteenth century, but Flora Thompson, recalling her childhood in the 1880s, mentions 'a superannuated potato-sack thrown down by way of a hearthrug . . . [or] brightly coloured hand-made rugs on the floor'.[100]

Whilst it must be accepted that carpets offer much comfort their excessive use in many old houses today may be out of character.

Ambrose Heal Collection—Floor-Cloth Makers

The following is a list of those manufacturers and retailers whose labels list floor cloths for sale. It is drawn from the Heal Collection in the British Museum and from Ambrose Heal's *The London Furniture Makers*.[101] I am indebted to Mrs Bernard Croft-Murray's notes on this collection in the British Museum.

Mid-18th century	Barnes and Sons, City Road, Moorfields
Mid-18th century	Biggerstaff's and Walsh's, Islington
1818	H. Buckley, 161 Strand and 'Manufactory' near Westminster Bridge
Circa 1810	Bulmer, 284 Strand
Mid-19th century	Carter and Company, 2 Cheapside near Paternoster Row
1790–1803	Thomas Cloake
1760–62	James Cox, near St. Martins Lee Grand in Newgate Street
1768	Gerard Crawley
Circa 1769	Crompton and Spinnages, Cockspur Street, Charing Cross
Early 19th century	Downing and Company, Knightsbridge and King's Road
1777–84	Gatfield and Co., St. Margaret's Hill, Southwark
Circa 1810	Hare and Co., 37 Newington Causeway
Circa 1810	John Samuel Hayward, 37 Newington Causeway, Southwark and 12 Leadenhall Street
Circa 1800	Matthew Heath, 18 Seething Lane, Tower Street
Mid-18th century	Thomas Iliffe, opposite the Hospital Gate, Newgate Street
Early 19th century	Morley's Original Floor-Cloth Manufactories, Knightsbridge and Kings Road
Mid-18th century	B. Philpott, Wardrobe Court, Great Carter Lane, near St. Paul's
Mid-18th century	James Platt, Newgate Street (succeeded by James Cox)
Circa 1760	Pope and McLellan's
Late 18th century	Joshua Russell, 10 Blackman Street, Southwark
Circa 1751	John Shepherd, opposite St. Clements Church, The Strand
1844	Smith and Barber, opposite the Horse Barracks, Knightsbridge
Early 19th century	William South
Early 19th century	Southgate and Mitchell, London Road, St. George's Fields; Warehouse No. 44, Newgate Street
Circa 1760	John Speer
Circa 1750	Francis Thompson
Mid-18th century	Thomas Tillinghurst, Swithin's Lane, near Cannon Street
Early 19th century	Walton's, 6 Newgate Street
Early 19th century	Thomas Weaver, 118 Long Acre (removed from Holborn)
Mid-18th century	Joseph Weston, Old Bethlehem, Bishops-gate
1763	Alexander Wetherstone, Portugal Street, Lincoln's Inn Fields
Mid-18th century	John White, Shoe Lane, Fleet Street

Notes to Chapter 6

1. Salzman, p. 146.
2. Henry Best, *Rural Economy in Yorkshire 1641*, Surtees Society edition, Durham, 1857, p. 107, 'For Makinge and Mendinge of Earthen Floores'.
3. J. Binns, *The Miseries and Beauties of Ireland*, 1837, pp. 1, 112.
4. Henry Aldrich (1647–1710), *Elementa Architecturæ*.
5. *Building News*, 3 September 1869, quoted by Innocent, p. 160.
6. Peate, *The Welsh House*, p. 173.
7. *Chambers's Encyclopaedia*, 1862, see 'carpets'.
8. Platt, p. 76 (see page 62, note 80).
9. Peate, *The Welsh House*, p. 172.
10. Translation quoted by Bax, p. 47. For the Latin original with the revolting details in full see Lloyd, p. 80.
11. T. Hudson Turner, *Some Account of Domestic Architecture*, London, 1877, 2nd edition, p. 93.
12. Innocent, p. 158.
13. Ware, p. 123.
14. Innocent, p. 161, quoting T. W. Troup writing mainly about Norfolk.
15. Ware, p. 123.
16. I am indebted to Mr James Chapman of Norwich City Architects Department for this information.
17. Morris (ed.), *The Journeys of Celia Fiennes*, p. 153.
18. Ibid., p. 268.
19. Further information on English limestones which are capable of being polished so as to appear like 'marble' may be found in 'The Use of Purbeck Marble in Mediaeval England', an unpublished thesis by James Ayres for the Institute of Education, London University, 1961.
20. Morris (ed.), *The Journeys of Celia Fiennes*, p. 12, written c. 1685.
21. Peate, *The Welsh House*, p. 174.
22. Joseph Wright, *The English Dialect Dictionary*, 1903, vol. IV, p. 527, see 'pitch'.
23. Peate, *The Welsh House*, p. 174.
24. This may be a folk memory distorting the historical use in Britain of imported flooring tiles. Henry Yevele is known to have used at Westminster Palace '8000 tiles of Flanders for paving floors'. See Salzman, p. 145.
25. Quoted by Dorothy Hartley, *Made in England* (1939), reprinted by Eyre Methuen, London, 1977, p. 136.
26. See *Scottish Home and Country*, the magazine of the Scottish Women's Rural Institutes, vol. XI, no. 3, March 1935.
27. Marie Hartley and Joan Ingilby, *Life and Tradition in the Yorkshire Dales*, Dent, London, 1968, p. 4.
28. Peate, *The Welsh House*, p. 172.
29. Addy, pp. 134–5.
30. S. R. Jones, *The Village Homes of England*, Studio, London, 1912, p. 114.
31. Hartley, *Made in England*, pp. 136–8 (see note 25, above).
32. Addy, p. 135.
33. I am indebted to Mrs George Morris of Washington DC for drawing my attention to these examples, both of which have since been illustrated by Fowler and Cornforth. The Crowcombe Court floor also occurs in Christopher Hussey's, *English Country Houses, Early Georgian 1715–1760*, Country Life, London, 1955.
34. Cornforth, pl. 110.
35. William Wordsworth, *Personal Talk*, London, 1888, quoted by Lloyd.
36. Loudon, 1842 edition, p. 344.
37. Addy, p. 26.

38. Turner, p. 92.
39. Richard Carew, *The Survey of Cornwall*, London, 1602, 1769 edition, pp. 66–7.
40. William Aiton, of Strathaven, *General View of the Agriculture of Ayr*, 1811, pp. 114–15.
41. Quoted by Emmison, p. 9.
42. Moxon, p. 155.
43. Information kindly supplied by Mr James Chapman of Norwich City Architects Department.
44. Moxon, p. 155.
45. Morris (ed.), *The Journeys of Celia Fiennes*, p. 345.
46. Innocent, p. 163 and fig. 52.
47. Best, p. 125 (see note 2, above).
48. *Chambers's Encyclopaedia*, 1862, see 'floors'.
49. Bax, p. 122.
50. Rodris Roth, *Floor Coverings in 18th Century America*, Smithsonian Press, Washington DC, 1967, p. 19, quotes Mrs John Adams writing from Paris in 1784, 'then a man-servant with foot brushes drives round your room dancing here and there like a Merry Andrew. This is calculated to take from your foot every atom of dirt, and leave the room in a few moments as he found it.'
51. Caroline Halsted, *Investigations or Travels in the Boudoir*, London, 1837, p. 17.
52. See S. W. Wolsey and R. W. P. Luff, *Furniture in England, The Age of the Joiner*, Arthur Barker, London, 1968.
53. Turner, p. 98.
54. Ibid.
55. Carew, pp. 18–19 (see note 39, above).
56. Fowler and Cornforth, pp. 216–17.
57. Roth, *Floor Coverings in 18th Century America*.
58. R. T. H. Halsey and Charles O. Cornelius, *A Handbook of the American Wing*, The Metropolitan Museum of Art, New York, 1924.
59. Quoted by Roth, p. 17.
60. I am indebted to Sir Robert Spencer Nairn of Nairn Floors International Ltd and to Miss Andrea Kerr of Kirkcaldy Museum and Art Gallery for this information.
61. I am indebted to Mr Anthony Davis and Mr Ronald Clarke of Coventry City Art Gallery and Museum for this information.
62. John Smith, *The Art of Painting in Oyl*, London, 1676, 1705 edition, p. 77.
63. Butcher's edition of *The Art of Painting in Oyl*, London, 1821, p. 22.
64. Photograph in the Fieldon Collection within the Ambrose Heal Collection at the British Museum, 30.2.
65. Letter from Charles Carroll of Annapolis, Maryland, 24 February 1767, to William Anderson, a London merchant, quoted by Roth, p. 12.
66. Ambrose Heal Collection, British Museum, 91.24.
67. Roth, p. 12.
68. Loudon, 1842 edition, p. 346.
69. Charles L. Eastlake, *Hints on Household Taste*, London, 1872, 3rd edition (revised), pp. 51–2.
70. Ambrose Heal Collection, British Museum, 30.24, the trade-card of Southgate and Mitchell.
71. Virginia Surtees, *Charlotte Canning*, John Murray, London, 1975.
72. Ambrose Heal Collection, British Museum, 30.30.
73. Ibid.
74. Ibid., 30.11, 30.12.
75. Illustrated in *The Art-Journal Catalogue*, p. 42.
76. The Hare factory is described in Rolinda Sharples's account of her visit in December 1816, a transcript of the manuscript being held by Bristol City Museum and Art Gallery.

77. Ambrose Heal Collection, British Museum, 72.103.
78. Ibid., 30.4. In 1804 Mr Booth at the same address, 19 New Spring Gardens, purchased floor cloth from Downing & Co. Receipt, Ambrose Heal Collection, British Museum, 30.9.
79. Wayne and Ruger of Charlestown advertised in 1768 that they sold 'Floor Cloths, painted as neat as any from London'. Roth, pp. 12–13.
80. Ambrose Heal Collection, British Museum, 30.4.
81. Little, *American Decorative Wall Painting*, p. 76.
82. *Chambers's Encyclopaedia*, London, 1862.
83. Ibid.
84. *Encyclopaedia Britannica*, 11th edition, 1910–11, see 'floorcloth'.
85. Fowler and Cornforth, p. 216.
86. These *Travels* were published in London in 1794 and are quoted by Roth, p. 29.
87. Halsted, pp. 18–19.
88. *Chambers's Encyclopaedia*, London, 1862, see 'list' and 'fillet'.
89. See Bax, p. 155, quoting Julius Hare's *The Story of My Life*, vol. I, p. 137.
90. Halsted, p. 9.
91. Ibid., pp. 10–11.
92. Ibid., p. 12.
93. Loudon, p. 344.
94. Lady Llanover (ed.), *The Autobiography and Correspondence of Mary Granville, Mrs Delany*, London, 1861, vol. III, p. 176.
95. Loudon, p. 345.
96. Ibid.
97. Halsted, p. 16.
98. M. E. B., *Hookies and Proddies*, information sheet published by Abbot Hall Art Gallery and Museum, Kendal.
99. Ibid.
100. Flora Thompson, *Lark Rise to Candleford*, Oxford University Press, 1939, Penguin edition, 1973, p. 19.
101. See page 61, note 48.

118. (*right*) Bedroom in Kennixton Farmhouse (c. 1620) from LLANGENNYDD on the Gower Peninsula, Wales. The straw mat resting on the purlins and supporting the thatch made secondary rafters unnecessary. The wood plinth on which the right-hand bed is placed is created by the charnel or recess in the ceiling (for hanging herbs and hams) in the room below. *In house re-erected at Welsh Folk Museum*

7 · Ceilings

Today the word ceiling is used to denote the overhead lining of a room with plaster, but in the past this was termed 'under drawing'. Mediaeval and Tudor documents generally use the word 'ceilings' to describe the wood panelling on internal walls.[1]

In simple, single-storey houses open to the roof the thatch covering was visible from within. This in most houses was considered perfectly adequate, but on occasion an attempt was made at greater finish. This 'finish' was always most easily accomplished first, before the thatch was made. One quite simple method adopted in parts of Wales was to lay a series of straw mats over the rafters which formed a base for the thatch and a lining to the roof-space [118]. Heavy-duty mats laid on the purlins from ridge to eaves had the further advantage of making rafters unnecessary. A still earlier method involved

the use of hazel sticks in place of the mats—in either case such provision did much to prevent stray straws or reeds falling into the house. In those parts of Scotland where turf roofs were usual a trickle of earth or even mud could be an annoyance and it became customary to line such roofs with divots of moss or grass laid on the rafters.

In nineteenth-century Ulster the inside of the roof of the bed outshot was lined with layers of newspapers pasted together and tacked in position across the underside of the rafters and whitewashed. This is probably a corruption of the use of mats of marram grass in the same position. Some years ago a rare example of such matting was found in a farmhouse at Shantallow, near Londonderry [119].[2] Despite the vestigial traces of the long-house in its overall planning it is of sufficiently high quality to suggest that it had been built for a 'planter', which would account for its resemblance to houses in the 'Highland Zone' of England.[3] The grass ceiling- and wall-mats probably owed their survival to being left *in situ* in a sealed loft, the occupants of the house being unaware of its existence. The loft was approached by massive stone stairs concealed behind double doors which had been papered over in about 1900.

Perhaps related to the grass-mat ceiling is the straw roof-lining found in Stradbally, Co. Waterford in 1962 [120].[4] On the other hand, the Co. Waterford example (now destroyed) may be so unique as to be related to nothing else. The lining was found only in the bedroom (measuring 13 by $15\frac{1}{2}$ ft (3.9 by 4.7 m)) of the single-storey thatch-roofed house. The straw of the lining was attached to boarding on the two sloping sides of the roof, the narrow portion of horizontal ceiling near the apex of the roof, and the gable area on the partition between bedroom and kitchen/living-room. The lining was divided into bands about 15 in (38 cm) wide and each band was made up of a single layer of wheat straw held in place by laths ($\frac{3}{4}$ in (1.9 cm) wide by $\frac{1}{4}$ in (.64 cm) thick). The lowest bands were apparently applied first and held with the bottom lath, and the lath of the next row up then held the top of the bottom row and the base of the next row of straws. 'This successive screening of the projecting upper ends of the straws in one zone by the lower ends of those in the zone above it was continued up the slopes of the roof and, presumably, across the ceiling as well.'[5] The ceiling was said to have been made in about 1869 by a man named Hannigan and despite its age 'was in an astonishingly perfect state of preservation. All the straws were as straight and tubular as if they had just been cut from the living plants. . . . They were moreover, incredibly clean and retained their original golden colour.'[6]

The steep-pitched roofs of East Anglia indicate that they were evolved for thatch. Because of the proximity of the Low Countries, pantiles probably replaced thatch in this region at an early date. It is likely that this sequence of events led builders to discover the advantages, in terms of insulation and wind-proofing, of laying the tiles on a layer of straw or reed. Whatever its origins, such lining was customarily used in East Anglia where it was a traditional practice to plaster the reed-lined ceilings of attic rooms.

As we have seen, upper floors could not develop until chimneys were installed and

119. Marram-grass roof-lining to the first-floor bed outshot in a farmhouse in
SHANTALLOW, NEAR LONDONDERRY, ULSTER. From the early nineteenth century such outshots
were more often lined with whitewashed newspapers. *Photograph: Ulster Folk and Transport
Museum*

120. Straw-lined ceiling (now destroyed) in a house in the High Street, STRADBALLY, CO.
WATERFORD, IRELAND. This remarkable ceiling is thought to have been made in the mid-
nineteenth century. *Photograph: Dr A. T. Lucas*

ceilings were in their turn dependent upon floors. It was therefore quite logical that early ceilings consisted simply of the joists that supported the floor above. Most ceilings of this type reduced the span that the joists bridged by means of a 'summer' beam, which was of considerable girth for strength.[7] Related to the summer beam, indeed often supporting one end of it, was the 'breast-summer' or 'bressummer' which was let into the face of a wall.

In Wealden houses that were jettied on two adjacent faces it was necessary that the joists be placed on two different axes at right angles to each other. This was made possible by means of the 'dragon beam' which was set at an angle of forty-five degrees to the joists and which is in effect a type of summer beam [121]. In early houses the joists are notable

121. Dragon beam in Bayleaf Farmhouse, fifteenth century. The dragon beam supporting two sets of joists was a necessary feature in houses with a jettied storey on two adjacent faces. The early date is indicated by the close spacing of the joists, their heaviness and the absence of chamfering or moulding.
In house re-erected at Weald and Downland Museum

for their great size and the close intervals at which they are tenoned into the summer or dragon beam. In some examples this interval can be as little as 1 ft (30.5 cm) between the centres of the timbers. Each tenon on each joist was tallied with a particular mortice in the summer beam by use of Roman numerals which were easily stabbed in with a carpenter's chisel. Some early floors and ceilings were constructed of alternate joists and planks laid on the same axis so that the upper face of the joist was in effect a floor 'board', and the lower face of the board took on the role of a lining to the ceiling. The effect of such ceilings and indeed their construction was similar to 'in and out' plank panelling. An example of such a floor has been recorded in a house, now demolished, at Dove Hill Houses, Sheffield,[8] but similar floors have also been located in Norwich.[9]

In mediaeval buildings, joists are usually found simply squared by means of the adze with no further attempt made to finish them. In Tudor and later buildings it became usual to chamfer these timbers and in important houses the joists were given elaborate

122. Ceiling of 151 Angel Street. HADLEIGH, SUFFOLK. Joists and their supporting summer beams were chamfered or moulded and provided with 'stops' of numerous kinds throughout much of the sixteenth and early years of the seventeenth century.
Photograph: Royal Commission on Historical Monuments

sections. The magnificence of Paycocke's at Coggeshall is underlined by the exceptional quality of these features. The degree of elaboration or simplicity of the joists often provides a clue not only to the likely age of the house, but also to its relative importance and the status of the individual rooms [122]. The mouldings and their 'stops' also provide clues as to the size and shape of the rooms where later partitions have confused the original planning. In timber-frame houses which have had stone or brick fronts added it is sometimes possible to find stops buried in the masonry indicating that the rooms were once larger.

With these methods of construction it was inevitable that the underside of the boards of the floor above should be visible from below. For this reason these boards between the joists were often decorated with painted designs [123, 124]. Where an upper floor was plastered it was the plaster that was visible and this may have given rise to 'underdrawing' wood floors with plaster panels. In Derbyshire, plaster floors were laid upon laths but farther south reeds were commonly used.[10] In Norfolk, 'The floors were solid, and were formed in this way: joists 4 inches by $3\frac{1}{2}$ inches [10.2 by 8.9 cm] were laid flatwise on the main beams and were covered with a layer of reeds about an inch in thickness: on this again were laid wide oak floor boards nailed through to joists through the reeds. This being done, the underside of the reeds was plastered between the joists, giving a good, sound proof floor and yet barely 3 inches [7.6 cm] thick.'[11]

Plaster on reed was very common in Norwich in the eighteenth and nineteenth centuries,[12] but I have also found an example of reeds used as laths attached to the underside of joists for a plastered ceiling in a derelict seventeenth-century house by the west end of Shepton Mallet Church, Somerset.[13] In the town of Stamford which has

123. Ceiling of John Knox's house in EDINBURGH. This painting, on the underside of the floor boards of the room above, probably dates from the late sixteenth or early seventeenth century and would thus post-date Knox. *Photograph by the author*

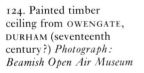

124. Painted timber ceiling from OWENGATE, DURHAM (seventeenth century?) *Photograph: Beamish Open Air Museum*

access to the fenland of East Anglia without being part of it, plaster floors of between 1 and 2 in (2.5 and 5 cm) thick were 'run' on a layer of straw or reeds which were laid directly across the joists. The plaster for this purpose was usually mixed with a little crushed brick so that in 1700 one hundredweight (50.8 kg) of plaster was considered sufficient to make one square yard (.84 square metre) of flooring.[14]

According to William Harrison, writing from Essex in the 1580s, reeds were widely used as a base for plastering, but he draws attention to a hazard that was considered to be attendant upon their use: 'In plastering likewise of our fairest houses over our heads, we use to laie first a laine [layer] or two of white morter tempered with haire, upon laths, which are nailed one by another, (or sometimes upon reed or wickers more dangerous for fire, and made fast here and there with saplaths, for falling downe,) and finallie cover all with the aforesaid plaster, which beside the delectable whiteness of the stuffe it selfe, is laied on so even and smoothlie, as nothing in my judgement can be doone with more exactnesse.'[15]

In East Anglia where wool wealth was combined with close contact with continental Europe through the Low Countries a number of timber-boarded ceilings have been located. In Norwich a wood lining of boards about $\frac{1}{4}$ in (6.3 mm) in thickness was used, running parallel to the joists and lying between them and the floor boards above (whose axis they opposed).[16] In very rare instances the joists were covered by narrow boards running parallel to the summer beam which remained visible. In the example at Lavenham, Suffolk [125], the boards are 'V'-jointed and only about $\frac{3}{8}$ in (1 cm) thick,

125. Boarded ceiling, late fifteenth century, in Garrads House, Water Street, LAVENHAM, SUFFOLK. The boards in this ceiling cover the joists but not the summer beam. The ribs, which have bosses where they intersect, serve to support the lining, each board being a mere $\frac{3}{8}$ in (9.5 mm) thick. *Photograph: Royal Commission on Historical Monuments*

which means that the narrow ribs planted on their face, together with the bosses at the intersections serve a structural function and prevent sagging.[17] Gwilt quotes a fifteenth-century example at Wingham in Kent and adds that this type of ceiling was usually decorated with distemper.[18] The Lavenham ceiling shows traces of such paint in the interstices of the moulded ribs and the carved bosses.

The use of plaster between joists probably gave rise to plastering the joists themselves, a fashion that was at its height in the first half of the seventeenth century. A number of examples of such plaster-clad timbers survive, of which Plate 126, from a house in Hitcham, Suffolk, is typical. A particularly good example was preserved in a ground-floor room in a house at Merchants Barton, Frome, Somerset, until the house was demolished by the town council in the late 1960s.

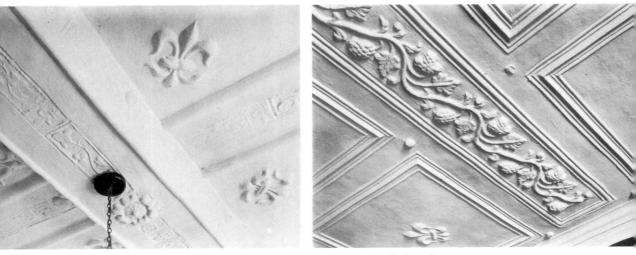

126. (*left*) Plastered timber ceiling in Brickhouse Farmhouse, Hitcham Street, HITCHAM, SUFFOLK, early seventeenth century *Photograph: Royal Commission on Historical Monuments*
127. (*right*) Plaster ceiling in 1 Duke Street, HADLEIGH, SUFFOLK, seventeenth century. *Photograph: Royal Commission on Historical Monuments*

The plaster ceiling obscuring, and indeed attached to, the joists was not general in vernacular houses until the seventeenth century [127]. The double layer created by floor and ceiling provided better sound insulation and on occasion in East Anglia this was improved by filling the cavity with chaff or in the Cotswolds with chopped straw[19]—a technique sometimes used in partitions.[20] Late seventeenth- to early eighteenth-century plaster ceilings on occasion carry rich mouldings dividing the ceiling up into compartments.

Despite the popularity of decorated plaster ceilings in vernacular houses in the seventeenth century they seldom occur in minor domestic buildings of the last three-

128. Plaster ceiling in a cabin in FRESHFORD, CO. KILKENNY, IRELAND. Despite the provincial grandeur of this ceiling, its location and date (late eighteenth century) are surprising to say the least. A Classical Revival ceiling in the other room of this house was doubtless installed at the same time. *Photograph: Lisa van Gruisen*

quarters of the eighteenth century. The extraordinarily elaborate though provincial plasterwork recently discovered in a cabin at Freshford, Co. Kilkenny, must be regarded as an amusing aberration [128].[21] The cottage no doubt provided the lodgings for the craftsmen employed on a neighbouring 'big house'.

The apparent lack of decorated ceilings in lesser houses of the last half of the eighteenth century is the more remarkable in view of the introduction of *carton-pierre*, an oriental substance which reached England via France. A rare instance of its use in a 'lesser' house occurs in J. T. Smith's *Nollekens and his Times*: 'Upon an investigation, in consequence of a report that there was a very fine copy of this work [the painted ceiling at

Whitehall] of Rubens, as a fixture in a house on the south side of Leicester-fields, I found that the curiously ornamented *papier-maché* parlour ceiling of No. 41 had been painted, though very indifferently by some persons who had borrowed groups of figures from several Rubens designs which they had unskilfully combined.'[22] Smith goes on to quote a conversation concerning the manufacture of papier mâché between Twigg, the well-known Covent Garden wit and fruiterer, and Mrs Nollekens.[23] Twigg is alleged to have remarked, 'I recollect the old house when it was a shop inhabited by two old Frenchwomen who came over here to chew for the papier mâché people.'

Because cornices were seen as an integral part of the wall in classical architecture Loudon asserted that without them 'no Room can have a finished Appearance'.[24] The mores of Classicism demanded a cornice but in smaller houses they were often left out on the grounds of cost. Ceiling decoration could be omitted without any sense of betrayal and it was stated that, '*Plaster Ornaments on Ceilings* have not hitherto been much introduced in cottages on account of expense.'[25] There were alternatives to the use of such plasterwork, and Loudon goes on to say that ornaments for ceilings could be obtained which were 'manufactured by Messrs Bielefelds and Haseldon at a very low price, of a description of papier mâché'.

It was not until the second half of the nineteenth century that decorated ceilings began to assume a popularity comparable with that which they had enjoyed in the seventeenth century. Gwilt observed that, '*carton-pierre*, a species of *papier-mâché*, has been re-introduced for cornices, flowers, and other decorations. . . . They have not all the delicacy of plaster cast . . . but their lightness and security with which they can be fixed with screws render them preferable to plaster ornaments.'[26]

The question of weight was always a problem for plaster 'stick and rag work' and it became a saying in the trade that 'if it stays up wet it'll stay up dry'.[27] Fibrous plaster became more popular than papier mâché in the second half of the nineteenth century and Gwilt states that, 'Mr Owen Jones has extensively used this material in his interior decoration.'

Notes to Chapter 7

1. Emmison, pp. 9, 13.
2. Desmond McCourt and E. Estyn Evans, 'A Late 17th Century Farmhouse at Shantallow near Londonderry', *Ulster Folklife*, vol. 14, 1968, pp. 14–23.
3. Barley, *The English Farmhouse and Cottage*, ch. 5, 'The Highland Zone'.
4. A. T. Lucas, 'A Straw Roof Lining at Stradbally, Co. Waterford', *Journal of the Cork Historical and Archaeological Society*, vol. 76, 1971, pp. 81–3.
5. Ibid., p. 83.
6. Ibid.
7. Nicholson, pp. 220, 230. Summer beams were also known as 'somers', 'girders' and 'dormants'. See also Innocent, p. 164.

8. Innocent, p. 163, fig. 52.
9. Information from Mr James Chapman, Norwich City Architects Department.
10. Innocent, p. 160.
11. Ibid., p. 161, quoting F. W. Troup.
12. Information from Mr James Chapman, Norwich City Architects Department.
13. The reeds no doubt came from the nearby Somerset Levels.
14. Royal Commission on Historical Monuments, *Stamford*, HMSO, London, 1977, p. LXIX.
15. Harrison, II, ch. XII, p. 235.
16. Information from Mr James Chapman, Norwich City Architects Department.
17. Herbert Cescinsky and Ernest Gribble, *Early English Furniture and Woodwork*, George Routledge, London, 1922, vol. I, p. 202 and fig. 205.
18. Joseph Gwilt, *Encyclopaedia of Architecture*, revised by Wyatt Papworth, London, 1876, p. 601.
19. E. Guy Dawber and W. Galsworthy Davie, *Cottages and Farmhouses in the Cotswolds*, Batsford, London, 1905, p. 15.
20. Innocent, p. 167.
21. I am indebted to the Hon. Desmond Guinness for drawing my attention to this example of Irish plasterwork.
22. J. T. Smith, *Nollekens and his Times*, London, 1829, 1919 edition, vol. II, p. 102.
23. Ibid., p. 174.
24. Loudon, p. 273, para. 566.
25. Ibid., p. 273, para. 568.
26. Gwilt, p. 679, para. 2251.
27. I am indebted to my father, Arthur Ayres, for this information.

8 · Stairs

In 1595 William and Mary Chapman completed the modernization of Hunt Street Farm, Crundale, Kent. The porch of their house commemorated the event with the inscription 'WC 1595 MC'. The work included the insertion of a fine brick flue and a framed oak staircase to replace the ladder that had previously been used.[1] One of the earliest dated examples of the floored-over hall is Kite House, Monk's Horton, where the alteration is dated 1574, although the fireplace is dated 1578.[2] It should be noted that in the traditional Wealden house the hall was placed centrally with floored-in rooms on either side, a feature reflected by the façade with its pair of jettied storeys. For this reason such houses needed two stairs or ladders, but when the hall was floored over one of these could be dispensed with.

Despite the existence of lofts for storage, access to which could easily be provided by means of a ladder, it was not until the widespread introduction of flues that the upper spaces of the house were sufficiently free of smoke for living purposes and only under such circumstances did the need for stairs become general.

In some of the 'highland zones' such as Devon there was a long tradition dating back to small Norman manor houses for first-floor living-rooms to be approached by exterior stone stairs. Boothby Pagnell in Lincolnshire boasts a fine example of the type. In these early examples the exterior stairs are usually in a straight flight whilst the interior ones are spiralled. Exterior stone stairs leading to a first-floor hall gave the occupants a defensible stronghold, but their survival in the 'highland zone' was merely traditional. It should be added that some external steps to the first floor provided access to rooms which, although part of the main body of the house, could remain separate from it. At Old Farm, Youlgrave, Derbyshire, these rooms were the quarters for the farm servants.[3] Dr Johnson describes old houses in Scotland which were 'very often [approached] by a flight of steps [outside] which reach(es) up to the second storey; the floor which is level with the ground being entered only by stairs descending within the house'.[4] John Knox's house in Edinburgh is of this type.

Because the ladder occupied very little space it long remained popular. Furthermore it could be slanted in several directions providing access to different rooms. A mud-built house which survived at Great Hatfield, East Yorkshire, until the late nineteenth century had a broad 'stee' or ladder to give access to the floored-over half of the house. This 'chamber' in the roof was barely 5 ft (152 cm) in height and was approached via the 'stee' through a hole in the floor which was covered by a trap door known as a 'throp hetch' or 'trap hetch'. The 'chaamer' in this instance was not created until the early nineteenth century and so is a very late example of what was probably an early form which persisted longest in the north of England.[5] A similar example is recorded by S. O. Jones's drawing illustrated in Plate 129.

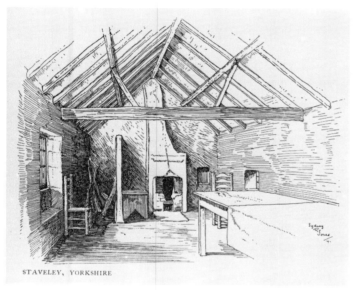

STAVELEY, YORKSHIRE

129a, b. Single-cell house with a sleeping loft (b), at STAVELEY, YORKSHIRE. Two drawings by S. R. Jones dated 1911. From such simple beginnings the first floor developed as did the need for a ladder to gain access to the sleeping loft. Such ladders were eventually replaced by stairs. The loft, not visible in (a), is positioned at the opposite end of the room to the fireplace. *Bath Public Library*

In Northumbria and Cumberland the peel towers used ladders in regions that were particularly exposed to the danger of attack from the Scots but elsewhere newel stairs in straight flights were built into the thickness of the wall.

The use of the ladder long persisted in Wales. Abernodwydd Farmhouse was originally built in the sixteenth century but modernized in the seventeenth century when the wattle and plaster flue was made and two attic rooms created. These two rooms are accessible by one ladder which may be sloped to reach either room [130]. The centrally placed flue probably occupies the site of a cross passage so that on one side of the fireplace a 'baffle' entry has been created whilst the other side of the flue provides space for the ladder. This re-use of the cross passage is found in most parts of England.[6]

The problems of exchanging a ladder for a stair of some type was as much a matter of

130. Bedroom in Abernodwydd Farmhouse, from LLANGADFAN, POWYS, c. sixteenth century (floored-in in the seventeenth century). Note the hazel rods used to support the thatch and the horns of the ladder by means of which the bedrooms were approached. The timber-framed flue has an infilling of wattle and daub which the fire has burnt to a crisp. Note also the wheels on the simple truckle bed. *In house re-erected at Welsh Folk Museum*

space as of cost [131]. The stair, which consisted of nothing more than treads set into 'stringers' and without 'risers' was simple to make but occupied a considerable amount of room. If space permitted, a straight flight constructed out of triangular baulks of timber laid on a pair of raking beams provided an effective and, in the days before carpet, a silent stair.[7] Addy recorded a most remarkable variant of the type at Hawkesworth House, Upper Midhope, near Penistone (dated 1671) [132] which occupied very little space at

131. The evolution of the staircase. The example shown on the right is based on fig. 137 in Loudon's *Encyclopaedia*. A surviving example in stone may be seen at Glastonbury Abbey

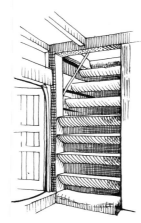

132. Wood staircase, the
first five treads of which
rise vertically. *Drawing:
James Ayres after a
photograph by Addy*

the expense of being awkward to use. He describes it as being made of 'triangular blocks
of oak' with gaps between them like a ladder: 'The first five steps are perpendicular and
the remaining steps incline slightly towards the top.'[8] According to Addy the handrail,
which was round in section, was original and the stairs were 'cased' in a corner of the
buttery backing onto the stud and plank panelling of the hall. The top of the stairs was
protected on one side by a timber-framed wall and on the other by 'an immense ark or
meal chest'. Another type of stair occupying very little space provided two treads (one for
each foot) on one riser—an example of the type in stone survives in the ruins of
Glastonbury Abbey—and Loudon recommends a wooden version of this 'economical
staircase'.[9]

In many parts of the country the chimney and the stairs were both placed in the area
once reserved for the cross passage. However, there was not always room for this
arrangement and either the stairs or the flue had to be located elsewhere. In general the
axial flue was at first favoured being a more efficient use of its heat than one placed on an
outside wall. It therefore became usual to place the stairs in a turret, a feature which was
often added to houses as part of their modernization. In Somerset and Devon the circular
newel stair, at first of solid oak baulks and later of stone, is placed in the back wall in its
own projection of stone or cob.[10] In Lincolnshire the Priory at Haydor has stairs
approached from the hall but housed in a wing rising to the attic. The newel stairs in this
example are of stone which, although remarkably old fashioned for their date (1620–30),
are nevertheless characteristic for such stone regions and will also be found in the
Cotswolds.[11]

In Essex where the simpler houses of the late sixteenth and early seventeenth century
were of two rooms chambered over (creating four rooms in all) the upper floor was
reached by a winding stair alongside the axial stack. At this time the staircase wing in East
Anglia and notably in Essex was always at the rear of houses in which the cross passage

was insufficiently generous to accommodate both a chimney and a staircase.[12] The central flue was easily added to existing structures, but whilst it provided an efficient source of heat it occupied a great deal of space. In a new house fireplaces built into the gables permitted the central staircase to become not only an object of beauty but one that delivered its passengers directly to more rooms than one placed off-centre. It should be added that such a staircase occupied no less and frequently more space than the flue that it had displaced, but with a new building the house could be made larger to compensate, an approach that was cheaper to build than a stair wing. Although the 'piano nobile' was not appropriate to smaller houses, the importance that such Palladian ideas of escaping rising damp gave to the first floor made ostentatious staircases fashionable, and this fashion was necessarily adopted on whatever scale the owner could afford. Furthermore, the central staircase brought with it that other great tenet of Classicism, symmetry. By the 1730s small farmhouses were built with symmetrical façades, a central door flanked by a window on each side with the whole ensemble contained by a pair of chimney stacks.

133. Staircase in Parsonage Farm, BOTTISHAM, CAMBRIDGESHIRE, 1725. The closed 'string' and sturdy balusters (one to a tread) are typical of early eighteenth-century provincial work in which some of the characteristics of the previous century were carried over. The polyhedra which surmount the newel posts are unusual. *Photograph: Royal Commission on Historical Monuments*

Winding or spiral stairs occupy less room than any other type and therefore have a longer history than most. The earliest spiral stairs were probably built of wood [134], the central newel or post of which was sometimes a single log of oak. When they were imitated in stone this feature continued to be employed, each masoned step incorporating a segment of the newel.[13] A remarkable spiral stair which survives in the dovecote of the thirteenth-century Priory at Hinton Charterhouse, Avon, has the lower sections of stone and the upper sections of wood.

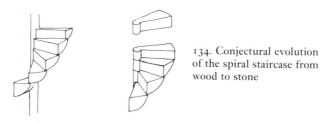

134. Conjectural evolution of the spiral staircase from wood to stone

Both the dog-leg staircase and the staircase rising round three sides of a well occupied about three times more space than the spiral stair.[14] Nevertheless, after about 1625 (by which time staircases were standard in the lowland zone) the framed staircase was usual but it often incorporated some 'winders' to save space [135].

135. Staircase in The Hall, CAXTON, CAMBRIDGESHIRE, seventeenth century. This is a particularly good example showing a newel stair rising around a small square well with finials below being reflected by pendentives above. *Photograph: Royal Commission on Historical Monuments*

In the north the staircase became a standard fixture somewhat later. In a house known as The Gables in the hamlet of Little Carlton near the Trent, two or three miles north of Newark, there is evidence for the use of ladders until the installation of the staircase in about 1700,[15] and as we have seen, ladders were in use in place of stairs in Yorkshire and Wales in the last century.

In the south-east the open newel may have evolved from stairs with a closed well. At Penshurst the stairway leading from the great hall to the solar rises round a walled-in well.[16] In many surviving examples this well is sealed by stud and plaster, as at Cookes House, West Burton, West Sussex (c. 1580), Fulvens House, Abinger Hammer, Surrey (c. 1625) and the sixteenth-century Augustine Steward House, Tombland, Norwich. A similar type of stair at Gaythorne Hall, Ashby, Cumbria, has the well walled-in with stone reminiscent of the Penshurst example.[17] Barley, when discussing an example of this type of stair at Rake House, Whitley, Surrey, argues that it is a 'new type'.[18] However, as it dispenses with the problem of counterbalancing the stairs it may well be the precursor of rather than the successor to the open well, examples of which are more numerous. With both the dog-leg (when not walled off) and the open newel it became necessary to provide some form of balustrading [136]. This was an opportunity that the

136. (*above*) Staircase in 21 Grove Terrace, HIGHGATE, LONDON, late eighteenth century. The narrow 'well', open 'string' and simple balusters of painted softwood with an unpainted mahogany handrail are typical. *Photograph by the author*

turners, a specialist branch of the woodworking trade, could not resist. Occasionally balusters or finials may be found that are square turned. Very often, and especially if they were worked on a raking plane, these were carved by hand and eye but sometimes examples may be found that were truly 'thrown' on a lathe. This was achieved by attaching the scantlings for the individual balusters securely to the outer face of a giant wheel. The wheel was then revolved at speed and one face of the balusters 'turned'. This process was repeated four times thus completing a set of square-turned balusters. Such work may be identified by means of a straight edge as each face of the baluster is slightly bowed.[19]

At the vernacular level, an alternative to the expensive work of the specialist turner [137] was the pierced flat baluster [138] which could easily be made by the joiner. It is

137. (*left*) Staircase, late seventeenth century, in the cob-built Westlakes Farmhouse, OTHERY, SOMERSET. *Photograph: Royal Commission on Historical Monuments*
138. (*right*) Staircase in the Old Rectory, CASTOR, CAMBRIDGESHIRE, oak, late seventeenth century or early eighteenth century. *Photograph: Royal Commission on Historical Monuments*

139. (*left*) Staircase in Collinfield Manor, KENDAL, CUMBRIA. The dog gate may have been moved from lower down the staircase. *Photograph: Royal Commission on Historical Monuments*
140 (*right*) Staircase in the Old Manse, BECKINGTON, SOMERSET, second quarter of the seventeenth century. In this example turned balusters on the lower levels give way to flat balusters (not visible) on the upper floors indicating their relative status. *Photograph by the author*

common to find cut and pierced balusters at the less visible top of the stairs, but the much grander turned variety at the foot of the stairs. Such balusters continued to be made well into the eighteenth and even the nineteenth century. They could more easily be given a raking plane than their more sophisticated three dimensional cousins. At the élite level the substitution of carved and pierced panels for balusters had a brief vogue in the third quarter of the seventeenth century and was followed by a longer lasting and more widespread fashion for balusters turned with the well-known barley-sugar design. In America such turning persisted until the close of the eighteenth century at a time when the grander houses in England had almost unanimously opted for wrought iron.

The introduction of the staircase resulted in the need for dog gates—just as dogs in church resulted in the necessity for altar rails. The well-known dog gate at Hatfield House is one of the most famous of the breed. On a much smaller scale the dog gate at Collinfield Manor, Kendal, Cumbria, is a good example [139]. Generally such gates were

141. (*left*) Staircase in a house at BOTTISHAM, CAMBRIDGESHIRE, second quarter of the nineteenth century. Such stairs are invariably combined with the scroll of the handrail and bottom step known as the 'cur-tail'. The fret-cut brackets are applied to the face of the 'open string'.
Photograph: Royal Commission on Historical Monuments
142. (*right*) Staircase in the Rectory at PAPWORTH ST. AGNES, CAMBRIDGESHIRE, probably 1830. By means of 'winders' a certain grandeur may be contrived within a small space. *Photograph: Royal Commission on Historical Monuments*

fixed at or near the foot of the stairs and the Kendal example may well have been moved to its present position to become a 'child gate'. This possibility is indicated because the balusters of the gate and the landing although of the same design are of different proportions.

Because the turner was a specialist and turning mechanical it is sometimes possible to locate work in different houses which may point to common authorship. Certainly the details of the staircase (second quarter of the seventeenth century) at Hassage Farmhouse, Wellow, Avon, bear a striking resemblance to the stairs of the Old Manse at Beckington, Somerset, ten miles away [140]. Another instance of stylistic relationship is the staircase of 1658 in the farmhouse at Brant Broughton, Lincolnshire, which is 'identical' to the one at Auburn Hall five miles away.[20]. It is possible that by the eighteenth century the staircase builder was becoming the specialist that he undoubtedly became in the nineteenth century; certainly many of the houses in Georgian Bath have almost identical staircases. The staircase immortalized by Beatrix Potter in *The Tale of Samuel Whiskers* at Hill Top Farm, Sawrey, Westmorland, has balustrading and a handrail which, though smaller in scale, are to the same design as the main staircase at Castle Bank, Appleby-in-Westmorland, which is forty-one miles (sixty-six kilometres) away by road, or thirty miles (forty-eight kilometres) by road and ferry across Lake Windermere. These Cumbrian staircases are of late eighteenth-century date but in many ways their wide, flat handrails would place them at least eighty years earlier if found in the south-east.

Despite the possibility that at least some staircases of the eighteenth century may have been built by specialists, the majority continued to be made by joiners. Batty Langley's *Builder's Jewel* (1754) is largely concerned with joinery and carpentry, containing sections on panelling and roofing timbers as well as Chapter V of the Supplement, 'Of Stair-cases'. He gives '11 different designs for stair-cases, from which the ingenious workman may form such others as his occasions may require'. These were 'circular', 'semicircular', 'octangular', 'triangular', 'trapezia', 'geometrical square' and 'eliptical', whilst his 'parallelograms . . . may be fit for any nobleman's palace'. In the century following Langley, Gwilt defined the 'Geometrical Staircase' as one 'whose opening is down its centre, or, as it is called, an open newel, in which each step is supported by one end being fixed in the wall or partition, the other end of every step in the ascent having an auxiliary support from that immediately below it, beginning from the lowest one, which, of course rests on the floor'.[21] Gwilt was here describing the structure of a wood stair but in masonry the problem was even more acute; 'one of the edges of every step [should be] supported by the edge of the step below, and formed with *joggled* joints. . . . The principle upon which stone geometrical stairs are constructed is, that every body must be supported by three points placed out of a straight line [which triangulate].'[22]

All writers on the subject of stairs make the point that the ideal ratio of riser to tread should first be decided and that these should later be adjusted to the circumstances of the house and the distance between the floors. Batty Langley urges that the '*headway* be spacious': 'That the breadth of the ascent be proportional to the whole building. . . . The height of the steps should not be less than five inches [12.7 cm], nor more than seven inches [17.8 cm], except in such cases where necessity obliges a higher rise. The breadth [horizontal depth from front to back of tread] of steps should not be less than ten inches [25.4 cm], nor more than 15 or 16 [38 or 40.6 cm), although some allow 18 inches [45.7 cm], which I think too much. The light to a stair-case should always be liberal.'[23] Batty Langley was of the opinion that a staircase should not be less than 3 ft (91.4 cm) in width but Gwilt felt that for better houses 4 ft (122 cm) was the minimum, whilst conceding that 'want of space in town houses often obliges the architect to submit to less in what is called the *going* of the stair'.

Even in quite small cottages, Loudon considered that stairs ought to open into the entrance porch. In our age of low relative mortality his main reason seems quite grotesque. He points out that if the stairs rise from the entrance lobby 'the bedrooms may be communicated with without passing through the back or front kitchen. This in the case of sickness, is desirable, and also in the case of death, as the remains may be carried down stairs while the family are in the front room.'[24] From the eighteenth century onwards the dog-leg stair has been usual in town houses and smaller houses elsewhere. The handrail is frequently a simple section of mahogany or oak, but the more elaborate 'toad's back' rail [143] was also used.[25] The balusters are often square with two to a tread, but in better houses three is usual. The handrail terminates in a scroll which is reflected by the bottom step, both being united by a cluster of balusters. This bottom step is known as the 'cur-tail' and is especially apt for dog-leg stairs.[26]

143. Section of a 'toad's back' handrail. *Drawing: James Ayres, after Gwilt, vol. I, fig. 875*

Notes to Chapter 8

1. Barley, *The English Farmhouse and Cottage*, p. 63.
2. Ibid., p. 63.
3. Ibid., p. 170.
4. Samuel Johnson, *Journey of the Western Highlands*, 1886 edition, p. 28.
5. Addy, p. 63. A good example of a 'chaamer' from Staveley, Yorkshire, is illustrated and described by S. R. Jones in *The Village Homes of England*, p. 118.
6. For East Anglian examples see Barley, *The English Farmhouse and Cottage*, p. 68.
7. Gwilt, p. 647, 'solid steps were housed into the carriage.'
8. Addy, p. 77.
9. Loudon, p. 79, fig. 137.
10. Barley, *The English Farmhouse and Cottage*, p. 111.
11. Ibid., p. 158.
12. Ibid., p. 73.
13. Innocent, pp. 168–70.
14. Barley, *The English Farmhouse and Cottage*, p. 73.
15. Ibid., p. 84.
16. Lloyd, fig. 819.
17. Barley, p. 114.
18. Ibid., p. 138.
19. I am indebted to Mr Arthur Ayres for this information.
20. Barley, *The English Farmhouse and Cottage*, pp. 219–20.
21. Gwilt, p. 648.
22. Ibid., p. 569.
23. Langley, p. 38. It should be noted that a staircase demands more headroom when descending than when ascending.
24. Loudon, p. 1141.
25. Gwilt, fig. 785.
26. Ibid., fig. 787.

9 · Paint and Painting

The Pigment and the Medium

Painting has been described as 'the art of covering the surfaces of wood, iron and other materials with a mucilaginous substance . . . acquiring hardness by exposure to the air.'[1] In the world of interior decoration nothing is so fugitive as paint and textiles nor so fickle in terms of fashion. Much of the evidence from the past has been either destroyed or obscured and much that has survived has either darkened or faded with age. With such an elusive topic it is perhaps appropriate, whilst avoiding the complexities of chemistry and optics, to look briefly at some of the fundamental facts concerning the painter's craft; and a craft it undoubtedly was before the introduction of plastic paints of recent years.

All paints consist of two basic ingredients, the pigment and the medium. Pigments may be natural or artificial, organic or inorganic. They may not be soluble in the medium, for then they would be dyes such as those used by the stainers or by painters, in glazes where the 'medium' would in effect be a varnish. In general the media used in paint have been drawn, until recently, from animal or vegetable sources. In addition to the pigment and medium, house paints usually include ingredients to help with the drying process as well as a basic 'covering' material to give more 'body' to the paint. Oil paints are made up of three parts: the base (i.e. white lead), the vehicle or medium (linseed oil) and the solvent (turpentine), and to these a 'drier' is sometimes added. With distemper the base is usually whitening, the medium water, and size provides the binding agent; to basic whitewash may be added numerous pigments.

The techniques used in employing these materials varied according to the surface to be painted. With wood it is necessary to 'prepare' the surface with size and with softwoods it is important to 'kill' all resinous knots. Undercoats were often executed in paint with a carrying agent that was 'lean' in character, with the final coats carried out in paint that was of a 'fatty' nature, a sound principle which is still followed.

The complex character of the chemistry of paint and the numerous methods concerning the craft of painting are endless and cannot be dealt with in detail here. Many books have been published on the subject, the earliest of which was probably William

144. Painted timber from an upper hall in a house in BISHOPRIC, HORSHAM, WEST SUSSEX, late sixteenth century, Before this house was floored-in the powerful zig-zag design would have been viewed distantly in the shadows of the roof timbers. *Photograph: J. R. Armstrong: Weald and Downland Museum*

Salmon's *Polygraphice, Or The Arts of Drawing, Engraving, Etching, Limning, Painting, Vernishing, Japanning and Gilding &c* (1672) which, whilst emphasizing the crafts of the fine arts (being dedicated to 'S^R. Godf. Kneller, Kt.'), does touch on aspects of house painting.[2] John Smith's manual *The Art of Painting in Oyl* first appeared in 1676 but it went through no less than six further editions or impressions and in 1821 was revised and re-issued by Butcher. This was followed in 1685 by the anonymous *A Short Introduction to the Art of Painting and Varnishing*, published by George Dawes. Another seventeenth-century publication that includes relevant information on painting is Stalker and Parker's *Treatise of Japaning and Varnishing* (Oxford, 1688). In the eighteenth century such manuals became quite common but one of the best known is probably Robert Dossie's *The Handmaid to the Arts* of 1758. Dossie is particularly withering in his reference to Salmon who 'took upon him to give instructions for the practice of almost all the arts and mysterious trades. . . . His collection would indeed have had considerable merit at the time it was published, if the valuable parts had not been confounded with such a heap of absurd stuff and falsities.'[3] In the nineteenth century, authors of such books abound but one of the most prolific was Nathaniel Whittock whose *The Decorative Painters' and Glaziers' Guide* of 1827 is particularly helpful. In addition to these books the numerous encyclopaedias are also a useful source of reference, among them *The Complete Dictionary of Arts and Sciences* edited by T. H. Croker and Others (London, 1764).

The early painters and decorators not only mixed their own paints, they also ground

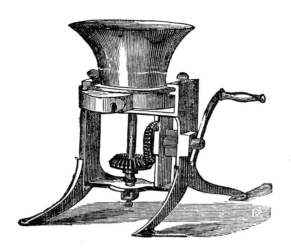

145. The painter and decorator's craft once included the grinding of pigment and the preparation of paint as these colour mills from the catalogue attached to Brodie and Middleton's *The Carver and Gilder's Guide* (c. 1880) testify. *Collection: James Ayres*

their own pigments. John Smith recommends 'A Grinding stone and Mulier; the stone it self ought to be Porphyrie, which is the best',[4] but any hard close-grained material that would not itself crumble and contaminate the pigment being ground, was used. In the 1705 edition of *The Art of Painting in Oyl* the muller is described as 'a pebble Stone of the form of an Egg'.[5] Such stones, which resemble truncated sugar loaves, are sometimes found in old houses and find a new use as door stops.

Dossie describes 'The operation subservient to the making and preparing of colours [as] sublimation, calcination, solution, precipitation, filtration, and levigation'.[6] It was levigation that necessitated the use of mullers [145].

Contrary to popular belief, oil paint was well known to mediaeval craftsmen.[7] However, it was but one of a variety of media known to them among which were water and size for distemper, milk and wax. The details of their methods are not certain as they, unlike later craftsmen, did not in general commit their knowledge to writing. Indeed it was the custom of the guilds to maintain secrecy over their 'mystery'.[8] Despite these difficulties it is possible to infer the methods used by mediaeval craftsmen by reference to later publications and even living craftsmen (excluding those trained only in art schools) where it is clear that the use of materials and tools has been passed down by word of mouth and example over many generations.

Oil paint must always have been valued for outdoor use, but before the Reformation it was less favoured for interiors, perhaps because of its frequently harsh appearance but also because oil paint darkens with age whilst the alternatives are remarkably stable, with an occasional tendency to fade. The use of oil paint was paralleled by gilding where only oil-based gold size is suitable for exterior work; for interiors 'water gilding' has always been considered best.

I. *The Drawing Room*, artist unknown, c. 1840, water-colour on paper, 16 in (40.6 cm) × 12.75 in (32.4 cm). This water-colour by an amateur provides abundant information on the appearance of a middle-class room of its period: the curtains, the height that the pictures are hung, the loose covers, the rag rug and the general colour scheme. *Judkyn/Pratt Collection*

J. Interior of house at COMPTON BASSET, WILTSHIRE, painted in 1849 by Elizabeth Pearson Dalby. *Salisbury and South Wiltshire Museum*

K. Window blind, mid-nineteenth century, Scotch cambric painted with the assistance of stencils. The whole blind measures 62.5 in (158.8 cm) wide × 102 in (259.1 cm) high. *Judkyn/Pratt Collection. Photograph: Derek Balmer.* *See pages 102–4*

Distemper is one of the most timeless of paints; it was in use as early as the twelfth century.[9] Ordinary whitewash consisted of whiting bound with size but for preference the 'binder' used was starch as it did not impair the colour of the whitewash. Blue (which in the nineteenth century was made by Reckitts) or 'blue-black', a carbon made from vegetable matter, was often added with a small quantity of turpentine to make the white less 'cold' in appearance. A related paint was limewash made from slaked lime mixed with $2\frac{1}{2}$ lb (1134 g) of rock alum for every pail of limewash, the alum taking the place of size or starch in whitewash. Another type of white finish was 'stucco whitewash' made from unslaked chalk lime slaked in boiling water and mixed with ground rice (although other cold water pastes were no doubt used).[10]

Distemper can be either 'white wash' or 'colour wash'. A variety of pigments were used for the latter including red ochre known as 'rodel',[11] yellow ochre of which 'Oxford ochre' was for long the best and most famous,[12] verdigris which produced a pale, greenish-blue which was apt to fade, and lime-blue made by precipitating sulphate of copper by means of milk of lime, using some heat.

The oils mixed with paints, in pre-Tudor times and after, included linseed, olive, walnut and poppy seed,[13] whilst the turpentines used in conjunction with these, included by Dossie, were 'the Common Venetian, Strasburg, Cyprus and Chio', of which 'Venetian', an exudate of larch, was most recommended.

Related to the turpentines were the lacquers, listed by Salmon: '*Gum-Lac*, called *Shell-lac*, *Gum-Animi* (It is either Oriental, coming from the *East Indies* or Occidental, coming from the West Indies . . .), *Gum-Copal* (. . . from Hispaniola, Cuba and other places in the Spanish West Indies), . . . *Gum Sandarack* (. . . brought from *Barbary* in long Tears or Drops . . .), *Benjamine* . . . *Rosin* . . . *Mastiche* (. . . Gum of the Lentisk-Tree growing in Chio, Ægypt and Syria . . .), *Gum-Elemi* [and finally the mysterious] *Olibanum* [which was] . . . the true ancient Incence but from what tree it is produced, Authors have not agreed.' However, Salmon goes on to say, 'but for myself being in the West Indies, I gathered it [olibanum] plentifully from the Floridian Cedar which is the Cedrus Baccifera'.[14] All of these lacquers were used in a variety of ways for both varnishing and japanning.

Wax as a medium, like milk, goes back to antiquity, and both were used in the Romano-Egyptian world. Nevertheless, wax as a medium is mentioned as an innovation by Edward Edwards in his *Anecdotes of the Painters* (1808) in connection with the Swiss artist J. H. Muntz who 'had a landscape painted in *encaustic* a process of which he seems to have considered himself the inventor; for he published a small octavo volume (1760) in which he demonstrated the operation, but it certainly does not deserve the attention of an artist'.[15] This assertion may have been possible in 1760, but mediaeval craftsmen knew the methods well and saw the virtues of the luminosity of this type of painting which gives a sense of the underlying material. The process is particularly effective for interior woodwork, for when polished the character of the wood emerges despite the undercoats of gesso[16] with which this type of work is usually associated. The wills of mediaeval craftsmen/painters show that wax was used rather than, or certainly in greater quantities than, egg tempera.[17]

Casein,[18] made from curds of milk, tended to produce an unpleasant smell which Butcher, in his edition of John Smith's *Art of Painting in Oyl*, claims to have overcome by means of a new recipe.[19] 'The very offensive and injurious smell . . . may be obviated by the following recipe—[which] will answer for inside work.' The materials used in this concoction were 2 quarts (2.3 litres) of skimmed milk, $6\frac{1}{2}$ oz (184.3 g) of fresh slaked lime, 4 oz (113.4 g) of linseed oil and 3 lb (1360 g) of whiting.

> Put the lime into a stone [stoneware] vessel, and pour upon it a sufficient quantity of milk to form a mixture resembling thin cream; then add the oil a little at a time, stirring it with a small spatula; the remaining part of the milk is then to be added; and lastly the whiting. The milk must on no account be sour. . . .
>
> The whiting, or ochre is gently crumbled on the surface of the fluid which it gradually imbibes, and at last sinks: at this period it must be stirred in.
>
> The paint may be coloured like distemper or size colour, with levigated charcoal, yellow ochre etc. . . . the quantity here prescribed is sufficient to cover twenty-seven square yards [22.6 square metres] with the first coat, and will cost about three halfpence per yard.

The above instructions make no reference to the need for preparing such paint over a low flame but this was probably necessary.

Today's plastic emulsion paints ('P.E.P.') are very similar to the casein paints of the past and produce similar results and when waxed resemble wax emulsion paint.

Apart from those outlined above various other paint-like substances were in use, many of which date back a long way. Mediaeval timberwork is often found bearing traces of a reddish, stain-like paint which has not been applied on the usual foundation of gesso. This is probably the same as the mixture applied to the South Door of York Minster as late as 1861 which consisted of rud (red ochre) and bullock's blood.[20]

The Use of Paint

In those periods of history noted for their archaeological zeal the use of colour is usually restrained. This was largely because exhumed sculpture and fragments of architecture had generally lost their original paint. Probably for this reason the Renaissance rejected the notion of painted architecture and sculpture. In countries like Germany where the mediaeval tradition permeated later idioms, the use of polychrome decoration lingered. Sir Henry Wotton in his *Elements of Architecture* (1624) referred to this with ambiguous emotions appropriate to the period of aesthetic change in which he lived: '. . . various colours on the *Out-walles* of *Buildings*, have always in them more *Delight* then *Dignity*;

Therefore I would there admit no *Paintings* but in *Black* and *White*, nor even in that kinde any *Figures* (if the roome be capable) under *Nine* or *Ten* foot high, which will require no ordinary *Artizan*; because the faults are more *visible* than in small *Designs*.'[21] It is clearly advisable, as Wotton acknowleges, that the treatment of interiors should be related to their scale, which, in my opinion, Wotton confused with size. Furthermore, the aspect of a room should, ideally, influence the colours selected to adorn it — dark tones in a room facing north would be sombre indeed. In small houses white paint is often advisable although it may be unimaginative. Loudon recommended 'the colouring of the Walls of rooms with water colours, or what is called distemper. . . . All the different colours are used for the walls of rooms but the most common after white are some shades of yellow, red, green or grey. As a general rule the ceiling should be of a lighter colour than the walls.'[22] The primacy of white is clear in this passage, but in one town, Norwich, it seems to have been used until the nineteenth century to the exclusion of all others.[23] This is possibly confirmed by Celia Fiennes who, writing in 1698, states that every year 'on Holly [Holy] Thursday when the Major [Mayor] is sworne in . . . they [the inhabitants of Norwich] newe washe and plaister their houses within and without.'[24] It should be noted that limewash provided a welcome disinfectant and that such decoration was probably but an extension of 'Spring cleaning'. Furthermore, whitewash was believed to be a useful fire-proofing agent when painted on thatch both inside and out.[25]

Before the Reformation and until the end of the Tudor dynasty surviving records (as existing fragments) of the internal treatment of walls are largely confined to the homes of prince or prelate. Salzman quotes the fashion in mediaeval interiors of marking out white walls with red lines to resemble masonry and also mentions the interior walls of the Tower of London which in 1337 were given a coat of whitening contrasting with the timber posts and beams which were painted with 'size and okkere'.[26] By the Perpendicular period the range of available pigments was quite considerable for the rich. The remainder of the population probably had to make do with decorating their houses with nature's pigments, chalk being the most common, with ochre as a possible alternative in some districts. Even in a Kentish yeoman's house of the quality of Synyards, Otham, the painting on plaster over the fireplace showing the lion and griffin of Tudor England is confined to earth ochres and lamp black on a white ground [146]. Mrs Little has found 'little evidence of paint in New England interiors during the seventeenth and early years of the eighteenth centuries',[27] a situation born of the high cost of importing pigments and media from England. Although the circumstances of Colonial America did not obtain in the mother country — our lesser interiors were probably always decorated with paint — the range of the palette was very restricted until the seventeenth century.

With the dissolution of the monasteries came the concomitant redistribution not only of wealth and lands, but also of materials and skills. One of the most remarkable survivals of a painted screen in a relatively modest domestic interior has recently been discovered

146. The lion and griffin painted in distemper on plaster, Synyards, OTHAM, KENT, early sixteenth century. *Photograph: Royal Commission on Historical Monuments*

at Cross Farm, Westhay, near Mells, Somerset. The screen is reproduced here in Colour Plate A for the first time. Paintings at this domestic level and of this period are so rare that it could be difficult to place for period, were it not for the presence of the guilloche pattern which suggests a date after about 1540. Mells was an important centre for the considerable estates of the abbots of Glastonbury and it is therefore perhaps unremarkable that this painting apparently dates from this period of great social change. The plank panelling is probably fifty years or more earlier as the chamfer 'stops' occur near the cill. By the time the painting was made a bench was apparently placed against the screen at which level the painting ceases. It was the clear intention of the artist to produce a rich effect by giving a subsidiary role to common pigments like white whilst affording a central place to exotic colours like verdigris. Red ochre is used in a secondary capacity whilst the whole design is delineated in lamp black. Thus all the colours were relatively easily obtained but the most expensive were used ostentatiously. It will be noted that the design is painted quite arbitrarily over the plank panelling despite its high relief and strong shadows. A similar disregard for the underlying surface may often be found in walls of stud and plaster where the design runs easily over either surface.

The room in which this remarkable survival stands measures 173 in (439.4 cm) by 120 in (304.8 cm) and includes a fine fireplace similar to the example in the nearby Priest's House at Muchelney. The room at Cross Farm was apparently the 'hall' of the house and was open to the roof, which is of raised cruck construction (as defined by Eric Mercer[28]). The screen divides the hall from the parlour (which served until recently as a dairy). The back is unchamfered and undecorated save for the whitewash which has probably been applied regularly over a considerable number of years.[29] A similar screen on the first floor of the Gate House at Glastonbury Abbey, 6 miles (9.6 kilometres) from Westhay, bears traces of painted decoration including a guilloche similarly treated to that at Cross Farm.

The guilds of painter/stainers combined two crafts, those who *painted* wood, plaster and other surfaces, and those who *stained* hangings, usually referred to in sixteenth-century wills as 'painted cloths', a cheaper substitute for woven tapestries. A typical reference to these painted hangings is 'the painted cloths in the hall being the halling' (1576). Contemporary descriptions show that the subjects depicted on such canvases were religious and temporal being mythological or classical, floral or arboreal with human or animal figures and sometimes just a simple text.[30] Thomas Gammige of Walden, Essex, who died in 1578 was a painter of such 'hallings'. In his widow's will of 1581 she mentions 'all my frames with painted pictures or stories in them, together with all my [grinding] stones, colours and frames, and all other things belonging to the art, mystery, science or occupation of a painter'.[31] The tradition for painted cloths persisted down to the eighteenth century and most surviving examples are elegant productions of that period. A number of public collections hold such works including the Victoria and Albert Museum and some provincial museums like Lewes and Luton.

In the closing years of the sixteenth century and until the Commonwealth the fashion for blackwork embroidery on clothes was reflected by the use of linear patterns in black on white for the decoration of interiors. A good example of this type of work came to light recently in Ivy House, Fittleworth, Sussex [147], and sections of the painted plaster are now preserved in the Weald and Downland Museum. In general, wallpaper remained a luxury in Britain until the mid-nineteenth century. It should however be noted that many of the examples of lining paper (in furniture) and wallpaper which survive from the first half of the seventeenth century are of this 'blackwork' type.[32]

By the early seventeenth century more pigments had become available to more people and despite what Entwisle has described as 'the "Black and White" vogue' and despite the rising influence of classicism as expressed by such as Wotton, polychrome decoration was used. Indeed it was used throughout the seventeenth century even for garden sculpture.[33] A good example of circa 1632 is a fragment of plaster painted with a portrait of Mary Frith (1584–1659), now in the Victoria and Albert Museum. Mural painting with figure work persisted at the higher social levels but for the most part died out elsewhere in the course of the seventeenth century. The best example of an eighteenth-century mural that I know of in a small domestic building (The George Inn, Chesham, Buckinghamshire) could be described as mediaeval in modern dress [C, D]. It has an unerring sense of pattern and respects the nature of the wall surface, unlike its more sophisticated contemporaries. Despite the vigour of the designs the room is small. The hunting scene measures only 90 in (228.6 cm) high by 72 in (182.9 cm) wide whilst the floral design occupies the adjacent wall and measures 120 in (304.8 cm) by 54 in (137.2 cm).

147. Decorative 'black work' painting, c. 1600, from Ivy House, FITTLEWORTH, SUSSEX. Such designs were also used in early wallpaper and furniture lining-paper as well as for the embroidery of clothes.
Photographs: J. R. Armstrong: Weald and Downland Museum

A number of murals painted in distemper survive from the early nineteenth century and I illustrate one that was recently discovered in the first-floor front room of 39 Grosvenor Place, Bath. This terrace was begun in 1791 to designs by John Eveleigh but the interiors designed by John Pinch the younger were not completed until after 1819. Number 39 was not occupied until 1828 when it was taken by Thomas Shew the architect and painter, and it was he who was probably responsible for painting this mural [M, N].[34] Whittock gives instructions for painting such murals in his *Guide* of 1827.

All of the painted decoration mentioned above is in distemper. At Phippens Farm, Butcombe, Avon [148], two rooms with complete mural schemes have recently been

148. Exterior of Phippens Farmhouse,
BUTCOMBE, AVON

discovered which were wallpapered over in 1920 [O and P]. The paintings are probably in distemper although the highlights appear to be in an oil-based paint. Both murals are executed in a blue grisaille. The wall-painting in the drawing-room [149]

149. Mural in the drawing-room of Phippens Farmhouse, BUTCOMBE, AVON, c. 1840 (detail). This relatively simple design was probably intended to imitate the contemporary though more expensive scenic wallpapers. Pictures and furniture would intrude quite arbitrarily over such painting. Painted in distemper in blue grisaille. *Photograph by courtesy of Mr and Mrs Charles Smith*

(which measures 177 in (449.6 cm) by 150 in (381 cm), height 102 in (259.1 cm)) is of simple pastoral and decorative subjects carried out with a fairly subdued tonal contrast, probably to allow for the intrusion of tall furniture and the arbitrary hanging of mirrors and pictures which have damaged the mural. The artist has painted a *trompe-l'oeil* dado imitating blue marble. The wall-paintings in the principal bedroom (232 in (589.3 cm) by 152 in (386.1 cm), height 100 in (254 cm)) are of a higher quality and in a better condition than those in the drawing-room. They contain much more activity, principally a stag hunt, and in the background may be seen a rather generalized view of nearby Blagdon church. It is painted on a dirty-pink ground and there is greater chiaroscuro here, but the treatment of the chimney breast [P] is low in key, most probably so as not to

150a, b. Mural in the principal bedroom of Phippens Farmhouse, BUTCOMBE, AVON, c. 1840, signed 'Walters' (details). Many of the figures that inhabit this landscape appear to derive from popular prints of the day. See also Colour Plates O and P. *Photographs by courtesy of Mr and Mrs Charles Smith*

compete with a mirror or picture. The artist considered this mural worthy of his signature which appears painted on a rocky outcrop as 'Walters' and may once have included his address. *The National Commercial Directory* for Gloucestershire, published by Pigot and Co. in 1830, lists Thomas Walters, Upper Maudlin Street, Bristol, under '*Painters*, House, Sign &c' but significantly he is not listed under '*Artists*, Portrait, Landscape and Miniature'. As a house painter he was undoubtedly responsible for the stencilling found in the dining-room and for the marbled fireplaces, and the pilasters in the entrance passage. The drawing-room mural which is of a different quality may be by one of the sons of Thomas Walters who were first referred to in the 1831 Bristol directory. By 1832, 'Geo. Walters, Ornamental Painted Baize manufacturer for table covers, mats, etc.' and 'Thos. Walters, Sign and ornamental Painter' are listed in the directory at 15 Narrow Wine Street. The earliest reference to the family occurs in the 1819 directory (as 'Walter') and the latest is in the 1847 edition, by which time paper hanging had become part of their stock-in-trade. Bristol Art Gallery possesses a delightfully innocent shipping picture signed 'Walters' and including the date 1827. The Phippens Farm murals are probably some ten years later. The size of the windows in the bedroom in relation to the ceiling height is such as to have given little or no space for curtains which would also have obscured part of the mural on the flanking walls. The reveals of the windows house shutters, but there is also evidence of the use of spring blinds and it is possible that these were painted *en suite* with the mural. The whole scheme is probably typical of wall-painting of this period and status although surviving examples are now exceedingly rare in Britain. Such wall-paintings were made in imitation of the contemporaneous though more expensive scenic wallpapers.

The use of water-based paints continued down to the present day with local variations in their use. In nineteenth-century Ulster it was fashionable to paint the lower part of the internal walls of cottages with a waist-high band of red ochre. Addy records an interesting local example of the use of colour in the north of England: '. . . it is the custom to decorate the inner walls of houses, and occasionally the outside stonework, by means of a colour obtained from the plant liver-wort. This substance, known as "archil", or "orchil", is mixed with limewash to give it a deep blue colour. . . . In the north of Yorkshire yellow-ochre sometimes competes with archil. . . . In Derbyshire the ceiling and the walls were sometimes decorated by a light green colour. This was done by putting copperas into limewash.'[35] In the second half of the seventeenth century it became more usual for 'wainscot' to be painted in oil-based paints. Today's fashion to strip paint from both furniture and panelling has all but expended itself. The fad was understandable as generations of painting had, more often than not, fudged the sections of mouldings. Gwilt rightly stressed that, 'In repainting old work, it should be well rubbed down with dry pumice stone.'[36] These stones were shaped to the sections of the mouldings on which they were to be used. Unless similar care is taken today with systematic painting and 'rubbing down' the expedient of stripping old work back to the wood may be regarded as preferable.

Stalker and Parker quote, with some misgivings, the use of paint to simulate, on wood, materials other than wood: 'Before Japan was made in England, the imitation of Tortoise-shell was much in request, for Cabinets, Tables, and the like; but we being greedy of Novelty, made these give way to modern Inventions: not, but that tis still in vogue, and fancied by many, for Glass-frames, and small Boxes; nay, House-Painters have of late frequently endeavoured it, for Battens, and Mouldings of Rooms; but I must of necessity say, with such ill success, that I have not to the best of my remembrance met with any that have humour'd the [tortoise] Shell so far, as to make it look either natural, or delightful.'[37] Surviving examples of this work appear to have been intended to be 'delightful' rather than 'natural', a notion confirmed by Loudon who argued that all woodwork should if possible be 'grained in imitation of some natural wood, not with a view of having the imitation mistaken for the original, but rather to create an allusion to it and by diversity of lines to produce a kind of variety and intricacy which affords more pleasure to the eye than a flat shade of colour'.[38] A remarkably good and early example of such an 'allusion' to graining is to be found on a fragment of oak panelling of circa 1600 from Hyde Abbey house, Winchester, and now in the Victoria and Albert Museum.[39] The panels in this fragment are painted in a linear 'blackwork' design on a white ground so characteristic of its period. The stiles and rails have been painted a yellow ochre on which a most informal and calligraphic rendering of crimson graining has been superimposed.

151. Painter and decorator's brushes illustrated in the catalogue attached to Brodie and Middleton's *The Carver and Gilder's Guide* (c. 1880). *Collection: James Ayres*

Celia Fiennes, describing Newby Hall near Ripon, Yorkshire, in 1697, remarks that 'the best roome was painted just like marble'.[40] Despite the appearance of such painting in the finest room in a grand house it was probably employed in houses of many social levels especially as the fashion declined in the early eighteenth century. Graining, marbling and even japanning was used to embellish quite small houses in eighteenth-century America and the practice must have been quite common in England where Stalker and Parker's instructions on how 'To counterfeit Marble' must have been invaluable.[41] Salmon's *Polygraphice* also gives instructions on the painting 'Of Marble and Tortoise Shell Japan' which should be finished 'before it is too dry, with a smaller

152, 153. The stiles and rails of this screen 74 × 103 in (188 × 261.6 cm) are painted to simulate marble, with decorative paintings symbolizing the seasons occupying the panels. Painted decoration of this type was popular for wainscoted rooms in the first half of the eighteenth century. *Victoria and Albert Museum*

pencil and one degree darker gently touch in the lesser veins and variety of Marble endeavouring as much as may be, to imitate, the exact foot steps of Nature, after this with a small pointed feather, and the deepest Colour, touch and break all your smaller Veins making them irregular, wild, and confused as they appear in real stone: let it dry for a day or two and wash it over with isinglass Size, or Parchment [size]. . . . Let it dry [again] for 2 or 3 days and then Varnish it over with the best white varnish.'[42] The treatment may be seen on the stiles and rails of an early eighteenth-century screen in the Victoria and Albert Museum [152, 153]. As can be seen, the naive drawing of the female figures and the accompanying landscapes imply that its original home was less than grand. It would however be a mistake to suppose that such an object was drawn from very far down the social scale.

In wainscoted rooms, overmantel and over-door pictures of a surprisingly primitive sort may be found in the houses of the gentry. Urchfont Manor in Wiltshire has an almost complete series of such overmantels. In grander houses decorative paintings by masters like Canaletto occupy such positions, and no less than thirteen of his works now at Windsor Castle were described as 'Door Pieces' by Joseph Smith in his catalogue of pictures acquired by George III.[43]

These paintings were apparently viewed as 'furnishing pictures' rather than considered as works of art [154]. Their position could have something to do with this attitude. As overmantel pictures they were exposed to the rising heat and fumes from the fire whilst as over-doors they were often so high as to be virtually out of sight. This explanation does not altogether apply in a number of surviving wainscoted rooms where every panel is painted with a decorative landscape. A George II room at the Manor Farm, Hughenden, contains a particularly successful example. Here the panels below the dado contain complete individual landscapes while those of the larger upper panels may be 'read' as individual compositions or as a continuous landscape. Wilsley House, Cranbrook, Kent, contains a room which reverses this idea by showing in the lower panels hounds chasing a hare and in the upper panels ships at sea,[44] and the stiles and rails of the panelling in this room are painted in imitation of marble. The lowly status of such painting may have had something to do with the fact that it was 'built in' and not easily available as part of the currency of art.

In the cleaning of 'Wainscotting, or any other Joynary or Carpentry Work that is painted in Oyl' John Smith recommended a mixture of water and 'well sifted' wood ash but added that 'if your painting be more Curious, whether Figures of Men, Beasts, Landskip, Fruitage, Florage, or the like then let your picture be gently scoured, and then cleanly washed off with fair Water: after it is well dry, let it be run over with Varnish made with white of Eggs, and you will find the Beauty and Lustre of your Picture much recovered.'[45]

The graining and marbling of wood panelling provided the setting for walnut furniture in which the forms were simple so as to reveal the 'figure' of the wood. With the

154. Fireplace with overmantel painting in the first-floor bedroom of the White House, FEN
DITTON, CAMBRIDGESHIRE. The brass fireplace with its Dutch tile surround is identical to one
recorded as being originally in a bedroom at Paycocke's, Coggeshall, Essex, by Basil Oliver in *Old
Houses and Village Buildings in East Anglia*, Batsford, London, 1912, fig. 21. *Photograph: Royal
Commission on Historical Monuments*

rise in the importance of mahogany, in which, except in Honduras mahogany, the grain is more noticeable by its absence, fashion shifted from simplicity of form to complexity, with an abundance of carved detail on high quality furniture. Furthermore, the influx of Huguenot weavers to England in the late seventeenth century had brought about the abundance of richly patterned brocades at a time when wallpaper was also available to the wealthy. This resulted in the flamboyant use of 'pattern' which was previously provided by but no longer demanded of paint. These trends taking place in the higher reaches of society were passed down the social scale where furniture continued to be made of walnut and oak rather than mahogany and stencilling took the place of wallpaper. In other words, the *effect* on design took shape without the material *cause*. The fashion for wainscoting declined amongst the élite. At the vernacular level its use continued, but whatever features the joiner added the walls were either painted in simple colours or were given 'interest' in the shape of wallpaper or stencilling in colours considerably less pungent than those used in marbling, graining or japanning. In New England 'pumpkin yellow' and 'Indian red' (as Dossie described it in England) continued the ancient use of easily available ochres.[46]

Where wide open spaces of coloured distemper were used on walls, notably in the first fifty years of the reign of George III, a less finite surface was created by means of distressing the paint with dry brush strokes and 'scumbling'. With oil paint on the other hand, the importance of glazes to give lustre to the surface cannot be over-emphasized. Dossie described the virtues of glazing in his own inimitable way. 'The property of *glazing* . . . is of so much importance . . . that no other method can equally well produce the same effect in many cases, either with regard to the force, beauty, or softness of the colouring.'[47]

The use of decorative painting was never totally out of fashion. In the third quarter of the eighteenth century, however, the archaeological researches of the Adam brothers brought about a re-assessment of the 'antique' and an awareness that, contrary to the notions of the Renaissance, the Greeks and Romans used painted decoration. The Classical Revival was about to reveal itself to the world in all its effete and painted details.[48] In a desire to obtain ever more exotic woods even painted marbling and graining were back in a big way [L]. By the early nineteenth century, with the publication of Whittock's *The Decorative Painters' and Glaziers' Guide* (1827), painters were simulating: Oak, Pollard Oak, Spanish Mahogany, Satin Wood, Rosewood, Bird's-Eye Maple,[49] Coral Wood (from Celon), Watered Damask Coral Wood, Red Satin Wood, Veined Marble, Sienna Marble, Verde Antique, Black and Gold Marble, and Porphyry [L, 155].[50] Whittock gives instructions for all of these in either oil or distemper. However, the eclecticism, the fickle liking for everything, so characteristic of Victorian taste, is foreshadowed in this volume and despite his observation that ancient Greece reached a 'high state of civilization and refinement' this is a historical statement rather than an aesthetic sentiment. He goes on to describe the 'Gothic' as 'The most beautiful and varied style of decoration'.[51]

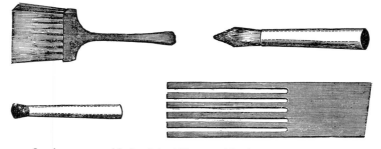

155. Implements used in 'graining' illustrated in the catalogue attached to Brodie and Middleton's *The Carver and Gilder's Guide* (c. 1880). *Collection: James Ayres*

Stencilled decoration in mediaeval England is well known. The word seems to have originated from the verb 'estenceler', to sparkle or cover with stars. It is known that Henry III favoured green walls scattered with gold stars.[52] Salzman in referring to work on St. Stephen's Chapel, Westminster Abbey, quotes the purchase of '6 dozen and 8 foils of tin for pryntes.' 'Pryntes' or 'doublettes' were apparently mediaeval terms for stencils although Salzman only found one instance of the use of these words.[53] Numerous examples of such work survive from mediaeval times to the seventeenth century. Addy states that in Derbyshire 'Before the introduction of wallpaper it was usual to decorate walls with patterns, such as green leaves with rather indistinct stems. This was done by means of a contrivance resembling a large stencil plate. The practice is ancient, whether the stencil plate was used anciently or not. The regulations of the *Feste de Pui* in London provided that the room for the feast was not to be hung with cloth of gold, or silk, or tapestry, but decorated with leaves and strewed with rushes',[54] a tradition that seems to have formed the basis for many stencil designs.

Walls were the main surface for stencilling but so long as the technique was popular it was widely used on many surfaces other than walls. The earliest-known example of English wallpaper dates from 1509 and carries a design rendered by stencil.[55] Indeed, although other methods such as woodblocks were used for printing wallpaper, stencilling long remained a popular method of producing quite complicated designs. Robert Dossie in his *The Handmaid to the Arts* (1758) recommends for wallpaper the use of 'thin leather or oil cloth stencils.[56] However, the type of stencilling with which this book is concerned was executed *in situ* directly onto the sized surface of wood or plaster as in all the examples that I have located so far. In the case of stud and plaster walls the designs run arbitrarily over both surfaces. Edward Batling's trade-card (at the sign of the Knave of Clubs, Southwark) of about 1690 makes it clear that wallpaper was then available 'in lengths or in Sheets, Frosted or Plain: Also a sort of Paper in Imitation of Irish Stitch,[57] of the newest Fashion, and several other sorts, viz Flock-work, Wainscot, Marble, Damask, Turkey-Work'.[58] If paper 'Hangings for Rooms' were available in London by the late seventeenth century, why was stencilling direct on walls so popular in both America and Britain over a century later? Taxation appears to be the answer.

Plain paper had been dutiable since 1694, but in 1712 an Act was passed which imposed a duty of 1d ($\frac{1}{2}$p) later increased to $1\frac{1}{2}$d on every square yard (.84 square metre) of paper 'printed, painted or stained'.[59] These taxes made wallpaper expensive and most surviving examples of 'direct' stencilling are to be found in relatively small houses or in the lesser rooms of larger ones. Again and again references to stencilling emphasize its cheapness. Robert Dossie refers to stencilling paper hangings as 'a cheaper method of ridding coarse work than printing'.[60] Loudon observes that, 'This mode of ornamenting walls of rooms is not unsuitable for cottages of the humblest description on account of its cheapness and because in remote places or in new countries, it might be done by the cottager himself, or by the local plasterer or house painter.'[61] It is clear that Nathaniel Whittock in *The Painters' and Glaziers' Guide* (1827) regarded stencilling as part of the house painter's craft [F]. Certainly a craftsman such as George Evans would have been capable of such work. He is described by Edward Edwards in his *Anecdotes of the Painters* (London, 1808) as follows: 'George Evans . . . practises as a house painter but frequently painted portraits. . . . Much cannot be said of his powers as an artist, nor will his portraits be much in request with posterity.'

A number of instruction manuals by writers like Dossie or Salmon survive from the eighteenth century although many are of much more recent date. *The Modern Painter and Decorator* by A. S. Jennings and G. C. Rothery,[62] published (in three volumes) as late as 1920, includes a chapter on 'Stencils and Stencilling', an art 'that deserves more attention than it usually receives'. It goes on to say that cartridge paper and occasionally 'thick lead foil is often used'; and 'Willesden paper which being specially treated in order to make it waterproof, is specially recommended for stencils as it does not require the application of either linseed oil or knotting shellac.' Linseed oil was particularly recommended as it made the paper transparent, enabling the craftsman to place each stencil with greater accuracy. The cutting of stencils demanded considerable skill [156a, b, c] and Jennings and Rothery recommended 'A very sharp knife, not unlike that used by shoe-makers, and called a "clicker's knife"', but they underline the importance of 'the use of various shaped punches' and surviving examples attest to the prevalence of these. The stencils once cut were held on the wall 'by means of specially made pins. These have handles sometimes of wood.' Distemper was apparently usual but oil paint was also used on occasion. In either case it was important that the paint should not be 'so liquid as to find its way underneath the stencil'. Guidelines were drawn on the wall surface and with the designs that were 'spotted or diapered, such as, for example, a fleur de lis . . . it will be a help if these guidelines are not only drawn vertically and horizontally, but also diagonally'. The instructions in *The Modern Painter and Decorator* are comprehensive and include recipes for suitable distemper: '. . . the use of dry colour ground in water . . . and thinned down with equal parts of turpentine and gold size. . . . in order to improve

M. (*above, left*) Mural in 39 Grosvenor Place, BATH. This terrace was begun in 1791 to designs by John Eveleigh but was not finished until 1819. The interiors were completed by John Pinch the Younger. This house was not occupied until 1828 when it was taken by the architect and painter, Thomas Shew, to whom these murals have been tentatively ascribed. Cupboard on right is shown in Colour Plate N. *Photograph: Delmar Studios. See page 167*

N. (*above, right*) Detail in cupboard on right of mural.

L. Oval panel showing a painter and decorator's samples of marbling and wood graining. *Museum of Lakeland Life. See pages 170–4*

O, P. Mural in the main bedroom at Phippens Farm, BUTCOMBE, AVON. The mural, which is signed 'Walters', was painted for James Shutter Williams who owned the house from 1819 until his death in 1862. *Photograph Delmar Studios. See pages 167–9 and Plates 150a, b*

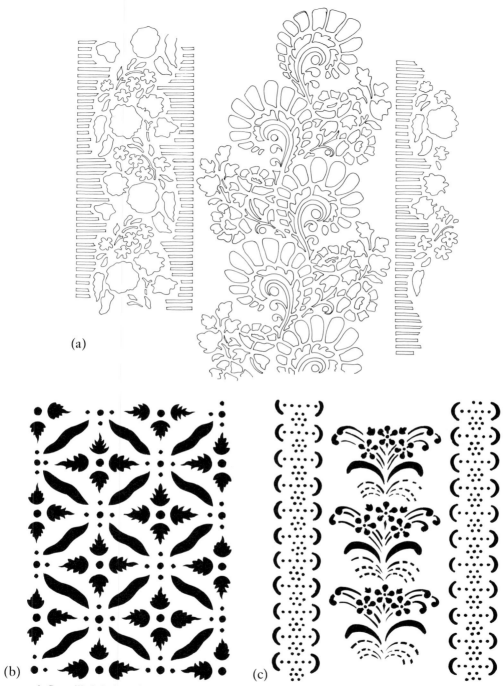

(a)

(b)

(c)

156. Stencilled designs found in the central house, Prior Park Buildings, BATH.
a. Design executed in dark and dirty pink on a pale pink ground (c. 1825) and found in a second floor room.
b. Design executed in dark dirty pink on a pale pink ground (c. 1825) and found in a large attic room.
c. Design executed in dark turquoise-blue on a dirty pink ground (c. 1825) and found in a small attic room.

the lasting qualities of distempered work, beeswax may be added with advantage. . . . the best wax is that to which a small quantity of cannuba wax has been added to stiffen it. One gallon [4.5 litres] of distemper will require about three ounces [85 grammes] of wax dissolved in about half a pint [.28 litre] of turpentine or less.' These instructions were first published in the 1920s but they clearly hark back to much older traditions. However, a final paragraph in this chapter concerns the innovation of 'spraying through stencils' which 'in addition to the great amount of time saved, . . . a gradation of colour may be obtained . . . [and] there is practically no risk of colour spreading beneath the surface of the stencil'.

It is clear from documentary sources and from surviving examples that stencilled wall decoration was widespread in both Britain and America from about 1790 to 1840 and it is likely that further research will show that the tradition did not completely die out between 1700 and 1790 (in either continent).[63] However, it is noteworthy that Robert Dossie's account of stencilling refers to its use exclusively as a means of decorating paper hangings. In both England and America wallpaper remained a superior form of wall decoration so long as it continued to be expensive. Poorer households had to make do with stencilled walls [157] such as the Manchester millworker's living-room so perfectly described by Elizabeth Gaskell in *Mary Barton* (first published in 1848):

> The room was tolerably large, and possessed many conveniences. . . . On the opposite side to the door and window was the staircase. . . . The other door, which was considerably lower, opened into the coal-hole—the slanting closet under the stairs; from which, to the fireplace, there was a gay-coloured piece of oil cloth laid. The place seemed almost crammed with furniture (sure sign of good times among the mills), beneath the window was a dresser with three deep drawers. Opposite the fireplace was a table, which I should call a Pembroke, only it was made of deal, and I cannot tell how far such a name be applied to such a simple material. On it resting against the wall was a bright green japanned tea-tray having a couple of scarlet lovers embracing in the middle. The fire-light danced merrily on this and really . . . it gave a richness of colouring to that side of the room. It was in some measure propped up by a crimson tea-caddy, also of japan ware. A round table on one branching leg stood ready for use, in the corresponding corner to the cupboard; and if you can picture all this with a washy but clean stencilled pattern on the walls, you can form some idea of John Barton's home.

In the mid-nineteenth century when the tax on paper was removed and it could be produced by the roll with improved machinery, wallpaper ceased to be exclusive and stencilling became relatively expensive and therefore fashionable and a subject worthy of discussion in the *House Decorator and Painter's Guide* (London, 1840).[64] As in mediaeval Europe, stencilling reappears as decoration in places of worship 'churches, chapels, ecclesiastical structures, Masonic temples, etc, where it may be regarded as being in

157. Stencilled matchboarding, c. 1840. The colour scheme is dark and light blue picked out with coral on a dirty-pink ground. Recently removed from a house in FRESHFORD, BATH. *Author's collection*

every way appropriate'.[65] In contrast, wallpaper had descended the social scale. William Bardwell's *Healthy Homes and How to Make Them* (London, 1854) lists minimum building and decorating standards and recommends that paper shall be hung on 'all the walls of the sitting and bedrooms of the dwelling with figured paper to the value of one penny per yard of approved designs.' According to Stalker and Parker painters preferred to price work by the yard but some customers insisted on asking for prices for the 'job' out of a 'mistaken piece of frugality . . . [thinking], if they can agree with a Painter by the greatt, their business is done; for by these means, they not allowing the Artist a Living price, he cannot spend both his oyl and labour, nor stretch his performance to the utmost extent of his skill.'[66]

The method of payment seems to have been set by convention. In *The Complete English Tradesman* (1727) Daniel Defoe warns shopkeepers not to spend too much money on 'painting and guilding, wainscoting and glazing' because 'the Joyners and Painters, Glaziers and Carvers must have all ready money: the Weavers and Merchants may give credit'.[67] A number of men trained as house painters successfully became 'easel painters'. Edward Edwards in his *Anecdotes of the Painters* (1808) states that George Evans and Joshua Kirby were so trained. The latter 'resided in the early part of his life at Ipswich, in Suffolk where he practised as a coach and house painter, and where he formed a lasting friendship with Mr Gainsborough'.[68]

For careful restorations of old interiors it is important that every attempt should be made to first establish the original colour scheme of a room and then to attempt to reproduce the paints that would have been used at that time. In much of America, and certainly on the eastern seaboard under the leadership of organizations such as the Society for the Preservation of New England Antiquities and the individual research of people like Nina Fletcher Little, this is now standard procedure and careful 'scrapes' are taken in the early stages of planning the restoration.[69] In Britain we have much to learn in this respect from American experience. The great danger with taking scrapes (or indeed with cleaning paintings) is that it is very easy to remove the glaze with the later accretion of paint. For this reason 'chipping' is to be favoured and solvents should be avoided.[70]

Notes to Chapter 9

1. Gwilt, vol. I, p. 693.
2. I have used the edition of 1701 but the British Library contains in addition to this and the first edition other copies dated 1673, 1675, 1681 and 1685.
3. Robert Dossie, *The Handmaid to the Arts*, London, 1758, 1764 edition, Preface, p. XX.
4. Smith, *The Art of Painting in Oyl*, 1705 edition, p. 1.
5. Ibid., p. 1.
6. Dossie, Section III. 'Levigation': to grind to a powder, especially with a liquid.
7. Salzman, pp. 157, 158. On p. 171 Salzman cites Horace Walpole's *Anecdotes of Painting in England* (1762) with its reference to the use of oil paint in England as early as 1239.
8. The treatise on *The Various Arts* by Theophilus (thought to have been written in the eleventh century) omits certain important chapters, some think because of pressure from the guilds (see Harvey, pp. 50, 54), whilst Cennino Cennini's *The Craftsman's Handbook* (1437) is too late to be considered characteristic.
9. Innocent, p. 1.
10. Kemp, ch. XVII.
11. Salzman, pp. 159, 170.
12. The ochre was quarried and ground in a windmill near Wheatley, Oxon. Yellow ochre was also found in Cumberland and Anglesea.
13. Harvey, p. 54. Dossie gives instructions on the preparation of 'Nut oil . . . [which] is oil of walnuts'.
14. Salmon, vol. II, ch. 2, Recipes VIII–XVI.
15. Edward Edwards, *Anecdotes of the Painters*, 1808, p. 15. Muntz worked for Horace Walpole at Strawberry Hill. Dossie in *The Handmaid to the Arts* mentions that 'Mr Muntz has published a treatise on the subject of painting methods', Preface to 1764 edition, p. XI. I have not been able to locate a copy of Muntz's book in the British Library.
16. Gesso is made of a mixture of whitening and size similar to whitewash except that the proportion of size is greater, though weaker solutions are usually used for the final coats.
17. Harvey, p. 164.
18. Related to casein paint was glue made from cheese. 'Mr Roubiliac, when he had to mend a broken antique [marble], would mix grated Gloucester cheese with his plaster, adding the grounds of porter and the yoke of an egg; which mixture, when dry forms a hard cement.' J. T. Smith, *Nollekens and His Times*, vol. II, p. 4. (See page 145, note 22.)
19. Butcher's edition of Smith's book, pp. 31–2.
20. Innocent, p. 159.

21. Sir Henry Wotton, *Elements of Architecture*, London, 1624, p. 96.
22. Loudon, p. 274.
23. I am indebted to Mr James Chapman of Norwich City Architects Department for this information.
24. Morris (ed.), *The Journeys of Celia Fiennes*, p. 149.
25. Innocent, p. 212.
26. Salzman, p. 159.
27. Little, *American Decorative Wall Painting*, p. 3.
28. Mercer, *English Vernacular Houses*, fig. 67.
29. I am indebted to Mr David Whitcombe, the farmer whose house it is, for permitting me both to see and photograph his house on numerous visits. Despite the incongruity of pebble dashing which shrouds the house it is a remarkable example of a 'long house' with a cross passage (the door to which is now blocked). One end, the floor of which is about 18 in (45.7 cm) lower than the 'hall', was always known by Mr Whitcombe's father as 'the bottom end'. It probably once housed cattle.
30. Emmison, p. 22.
31. Ibid., p. 78. The reference to frames probably means straining frames for painting such hangings on, like those used in the nineteenth century for painting window blinds.
32. E. A. Entwisle, *The Book of Wallpaper* (1954), Kingsmead Reprints, Bath, 1970, pp. 24–7.
33. In 1698 Celia Fiennes noted that the brick pillars to Patshull Park near Shrewsbury were surmounted by 'stone heads on which stood a Turkey Cock on each, cut in stone and painted proper'. Morris (ed.), *The Journeys of Celia Fiennes*, p. 229.
34. For details of the designers responsible for Grosvenor Place see Walter Ison, *The Georgian Buildings of Bath* (1948), Kingsmead Reprints, Bath, 1969.
35. Addy, p. 133–4.
36. Gwilt, p. 694.
37. Stalker and Parker, p. 79.
38. Loudon, p. 277.
39. W 123 1937.
40. Morris (ed.), *The Journeys of Celia Fiennes*, p. 85.
41. Stalker and Parker, p. 82.
42. Salmon, ch. XV, items III, IV, V.
43. Quoted by Margaret Jourdain, *English Interior Decoration 1500–1830*, Batsford, London, 1950, pp. 33–4.
44. Ibid., p. 56.
45. Smith, *The Art of Painting in Oyl*, p. 73.
46. Little, *American Decorative Wall Painting*, p. 1.
47. Dossie, Part I, ch. 2.
48. Richardson and Eberlein have noted in *The Smaller English House of the Later Renaissance*, London, 1925, p. 31, that the new style did not find favour with all; Chambers for one 'professed contempt for the macaronic attitude of the Brothers Adam'.
49. Not simulated until about 1817 at which date George Morant of New Bond Street sent J. B. Papworth a sample. See Jourdain, pp. 68, 76.
50. Taken from the index of Whittock's *Guide*.
51. Whittock, pp. 104, 115.
52. Salzman, p. 159.
53. Ibid., p. 167.
54. Addy, p. 134.
55. Found in Christ's College, Cambridge. Entwisle, pl. 1 and 2.
56. Dossie, 1764 edition, vol. II, part VI, appendix.
57. Probably the seventeenth-century term for Florentine stitch used to produce the then fashionable and well-known zig-zag pattern.

58. Trade-card for Edward Batling, Ambrose Heal Collection, British Museum.
59. Entwisle, p. 57.
60. Dossie, vol. II, part VI, appendix.
61. Loudon, pp. 277–8.
62. A. S. Jennings and G. C. Rothery, *The Modern Painter and Decorator*, Caxton Publishing Co., London, 1920, vol. II, p. 85.
63. Francis Reader, 'Mural Decoration', *Archaeological Journal*, vol. XCV, 1938. See also James Ayres, *British Folk Art*, Barrie and Jenkins, London (Overlook Press, New York) 1977, pp. 107–10.
64. This book gives advice on the decoration of very grand interiors. On the title page the authors, H. W. and A. Arrowsmith, declare themselves to be 'Decorators to her Majesty'.
65. Jennings and Rothery, vol. II, p. 69.
66. Stalker and Parker, pp. 79, 80.
67. Daniel Defoe, *The Complete English Tradesman*, London, 1727, p. 258.
68. Edward Edwards, *Anecdotes of the Painters*, London, 1808, pp. 31, 44.
69. It should be added that in a number of restorations x-ray cameras are used to establish whether or not nails are old and woodwork original. This was done when investigating the staircase of the Paca House in Annapolis, Maryland. See the magazine *Antiques*, New York, January 1977, p. 163.
70. Morgan Phillips and Christopher Whitney, 'The Restoration of Original Paints at the Otis House', *Old-Time New England*, the bulletin of the Society for the Preservation of New England Antiquities, vol. LXII, no. 1, Summer 1971, serial 225.

10 · Furniture

In *The Boke of Husbandrie* by John Fitzherbert (c. 1523) may be found a formidable list of household chores and farming duties under the heading *What markes a wyfe shulde do in a generalytie*. The tasks for the day are listed in order from sunrise to sunset. Thus in the morning the 'wyfe . . . than first swept thy house dress up thy disshboard and set all things in gode order within thy house'. From such references one may infer that a 'disshboard' was more than a utilitarian article for storage—it was a basis for the display of plate, the 'consumer durables' of their day. The furnishing of a home has probably always, and at all social levels, played this dual role. Even with the poor, where possessions were meagre, a few 'treasures' held more than a material significance. Robert Roberts's *The Classic Slum* sums up this seeming contradiction where 'For many in the lowest group the spectre of destitution stood close; any new possession helped to stifle fear.'[1] In pre-Reformation England possessions were few. This was partly because the élite maintained for their pleasure, as did the poor out of necessity, an active outdoor life. These conditions long persisted, resulting in furniture designed to fulfil many uses:

> The chest contriv'd a double debt to pay
> A bed at night, a chest of drawers by day.[2]

It would be a mistake to presume that the standard of furniture, any more than the standard of life, was consistent throughout the British Isles before the coming of the railways [158]. Even after their intrusion it was only the standardization of the measurement of time that arrived immediately. Loudon, writing just before the full impact of the 'Age of Steam', describes 'Two Ploughmens Cottages in a Village near Salisbury': 'The Interior of these cottages, it will be observed, is very different from that of either the Scotch or Northumbrian ones: irregularity and variety characterise the former much as plainness and simplicity do the latter. The one gives the idea of the cottage of a serf and the other of that of a free man.'[3]

This inequality, together with the use of different materials, accounts for certain regional characteristics in the type and design of furniture.

158. Lakeland interior by Emily Nicholson, early nineteenth century. This water-colour illustrates the importance of knitting in the cottages of Northern England as well as showing the influence of regions adjacent to Cumbria. The chimney, although of stone, is of a type known in Scotland where they are constructed of timber. The spindle-back chair on the right is a Lancashire type. *Museum of Lakeland Life and Industry*

Vernacular furniture in Britain is a formidable subject to look at in one chapter and I shall therefore use the remaining pages to discuss those aspects which are particularly characteristic such as perishable and painted furniture, built-in cupboards and beds, and the persistence of the dowelled through-tenon.

* * *

Much early furniture was either immovable because of its size or weight, or was a fixture which may be 'read' as part of the architecture. The Archbishop's throne of Purbeck marble at Canterbury is a fine example of such 'dormant' furniture. At the domestic level there are the stone beds and 'dresser' of the Stone Age settlement at Skara Brae, Orkney [159],[4] which are strikingly similar in form to the seventeenth-century fixed wood furniture of mediaeval type from Åmlid, Valle, Setesdal, Norway [160]; a reversal of the classic use of stone in the image of wood. The 'found object' too would on occasion fulfil a household need, such as the vertebra of a whale used as a stool[5] or the log of wood which traditionally provided a seat on one side of the central or 'roundabout' hearths still used in Co. Antrim within living memory.[6] Sometimes the basic structure of the house would

160. (*right*) Living-room of a farm in ÅMLID, VALLE, NORWAY. Although of a mediaeval type this example is not earlier than second half of the seventeenth century. *In house re-erected at Norsk Folkemuseum, Oslo*

159. Hut 7, SKARA BRAE, ORKNEY. This settlement is Neolithic but on these remote islands could be as late as 300 BC. *Photograph: Department of the Environment, Edinburgh*

serve the needs of its occupants. The single-room mud houses of Athelney, Somerset, were contrived so as to provide a bench around their perimeter created by the central trough which was their floor.

None of these exotic if rudimentary examples of furniture provided the storage space which only the chest, and its descendant the chest of drawers, could offer. In its earliest form as the trunk, it was as its name implies, a 'dug-out' tree trunk. The hewn quality of such articles for daily use, sculptured out of the solid, characterizes not only the surviving examples of 'trunks' of this type but also the constituent parts of much early carpenters' and even joiners' work [161]. Quite apart from the influence of the 'dug-out' the early abundance of timber encouraged its lavish use, and the influence of the mason confirmed it.

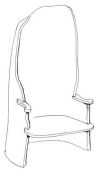

161. Late eighteenth-century (?) chair made from half a log of elm. *Museum of English Rural Life*

The 'dug-out' trunk was followed by the six-board chest. Most examples of the latter have suffered the consequences of damp floors and are today usually much lower than when first made. In fact the end-boards were often made from the fifth board sawn in half.[7] When seen on elevation such a chest conforms to a double square, a rather sophisticated visual trick which was probably nothing more than serendipity occasioned by the economical use of materials. The construction itself was far from sophisticated; nails held the timber fast and prevented its natural movement. Most examples will be found to be badly split.

Some early types of furniture have persisted longest in those utilitarian roles where they are least subject to the whim of fashion, the butcher's chopping block being a good example. Similarly the meal chest known as the 'ark', with its movable pegged, horned tenons and its roof-like lid, continued to be made in Wales into the eighteenth century.

Early in the thirteenth century a species of chest, common to most of Europe and known in Germany as a *stollen*[8] chest, was devised which retained the wide stiles of the ark but had a flat lid and panelled ends which permitted a certain amount of movement and were therefore found to be structurally more effective than the butt joints and rigid nailing of the six-board chest. This type may be seen as transitional and the immediate antecedent of the fully framed chest.

The framed chest was the result of much labour with its many mortices and tenons, and its stiles and rails grooved to accommodate panels. For this reason the top and back and sometimes the ends as well often remained simple slabs of wood and the single element which maintained the sound principles of frame and panel construction was the front. Even the plainest of framed chests has stiles and rails with bevelled edges surrounding the panels thus producing the familiar mason's mitre; elaborate examples were given rich mouldings. The mason's mitre is a subject about which much could be written. The mitre produces that dubious feature in a structure known as the 'feather edge'. A feather edge does not long survive in stone.[9] For this reason all junctions in masonry are kept as near the right angle as possible. The familiar mason's mitre results from the bevel worked on one piece of stone (usually horizontal) being given a 'stop' to provide the 'return' for the bevel worked on another stone member placed at right angles to it, as shown in Plate 64.

In timber the feather edge is possible and therefore the 'true' mitre has been used since the late sixteenth century, for non-structural purposes as it is a weak joint. Mediaeval carpenters and joiners seem to have recognized this weakness and despite the great expense of working the mason's mitre in wood its use long persisted. Furthermore 'end grain' makes a bad glue joint. Throughout much of the seventeenth century the decadent mitre became something of a vice among designers, if not craftsmen, who began to enjoy a profusion of applied mouldings relishing its use, whilst significantly resisting its charms for structural purposes. Even the later Louis XIV rooms elaborately panelled in wood employ the sound principle of construction of the mason's mitre despite the frivolous nature of their ornament. The strength of the mortice and tenon remained important for the framing of heavy mirror glass; the weak mitre was strengthened in bulky picture frames by means of a diagonal 'key' dovetailed into the back of the joint. Moxon, in his *Mechanick Exercises* (1677), describes the 'Mitre Square and its use' and remarks that 'thus Picture Frames and Looking Glass-frames are commonly made'.[10]

The detailed treatment and decoration of chests may be related to the panelling that is contemporary with them. Both obeyed the structural standards of their time and the aesthetic fashion of their day.

The great disadvantage of the chest was that nothing could be put on its surface without impeding access, and having gained access it was often necessary to delve deep to find one small object. These two disadvantages were overcome in one by the chest of drawers.

Today the word 'plank' and 'board' are synonymous but originally there seems to have been a distinction between them, the plank being considered heavier than the board. Undoubtedly the cup-*board* uses lighter timber than the plank of a trestle table. In sixteenth-century documents a 'table' was either a movable panel-painting[11] or what we would now call a table top—'a table lying on two trestles'. In joiner's work it was described as a 'table with the frame'.[12] 'Refectory tables', as they are known today, were often considered as fixtures or tables 'dormant'. Addy, describing the furnishing of Hawksworths House, Upper Midhope, West Yorkshire, notes that the table though movable is so large that it must have been constructed *in situ* when the house was built in 1671.[13] In his plan of the house, Addy located the main long-table in its traditional place alongside the lateral screen. Against this screen is a fixed bench; on the other side of the table are two long forms and at its head, a joint stool. This arrangement is not just a trivial matter of decor. The regular accommodation of a large number of individuals at table is not simply a reflection of the larger families of the past but indicates the continuation of the ancient tradition of the family of the house co-existing with the un-married farm servants at mealtimes. In the south this would be considered a late survival of an earlier tradition. Even in this example the family, as Addy's plan shows, has deserted the traditional table for a round one near the fire. At this social level it was not until the eighteenth century that the divorce, all-be-it under one roof, of family and servants was made absolute.

By the late sixteenth century, tables were more numerous and various and in the second half of the seventeenth century the introduction of coffee, tea and chocolate accelerated this trend. Presumably so as to prevent rooms becoming congested with furniture, the gate-leg table was devised and became common in the late seventeenth century. It may be a development of the so-called 'credence' table of the early part of the century which also has a 'gate' leg, but hinged table tops were in use much earlier.

In the eighteenth century the tilt-top table, often supported on a column and tripod,

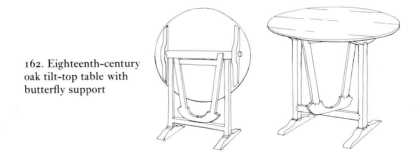

162. Eighteenth-century oak tilt-top table with butterfly support

possessed a similar space-saving virtue. J. T. Smith in *Nollekens and His Times* (1829) writes of the popular taste of 'the same class of persons, who in my boyish days would admire a bleeding-heart-cherry painted upon a Pontipool tea board [of tin plate], or a Tradescant-stawberry upon a Dutch table.' In a footnote Smith provides further information on the 'Dutch' table: 'This description of table, the pride of our great-grand-mothers, in which the brightest colours were most gorgeously displayed, was first imported from Holland into England in the reign of William and Mary. The top was nothing more than a large oval tea-tray, with a raised scalloped border round it, fixed

163. Hinged table, ULSTER, nineteenth century. The hinged table attached to the wall was popular in Ulster. In this example the table is given the added advantage of a rail along which it may travel. Note the Connecticut clock which became such a typical feature of cottage interiors throughout the British Isles following the 1851 Exhibition. *Photograph: Ulster Folk and Transport Museum*

upon a pillar, having a claw of three legs. They are now and then to be met with in our good old-fashioned family mansions, and brokers' shops. They were formerly considered by our aunt Deborah to be such an ornament to a room, that in order to exhibit them to advantage, they were put in the corner of a waiting-parlour for the admiration of the country tenants, when they brought their rents, or sat waiting their turn for an order for coals in a severe winter.'[14] Despite Smith's assertion that such 'Dutch' tables with a scalloped border, today known as a 'pie crust', were found only in 'mansions', they undoubtedly had a wide social distribution. Their basic feature of a tilt-top on a tripod stand continued in use well into the nineteenth century.

Before leaving the subject of tables it should be remembered that not all homes had one. They tend to be absent from the black houses of the Outer Hebrides. Fynes Moryson, writing in the eighteenth century, says that the Irish country people 'have no tables, but set meat upon a bundle of grass as napkins to wipe their hands. . . . I trust no man expects among these gallants any beds, much less feather beds and sheets.'[15] In such houses the table was often a simple, thin slab of wood, circular or sometimes rectangular, which hung on the wall when not in use [164]. At mealtimes the family would sit in a circle and place this board upon their knees.[16]

The upholstered comfort of today's chairs bears little relationship to the past when to have a back to one's seat of wood signified status, a cushion was a luxury enjoyed by a minority.

164. Table, 20 × 12 in (50.8 × 30.5 cm), cut from solid bog-wood, CO. ARMAGH. Such tables were placed on the knee when in use and hung on the wall when not. *Drawing: James Ayres, after Emyr Estyn Evans*

With smoke-filled interiors seating was kept low, and with uneven floors three legs were customary for stools and even tables—the so-called 'cricket' table being characteristic. In fact the word cricket may once have meant 'stool'. Moxon, in describing the use of the draw knife, says that it was 'seldom used about *House-building* but for the making of some sorts of Household-stuff as the Legs of Crickets, the rounds of Ladders, the Rails to lay Cheese or Bacon on &c.'[17] In all these instances the draw knife would be used to taper the ends of small scantlings of wood to produce what in effect is a tenon without a shoulder. Since this type of joint is weak it was usually compensated for by means of wedges and was later extensively used for the so-called Windsor chairs made with or without turned members. When Windsors or indeed stools had thick seats the additional support afforded by stretchers was unnecessary and they were often dispensed with. In fact the Windsor chair is nothing more than a stool with a back added, the legs and back being unrelated structurally, unlike the 'stool-chair' or 'back-stool' described and illustrated in Randle Holme's *Academy of Armory* (written between 1648 and 1649) where the 'back-foot' as it is traditionally termed,[18] is one continuous piece of wood forming leg and back.

One of the earliest references to the 'Windsor chair' is the 1730 advertisement for John Brown of St. Paul's Churchyard, London, who sold 'All sorts of Windsor Garden Chairs of all sizes painted green or in the wood'.[19] Jane Toller has shown that such chairs probably derived their name from those made in the vicinity of the royal borough which were shipped to London via the River Thames in large numbers. Unfortunately very few were labelled or branded but some bear the name 'Richard Hewitt, Chairmaker at Slough in the Forest'. At that time Slough was little more than a hamlet in the parish of Upton and it is likely that the chairs from this area became known by the name of the only place of consequence in the district. Some labels make reference to 'Windsor Forest'. Hewitt's workshop was only two miles from Windsor and just as he sent his goods via the Datchet road to the Thames for onward shipment to London so the Wycombe makers sent their products to Marlow which is also on London's river.[20] If such a hypothesis is to be accepted it is necessary to find evidence of dealers (although they often claimed to be manufacturers) located on or near the Thames, downstream, in or near London. The Ambrose Heal Collection of trade-labels contains just such evidence. A good example is a label dating from the second half of the eighteenth century for 'Lock[n] Foulger—Chair Maker at Wallam Green Makes all sorts of Windsor Chairs, Garden Seats, Rural Settees &c. Wholesale and Retail.' Another is 'William Webb, Near the Turnpike, Newington Surrey, Maker of all Sorts of Yew Tree Gothic and Windsor Chairs, China and Rural Seats, Single and double angle, and Garden Machines, Childrens Chaises on the most reasonable terms. NB for Exportation.' William Webb is listed in the directories between 1792 and 1823. In 1817 (R.) Webb and Bruce are located in the King's Road, Chelsea, but by 1823 they had moved to Hammersmith.[21]

165. Two Welsh stick-back chairs. Early chairs of this type were given three legs to provide stability on uneven floors. It will be noted that the left-hand example was originally of this type. The comb-back is probably the earliest type of stick-back chair. Hoop-back chairs require relatively sophisticated techniques in bending wood

Although chairs of this type are now inseparably associated with the town of Windsor they were in fact made in many parts of England as well as Scotland, Ireland and Wales. The Windsor chair is probably ancient and although none are known to survive from before the eighteenth century, certain types related to them do.[22] By about 1725[23] the Windsor chair had migrated to America where the use by colonial craftsmen of woods such as pine and hickory resulted in a mutation that must be seen as a distinct species. In England the traditional woods were elm for the seat, beech for the legs and stretchers, with ash for the back. In a 'comb-back' the 'comb' is often of the same wood as the seat— elm. In high quality examples yew was used for the legs, stretchers and back which in exceptional examples were elaborated with 'Gothick' details. All chair backs sustain considerable leverage. Some Windsor chairs solved this problem by making seats with an additional dovetail extension at the back known as a 'bob-tail' from which sprang two extra 'sticks' for support. The addition of arms provided supplementary support to the back. The sticks in an English hoop-backed chair are generally wedged like the legs but in many American examples (and some English) they will be found to be dowelled with tiny 'trennells'. The use of bent wood in the construction of such chairs required very special skills. One labelled Windsor chair, said to have been used on board ship by Captain James Cook on one of his voyages, bears the label '. . . Pitt, wheelwright and chairmaker'.[24]

The bodgers of Berkshire worked in the beech woods turning the legs 'green' on pole lathes. Once seasoned they became slightly elliptical in section which increased their strength when driven into the hole that was drilled through the seat to receive them. The bodger's craft was confined exclusively to producing the turned legs and other turned elements in Windsor chairs. Bodgers, working in the traditional way as a band of craftsmen using temporary workshops in the beech forests, survived in the county until the late 1950s, one of the last of the tribe being H. F. Goodchild of Naphill.

Yew-wood chairs were left unpainted and unlike their less exalted brethren more often bear the brand of their maker, for example Amos of Grantham.[25] It was probably usual for the more ordinary sort to be painted; dark green and blue were popular in England but an earth red was also used in Wales. Windsor chairs were used at all social levels from cottages to stately homes where they are found in summer houses and gardens. According to pictures by artists such as Thomas Robins (1716–70), they were often painted white. By Loudon's day the fashion for painting Windsors was declining. They were 'frequently stained with diluted sulphuric acid and logwood; or by repeatedly washing them over with alum water, which has some tartar in it; they should afterwards be washed over several times with an extract of Brazil wood.' This process produced an effect resembling mahogany and the final oiling and rubbing 'with woolen cloths' completed the deception. Loudon credits a 'Mr Dalziel under whose direction most of them have been prepared [with] preserving the character of simplicity' in these chairs. There is probably some bias in this statement as Dalziel was responsible, together with Edward Buckton Lamb, for the furniture designs that appeared in the volume. Other nineteenth-century makers in the region included Thomas Widgington (who set up a workshop in High Wycombe, away from the beech woods, in 1801), Samuel Treacher, and later in the century Daniel Glenister, Walter Skull and Benjamin North.[26]

Why has the Windsor chair been successful for so long? For a chair constructed of wood to be comfortable without the benefit of upholstery the fewer right angles in its design the better. This requirement resulted in the development of the specialist craft of chair-maker in high-class work. The more widely available joiner-made rural chair retained the rectilinear appearance of an earlier age of discomfort. The Windsor chair was at first almost alone in providing at a low cost the comfort offered by more 'fluid' lines.

The chair illustrated in Plate 166 is related to the Windsor and was known as such. The earliest illustration of the type that I know of occurs in Loudon.[27] They were and are commonly found in kitchens.

Related to the Windsor chair in some of its details is the early nineteenth-century so-called 'Mendlesham' chair, named after Mendlesham in Suffolk where its chief makers,

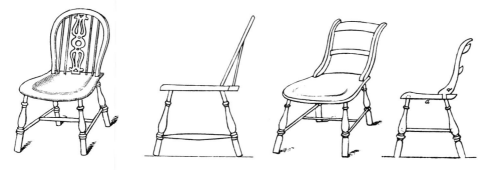

166. Windsor chair and related design from Loudon's *Encyclopaedia*. The Windsor chair has enjoyed a long period of success and wide social distribution. *Bath Public Library*

Daniel and Richard Day, were located. A simpler variant of these chairs was also made in Essex, but in either case they were more often than not made either of fruitwood (apple or pear) or of yew [167].[28]

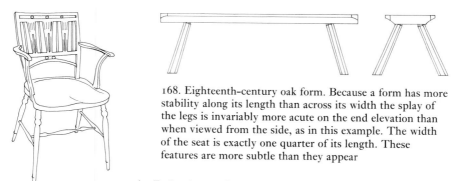

168. Eighteenth-century oak form. Because a form has more stability along its length than across its width the splay of the legs is invariably more acute on the end elevation than when viewed from the side, as in this example. The width of the seat is exactly one quarter of its length. These features are more subtle than they appear

167. Early nineteenth-century East Anglian 'Mendlesham' chair

In the seventeenth century and before, the chair retained its status as the seat of the master of the house, a significance that it has not entirely lost. The majority of people sat on stools or forms. As level floors were introduced so stools and chairs abandoned the use of three legs in favour of four. Examples of furniture brought up to date in this way survive. On simple stools the legs are usually set at an angle to enhance stability. On rectangular-seated, four-legged stools this angle is consistent when viewed from either elevation. However, with forms the stability is greater on the long axis than on the narrow axis and it will generally be found that the angle of the leg is more acute when viewed from the end elevation than when seen from the side [168]. Simple boarded stools and forms made by carpenters were eventually succeeded by 'joint-stools' and forms which employ the shouldered mortice and tenon of the joiner. Once one pair of legs was extended upwards to create a back the familiar back-stool was arrived at.

As the joiner deferred to the subtleties of the cabinet-maker so he in turn, towards the close of the seventeenth century, gave ground to a new breed of woodworkers known as chair-makers. Their products are distinguished by their departure from the use of the right angle, as a consequence of which chairs assumed a less 'wooden' appearance. Undoubtedly much country furniture continued to be made by general joiners and cabinet-makers, but their wares are noteworthy for their more rectilinear appearance and the persistence of the dowelled through-tenon. Notwithstanding the early character of much provincial furniture in Britain, most craftsmen seem to have responded with interestingly various degrees of success to prevailing fashions. The chair illustrated on Plate 169 is a characteristic example of the hybrid with its mediaeval construction employing dowelled through-tenons.

Many articles of furniture, and most notably chairs, employ turners' work. The turners long remained a separate group of craftsmen making drinking vessels and trenchers. Until the sixteenth century earthenware cups were extremely rare. As late as 1552 the Drapers' Company was still using turners' work for cups at their feasts 'with

169. Chair, ULSTER, early nineteenth century, mixed hardwoods including oak. In its interestingly debased way this chair shows the influence of designers like Hepplewhite and Sheraton and the persistence of the early tradition of sound construction. The 'back feet' are not simply morticed and tenoned into the back rail but are given the additional strength of dowels. Country furniture showing metropolitan influence is found throughout the British Isles.
Ulster Folk and Transport Museum

170. Buffet chair. Detail of a painting by Jàn Steen (c. 1626–79), Munich. Such chairs may have reached the British Isles via Scandinavia but the Low Countries are a more likely source for this design. *Photograph: The Courtauld Institute*

ashen cups set before them at every mess'.[29] The turners in London received their charter as a guild in 1604 and four years later had extended their activities to include chairs and wheels.[30] A number of 'thrown' or turned chairs and stools survive from this period and were known in their day as 'buffets' or 'tuffets'—Little Miss Muffet sat on a tuffet, not a 'stump' of grass.[31] Chairs of this type usually have three legs for stability and are triangular on plan up to the seat level, with the back and arms forming a rectangle above. Such chairs and stools endeavour to counteract their structural weakness by multiplying their members. Randle Holme illustrates a stool of this type and states that 'Wrought with Knops and rings all over feet. These and the chairs are generally made with three feete.'[32] It is likely that chairs of this type reached Britain from the Continent via the Low Countries [170] but it has also been suggested that they originated in Byzantium and reached our shores via Scandinavia.[33] Whatever the truth of this, they were undoubtedly to be found in fairly large numbers in the Welsh Marches in the mid-eighteenth century. Writing from Strawberry Hill to George Montagu on 20 August 1761, Horace Walpole reported that, 'Dicky Bateman has picked up a whole cloister full of chairs in Herefordshire. He bought them one by one, here and there, in farmhouses, for three-and-sixpence and a crown apiece, they are wood, the seats triangular, the backs, arms, and legs, loaded with turnery. A thousand to one there are plenty up and down

Cheshire too.'[34] These early seventeenth-century 'thrown' chairs may be considered by some to be too grand for the minor interiors with which we are concerned. However, in Walpole's day it is clear that they were found in 'farmhouses' although from his social position in the eighteenth century he probably underestimated the status of the early seventeenth-century houses in Herefordshire where they were found. Significantly, these chairs were 'picked up' by Dicky Bateman 'one by one' and each was probably the one and only 'master's chair' in the house. Some of these chairs were relatively simple and without arms such as the example portrayed by Frederick Daniel Hardy (1826–1911) in his (185?) painting of *The Interior of a Sussex Farmhouse* [33].

It is more than likely that the rush-seated ladder-back chair came into this country somewhat later in the century from the Low Countries [171]. Many Dutch paintings show ladder-back chairs in modest interiors but in *A Tea Party* by Nicolaes Verkoje (1673–1746) they are shown in elegant surroundings.[35] They are described in the late

171. The parlour, KINGS WESTON, GLOUCESTERSHIRE. Water-colour drawing by S. H. Grimm, late eighteenth century. Simple country furniture had a wide social distribution. *Kay Collection, British Library, Department of Manuscripts*

seventeenth-century inventories as 'Dutch matted chairs' or 'Dutch Flagg chairs'.[36] The reference to the flag may suggest the use of irises as a substitute for rushes. In America, Indian corn was sometimes used as an alternative.[37] The front legs of the characteristic chair of this type are of a form that could be termed a 'suppressed cabriole', but early (i.e. early eighteenth-century) examples probably had simple turned legs such as those illustrated by Grimm in the Saracen's Head, Southwell [12]. The ladder-back consists of three or four 'rungs' of ash which are shaped on elevation and bent on plan. In some examples the back consists of a series of vertical spindles and these were particularly popular in Lancashire and Cheshire. The sections of some of the turned members in these chairs is often rich not to say voluptuous and this is notably true of their front stretchers.

172. Eighteenth-century wainscot chair in oak. *Kalman Collection*

As has been noted, chairs of the Windsor type were used in Scotland, but in some crofting areas where timber was scarce little more than small trees or driftwood was available out of which to construct furniture. These conditions encouraged the development of chairs made from a 'patchwork' of timbers [173]. 'Knees' from small trees were used in 'Sutherland' chairs to provide the 'armature' for seat and back. The seat of a simple chair is normally made out of one slab of wood. Not so in some parts

173. Group of chairs: (a) Sutherland ladder-back, (b) Invernesshire chair, (c) bog-wood chair from the Isle of Harris, (d) Argyle chair, (e) child's chair from Invernesshire, (f) rush-seated chair from North Uist. *Highland Folk Museum*

of Scotland, such as Argyll, where a 'knee' was used to provide the rear portion of the seat and onto this was 'housed' a smaller, straight section of timber. Birch is a wood that grows well in cold climates and it was favoured in Scotland as well as in Scandinavia. These 'patchwork' chairs use a variety of hardwoods including birch and the fruitwoods. In addition, ash and other timber with great strength along the grain were used for such chairs. Another very distinct type is the Inverness-shire chair with its unusual protrusion of the seat behind the back and the front stretchers shaped in a manner reminiscent of late seventeenth-century English chairs. The 'Orkney' chair which combines straw rope and wood is well known by the many reproductions that have been made of it [174].

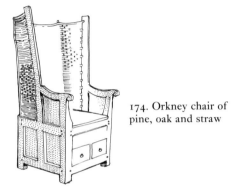

174. Orkney chair of pine, oak and straw

In Ireland the English strategy or policy of deforestation, which made military as well as commercial sense, providing fuel for the iron furnaces of Cumbria, resulted in a lack of timber. Elegant furniture apart, very little Irish furniture dates from before the Famine [175]. Because the native oak forests were destroyed by the late seventeenth century, the mass of furniture in Ireland came to be made from imported softwoods or bogwood.[38] In Co. Antrim the successor to the three-legged 'creepie' was a characteristic low, four-legged chair which, like its counterpart in the crofting communities of Scotland, was constructed out of a minimum of timber [176]. Although apparently in one piece the seat is in fact very thin. It is framed to give an appearance of thickness (as well as to provide strength) and supported by two lateral battens into which the legs are thrust. Such chairs were usually painted a dark red or green.

Many of these chairs from the cabins of Ireland or the crofts of Scotland were home-made. They are invariably low-seated because of the smoky conditions in the simple homes for which they were designed.

> By sitting low, on rushes spread,
> The smoke still hover'd overhead;
> And did more good than real harm
> Because it kept the long house warm.[39]

175. Living-room in a CO. DOWN farmhouse. The fielded panels of the cupboard to the right of the fireplace are typical of nineteenth-century Ulster. *Photograph c. 1910 by R. Welch: The Ulster Museum*

176. Creepie, rush pess and chair, and three other chairs all from ULSTER

The mediaeval tradition of placing or fixing a bench against the lateral timber screen in the hall is the probable origin of the settle. Certainly by the eighteenth century the settle often occupied a similar position in the house. Loudon in fact describes settles as 'benches' and even illustrates a 'Grecian Bench'.[40] Unlike the screen and form it was not so draught proof, a deficiency that was met by the provision of a curtain. 'On the back there might be a towel roller, or in a superior kind of cottage, the back of the settle might be ornamented with prints or maps in the manner of a [movable] screen . . . there might even be book shelves fixed to the back, and a flap might be hung to it, with a jib bracket to serve as a reading or writing table.'[41] When 'box' seated, the space in the settle was used for storage, with access by means of a lid in the seat or drawers in the front. Occasionally the back took the form of a cupboard, traditionally used for hanging sides of bacon, and in Wales the back of the settle was sometimes the side of a box bed [177a]. The Scottish equivalent of the settle was the 'seise' which provided no draught-proofing whatsoever [178].

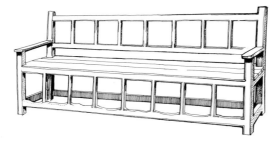

178. Late eighteenth/early nineteenth-century seize or settle from a croft in NORTH UIST. This kind of bench was also known as a deece or deas (from the dais of a hall where they originally stood). *Highland Folk Museum*

The settle-bed of Ulster was common in the province [179, 180] but was not apparently used elsewhere in the British Isles although it is found on the north-east seaboard of North America in both Canada and the United States.[42] The planks forming the seat and front are fixed to one another to form an 'L' section which is hinged to open out forming a trough-like space which usually measures about 72 in (183 cm) by 36 in (91.4 cm) by 18 in (4.7 cm) deep. In principle these settles when opened as beds are the same as the stone beds of Skara Brae on Orkney or the similar wooden beds of mediaeval type found in Norway. In all cases these beds were filled with heather, straw or some such material which would provide a mattress. Rather similar is *la veille*, also known as *la filyie*, of Jersey which, though not a bed, was a seat in the shape of a box 'filled with dried bracken, and that covered with a piece of carpet'.[43] The type of mattress was related to pocket, class and region. The rich could afford feathers or combed wool but many had to make do with flock or straw. In Harrison's day servants were fortunate if they had so much as an undersheet 'to keepe them from the pricking straws that ran oft through the canvas (of the pallet) and rased their hardened hides'.[44] Writing in 1664, John Evelyn

177a, b. Kennixton Farmhouse from LLANGENNYDD on the Gower Peninsula built in about 1630. A recess in the ceiling above the fireplace known as the charnel was a dry space for hanging bacon and herbs. The back of the settle opens into a cupboard bed. *In house re-erected at Welsh Folk Museum*

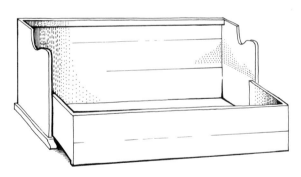

180. Settle-bed from ULSTER shown open

179. Settle-bed, ULSTER, eighteenth century (?), fir, painted, 72 in (182.9 cm) wide by 58 in (147.3 cm) overall height, by 21 in (53.3 cm) front to back. The seat folds forwards to create a trough in which a bed could be made. The height of the 'seat' is 32 in (81.3 cm) which suggests that this example may have been used as a sideboard during the day. The mediaeval character of the design with its sledge feet and the primitive dovetails used in its construction make its date uncertain. Such settle-beds are common in Ulster (and North East America) but are not found in other parts of the British Isles. *Ulster Folk and Transport Museum*

recommended beech leaves 'gathered about the fall and somewhat before they are frostbitten'.[45]

The box or cupboard-bed was probably once widespread in the British Isles where surviving examples will now be found only occasionally in the north of England [181] and in Wales, more often in Scotland where they may have been unusual until the eighteenth century [182].[46] Such beds were once common in Scandinavia and they are also found in Brittany. They may be either free-standing or built-in and may derive from the bed alcoves that were built into the thickness of walls. Undoubtedly box beds were kept snug by the warmth of the human body. Some are provided with ventilation, but those that are not gained air, one may presume, through an open door. In those parts of Scotland where wood was scarce such beds were often screened off by curtains rather than doors. In small one-room cottages they provided a bedroom with some privacy and it was probably for this reason that they were made well into the nineteenth century. Loudon illustrates 'An Improvement in the Box Bedsteads used in Scotch Cottages'.[47]

181. Bed-cupboards built into a house in WAITBY, CUMBRIA, oak, late seventeenth century. The turned balusters which fill the top panels of the doors provided ventilation.
Photograph: Royal Commission on Historical Monuments

182. Bed-cupboard from BADENOCH, SCOTLAND, fir, dated 1702 and initialled D. MP, 71 in (180.3 cm) wide, by 58.5 in (148.6 cm) high, by 48 in (121.9 cm) deep. Bed-cupboards are found throughout much of peasant Europe and are either built-in or free standing as is this example. In contrast to England and Wales pine and fir were extensively used in Scotland.
Highland Folk Museum

183. Bedroom of the Weaver's House from BALLYDUGGAN. The nineteenth-century beds are of a type that are common in North America. *In house re-erected at Ulster Folk and Transport Museum*

In Ulster the 'bed outshot' was a reasonably standard feature, built into the wall running at right angles to the fire-hood wall.[48] In some examples a proportion of the interior depth of these alcoves is accommodated in the wall thickness.[49] Despite the generally rudimentary roof-lining elsewhere in the house, the *cailleach* or outshot was invariably lined with newspapers pasted together and whitewashed. Judging by the dates of these newspapers this is probably an early nineteenth-century innovation in place of the woven grass mats once used to line bed outshots. In Ulster these beds were often reserved for visitors, the family sleeping on the floor, with mother and father side by side in the centre, the youngest daughter next to the mother and son next to the father, and so on in gradually increasing ages.

From early times most people slept on half-headed bedsteads. These resemble modern bedsteads except that the primitive mattress was supported by interwoven ropes that passed through drill holes in the surrounding frame. On these, as on many bedsteads, the mortice and tenon was often held by means of bolts which could be undone to dismantle the bed [183]. In Kennixton Farmhouse from the Gower Peninsula,

184. (*left*) Cupboard with stone shelves built into the gable wall of a ruined croft. The timber architrave would have facilitated the hanging of a wooden door. In thick-walled stone or cob houses such built-in storage is common to much of the British Isles. *Photograph: Highland Folk Museum*
185. (*right*) Cupboard built into the central room of Heaning Farmhouse, WINDERMERE, CUMBRIA, oak, dated 1681, initialled IDO. 'The great rebuilding' took place in Cumbria later than in many other parts of England. Furniture built into Cumbrian houses of this period of redevelopment is reasonably common. *Photograph: Royal Commission on Historical Monuments*

now re-erected at St. Fagans, the divan bed is in fact on top of the recess in the ceiling of the room below. This recess, known locally as a 'charnel', was near the fire and not only made the bed warm but also, in the room below, provided a dry space in which to hang bacon and herbs. This feature is also recorded in Yorkshire in Langstrothdale and in the Dales around Sedbergh.[50]

One of the most important uses of the enclosed cupboard was for the storage of food. By building it into the thickness of a stone wall and equipping it with a wooden door, reasonably cool temperatures could be maintained [184]. These cupboards are found in most parts of the British Isles but in the seventeenth century they were particularly popular in Cumbria [185]. By building them into the warm wall of the chimney items like

186a, b. Food cupboard from ACHARACLE, HIGHLAND, SCOTLAND, fir and wicker, late nineteenth century, 30 in (76.2 cm) wide, by 67 in (170.2 cm) high, by 15 in (38.1 cm) deep. Ventilation was a necessity in food cupboards and despite the late date of this example its use of wicker points to its being an early type. *Highland Folk Museum*

salt or herbs could be kept dry. The use of such a cupboard for valuable herbs may be inferred by their small size and the presence of a lock. Food is preserved better with ventilation and such provision may help to distinguish between a food cupboard and a wardrobe. In early times when cupboards were known as 'aumbrys' the needs of ventilation were probably met by the use of woven wickerwork. A late example of the type is the remarkable cupboard from Acharacle, Highland [186a, b]. The alternative was to frame up panels of turned spindles, as in the cheese cupboard [187a, b] from Strathnairn (a fertile dairy farming region), or to pierce panels of wood with drill holes, as in the front of a built-in cupboard of the seventeenth century recently removed from Blue Barnes, North Essex [188].[51]

The 'court cupboard', as it became known in the sixteenth century, consisted of open shelves and occupied an esteemed place at court where it was used to display the 'plate'.[52] Towards the close of Elizabeth I's reign the upper half of some of these cupboards was partially enclosed. In the course of the seventeenth century this process was completed

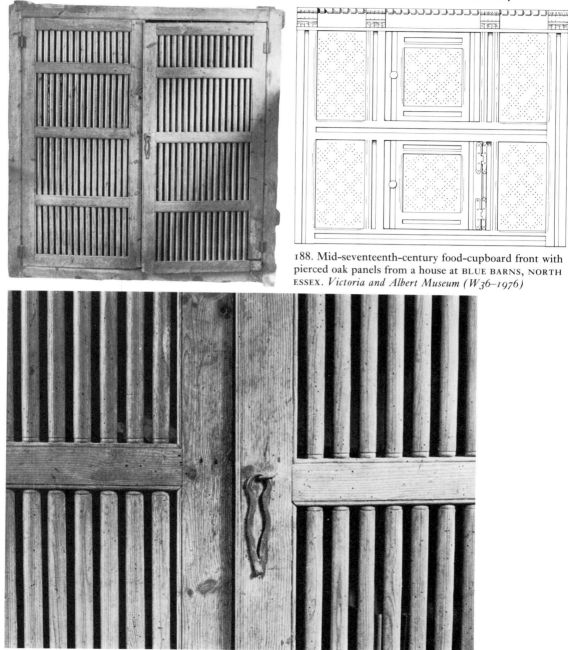

188. Mid-seventeenth-century food-cupboard front with pierced oak panels from a house at BLUE BARNS, NORTH ESSEX. *Victoria and Albert Museum (W36–1976)*

187a, b. Cheese cupboard from STRATHNAIRN, SCOTLAND, pine, early nineteenth century. Strathnairn is a fairly prosperous dairy farming area. *Highland Folk Museum*

189a, b. Two oak press cupboards built into the north wall of one room in Common Farm, WINDERMERE, CUMBRIA. The earliest of the two is dated 1628 and the other 1715. The Jacobean tradition was long preserved in the Lake District. *Photograph: Royal Commission on Historical Monuments*

with both levels fully enclosed by doors, thus creating the 'press-cupboard', but with vestiges of the original form surviving in the columns or pendentives to the upper section which also retains a narrow shelf [189a, b]. In Wales these pieces of furniture were taken a stage further by the addition of a third tier—they are known as 'tridarns'. These objects may be seen as the natural predecessors of the ubiquitous dresser without which no home from the eighteenth century onwards was complete.

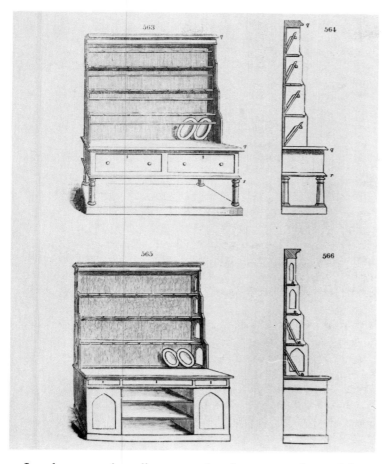

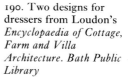

190. Two designs for dressers from Loudon's *Encyclopaedia of Cottage, Farm and Villa Architecture. Bath Public Library*

Loudon unequivocally asserts that dressers are 'essential to every kitchen, but more especially to that of the cottage to whome they serve both as dressers and sideboards' [190]. Most of the nineteenth-century examples that will be found built into the kitchen of the average town house are made of deal. However, in the country, when the hall served the double function of kitchen and main living-room, oak was favoured and every attention was given to the finish befitting furniture for a living-room. In the north of England in the late eighteenth and early nineteenth century dressers were often embellished with mahogany cross-banding and given ivory escutcheons. Probably the simplest of all the oak dressers was made in the region of Bridgwater, Somerset. It was not made up in the usual way of two sections—shelves and base—for the sides were composed of a pair of boards running from floor to ceiling.[53] Not all dresser shelves were given boarded backs as the wall of the house was often adequate. In

191. Living-room in a house in DRUMAGHLIS (TOWNLAND), NEAR BALLYNAHINCH, CO. DOWN.
The pyramids of inverted bowls on the bottom shelf of the dresser and the forward-sloping plates
are typical of Ulster. *Photograph c. 1910 by R. Welch: The Ulster Museum*

England and Wales the shelves are usually equipped with a groove; the plates were
slotted into this and leant against the back. An alternative method, occasionally found in
England and Wales but common in Scotland and Ulster, was to fit battens of wood on to
the front of the dresser between the shelves so that the plates could be leant forward. The
favourite crocks that were displayed on these shelves were willow pattern and other
'Staffordshire blue'. In Ulster the bottom shelf of such dressers was usually reserved for
pyramids of inverted soup bowls [191].

In Ireland and Scotland dressers were generally constructed of softwoods. Indeed, the
more widespread use of conifer for the furniture in small traditional interiors in these two
countries produces an effect markedly different from equivalent interiors in England and
Wales. The dresser often occupied the wall facing the fire, and in one-room cottages its
position was advanced away from the wall, screening off a small bed-space [192]. In the
so-called black houses of the Hebrides and elsewhere in Scotland the dresser often stood
against an outer wall. So that it could fit in that position the top (when viewed from the
side) was angled parallel to the roof timbers [193]. This is characteristic of some late
Gothic, South German softwood furniture; a comparison which is coincidental, few
surviving Scottish dressers being earlier than the nineteenth century.

192. Single-room cottage from
RHOSTRYFAN, GWYNEDD, dated 1762.
The dresser backs onto a partition
which creates two small bedrooms with
a loft over. *Re-erected at Welsh Folk
Museum*

193. Dresser from a croft at EOCHAR,
SOUTH UIST, OUTER HEBRIDES,
SCOTLAND, fir and pine, mid-
nineteenth century, 46 in (116.8 cm)
wide, by 69 in (175.3 cm) high, by 22 in
(55.9 cm) front to back. Dressers of this
type customarily stood against an
outside wall of the 'black house' with
their backboards rising to the level of
the wall plate. The hood is angled to
run parallel with the rafters of the roof.
Highland Folk Museum

Most furniture from small domestic interiors in England was made from oak, fruitwood, ash and elm. In Scotland softwood with some birch was widely used together with some woods common to England and Wales. In Ulster the picture is similar to that found in Scotland with the addition of some bog oak. Compared with continental Europe remarkably little of this furniture was painted after about 1700, the ubiquitous stick-back chair and the settle-beds of Ulster being exceptions and exceptions that were simply painted one colour. Decorative painting, used to such good and florid effect in much of peasant Europe, seems to be almost unknown in post-mediaeval Britain, though it may have persisted into the seventeenth century as a survival, and is found on the inner side of the lids of sailors' chests and on the furniture traditionally used in the cabins of canal boats.[54] As Eric Mercer has observed, 'Early timber furniture has survived less well, but its direct successors in eighteenth- and nineteenth-century Scandinavian peasant houses reflect its qualities.' Among these qualities was the love of colour. 'The important difference however is that in early years even the best furniture of kings was often painted, while later painting was usually confined to the furniture of lesser men or to the less important furniture of the great.'[55] Only under the influence of Robert Adam did this trend fleetingly reverse itself. In many towns outside London the fashionable materials of the eighteenth century, such as walnut or later mahogany, were used for much furniture which is otherwise provincial in style and construction. Some upholstery was used in such work and fruitwood chairs with 'drop in' seats are quite common.

Apart from wood other materials were used for furniture. As we have seen, the vertebra of a whale provided a convenient stool but such an object was obtainable only in certain coastal regions. More widespread was the use of woven wickerwork, a tradition going back to Roman Britain if not earlier.[56] In the cathedral on the island of Iona wickerwork coffins were found in the crypt.[57] In areas such as the Outer Hebrides, where timber was so scarce, wickerwork chairs [194] were much used and where wickerwork was unavailable straw rope provided an alternative which was also used in timbered regions. 'In Monmouthshire, easy chairs with hoods, like porters' chairs in gentlemen's halls, are constructed of straw matting on a frame of wooden rods, or of stout iron wire; and [some] chairs . . . are made entirely of straw in different parts of England in the same way as the common beehives.'[58] A 'lip-work' chair from Wales of the type described by Loudon is illustrated on Plate 195 and they are also well known in the west of Ireland.[59] These chairs are thought to have been common in Scandinavia, the word 'lip' corresponding to the Danish *løb*.[60] The word also occurs in English dialects as 'leap', to mean basketwork. In Wales these chairs were known as *cadair telynor* or harpist's chairs. In at least one example this type of chair, whose design was born of straw rope, was translated into wood [196]. Rushes were also used to make furniture, and the drum-like 'pess' is still made in East Anglia [197]. It is a type of hassock. In fact the latter may well be related to the pess as the word 'hassock' has been thought by some to derive from the Welsh for sedges which is *hesg*.[61]

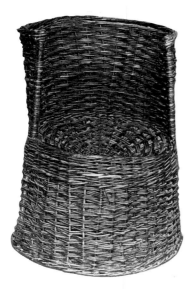

194. Wickerwork chair of the type once made on SKYE. Although of a traditional type this example was made in the Highland Homes Industry Factory at Kilmuir in 1936; 22 in (55.9 cm) diameter by 30 in (76.2 cm) overall height, the level of the seat being 16 in (40.6 cm). In areas such as the western and northern Isles of Scotland, as in Ulster, the scarcity of timber encouraged the production of furniture made from driftwood, wicker or straw rope. *Highland Folk Museum*

195. Welsh lip-work chair. Seating furniture of straw rope was once made in many parts of the British Isles from Ulster to East Anglia. *Welsh Folk Museum*

196. Chair from Blaencrymlin Farm, BLACKMILL, NEAR BRIDGEND, GLAMORGAN

197. Two rush pesses. *Stranger's Hall, Norwich*

The dominance of 'easel painting' must be seen as a product of the Renaissance. Before then the movable panel painting was the exception and the painter's craft ranged over a wide variety of surfaces integrating him more fully with his public and the home. Overdoor and overmantel pictures (described elsewhere) were among the last examples of the painter's craft united inseparably with their architectural setting. However, by the late seventeenth century movable pictures, both paintings and prints, were to be found in many homes. Early picture frames followed architectural practice and included a cill like a window and the familiar mason's mitre. The widespread appearance of easel paintings by the early seventeenth century promoted the development of the picture frame as an object removed from architecture. In the second half of the century a common and simple type of frame which derived from the Continent employed ebony worked with a 'wriggled' moulding. Quite how this moulding was achieved I do not know despite Moxon's description 'Of the Waving Engine': 'And as the Rounds of the Rack ride over the round edge of the flat Iron, the Rack and Riglet will mount up to the Iron, and as the Rounds of the Waves on the under side of the Rack slides off the Iron on edge, the Rack and Riglet will sink, and so in progression . . . The Riglet will on its upper side receive the form of several waves.'[62]

By 1688 Stalker and Parker were recommending lightweight simulated ebony frames which 'are usually made of stained Pear-tree, with narrow mouldings for little pieces, which increase in bredth, as the size of your picture does in largness; they are made with Rabets, and are afforded for 6, 8, and 12 pence, or more, according to their several dimensions.'[63]

These frames long remained popular and today are known as 'Hogarths'. The elaborate, carved wood frames of the seventeenth and eighteenth centuries, with their resplendent water gilding are generally outside the scope of this book. In the early nineteenth century, frames with a simple section were sometimes painted to simulate bird's-eye maple and at about the same time rosewood and bird's-eye maple veneer was also used. Original examples of the painted bird's-eye maple are now very rare. Another favourite of the second half of the nineteenth century was the 'Oxford' frame; it is described in *The Practical Carver and Gilder's Guide* (c. 1880):[64]

These frames have become favourites within the last few years. They are made of oak, with cross corners, and are made up in fancy patterns, some of which are finished with ultramarine on the bevels. They can be had of the wholesale houses of the following sizes:

$4\frac{1}{4}$ in. by $3\frac{1}{4}$ in.	[10.8 cm. by 8.3 cm.
7 by 5	17.8 by 12.7
8 by $6\frac{1}{2}$	20.3 by 16.5
$10\frac{1}{2}$ by $8\frac{1}{2}$	26.7 by 21.6
12 by 10	30.5 by 25.4

14	by 12	35.6	by 30.5
16	by 14	40.6	by 35.6
18	by 16	45.7	by 40.6
21	by 14½	53.3	by 36.9
23	by 18½	58.4	by 47
29	by 21	73.7	by 53.3]

The *Gilder's Guide* adds that 'Oxford frames are suitable for sacred subjects, mottoes, views in the Holy Land, &c., but are used for portraits, and many other pictures look well in them.' In the nineteenth century many frames were made up to imitate carving of a 'composition' similar to gesso with 'slips' of 'German gold'—a substitute for the real thing.

In the seventeenth, eighteenth and early nineteenth centuries pictures were generally hung rather high [I] in relation to the average height of individuals. The interior of the Reverend Richard Kay's parsonage recorded by his protégé, the German artist S. H. Grimm, shows this feature clearly [198]. Apparently this enabled pictures to

198. *The Harvest Children at Prayers, Kirkby Parsonage with the Green Dale Oak Cabinet [from Welbeck Abbey], Nott.* Water-colour drawing by S. H. Grimm, late eighteenth century, 13.5 × 10.5 in (34.3 × 26.7 cm). Pictures were commonly hung high in the eighteenth century. *Kaye Collection, British Library, Department of Manuscripts*

be viewed more easily when the company was standing. The excessive height at which pictures were hung was sometimes compensated for by tilting them forward, and the two methods of hanging often co-existed in the same room as is shown in the drawing of Pepys's library.[65] In panelled rooms pictures would often be shown hung arbitrarily across stiles and rails and not kept within panels, a feature which is well illustrated in the 1762 group portrait of *The Family of Thomas Bateson*, attributed to Philip Hussey (1713–83).

At Newby Hall, Yorkshire, in the late seventeenth century the pictures were 'not set up, the house being in mourning for his Lady and her mother the Lady Yorke',[66] but it is not known how general this practice was in lesser households.

In the eighteenth century cheap prints became available to many people, but by the nineteenth century they were truly ubiquitous. Mirrors however remained expensive which is why they were so lavishly used by the rich in the eighteenth century. Their more general distribution did not occur until the nineteenth century.

It was often found aesthetically advisable with large numbers of small prints to hang them in 'constellations' [200]. There was in general no objection to picture wire or cord

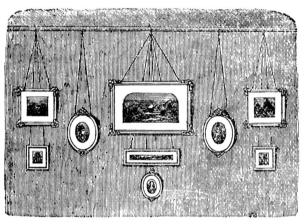

200. An 'Arrangement of Pictures' illustrated in Brodie and Middleton's *The Carver and Gilder's Guide* (c. 1880). *Collection: James Ayres*

being visible, but it was recommended that, 'The colour of the cord should correspond with the paper or the paint in the room as much as possible, so as not to be noticed, as it is no ornament to see cords on the walls.'[67] Picture chain, used in grand establishments, was generally used for heavy pictures and mirrors and kept to a minimum length. Clearly in a matter of this nature there was considerable individual variation: '. . . much depends on taste; some will have the bottom edge of the frames all round a room to range exactly, while others prefer to see the line broken.'[68]

199. *Interior of a Cottage on Boxley Hill, Maidstone.* Water-colour drawing c. 1840 by Arthur Vine Hall (1824–1919). By the nineteenth century the yeoman's house of the sixteenth century was considered to be 'a cottage'. This drawing shows that the early tradition for sparse furnishing was preserved in the second quarter of the nineteenth century. The mirror hanging on the extreme left was clearly made for a much grander establishment. Employers in 'the big house' often gave generous wedding presents to the villagers who had been 'in service'. *Collection of Mrs Polly Rogers*

By the early nineteenth century pictures were fairly general even in small cottages. Loudon in writing about 'Pictures, Sculptures, and other internal Ornaments' observed that, 'There is no cottage or dwelling, however humble, in which there will not be found some object purely ornamental. Later in the century this trend was firmly established: 'There is now scarcely a cottage where its inmates do not look with pride and pleasure upon some humble effort of art, that adorns the walls of their home, and from the artisan to the titled nobility of our land, the work of the artist and engraver is admired and valued.'[69]

However, not all pretty things were necessarily regarded as 'purely ornamental'. Hanging shelves and spoon racks were both decorative and useful, and following the 1851 Exhibition the astonishingly cheap and attractive Connecticut clock found its way into almost every home in the British Isles. Superstitions, often of ancient origin, resulted in household features that were not merely pretty but were of fundamental importance to those who owned them. In *John Ashby of Tysoe* his daughter, M. K. Ashby, describes an interior which contains an apparently innocuous collection of nick-nacks: 'On the mantle-piece were china figures of old-fashioned policemen, pale blue-and-white, and small lions with crinkled manes. On the wall above were hung long hollow glass walking-sticks, twisted like barley sugar, one of them filled with tiny coloured balls like a confectioner's hundreds and thousands.'[70] These walking-sticks were more than nick-nacks. They were hung in a house to absorb disease which, so the superstitious believed, could be wiped off the glass with a cloth.[71] Such features and objects like the witch-posts of Yorkshire, the Bridget's crosses of Ireland or the glass balls that were thought to repel witches, may have been decorative but their primary purpose concerned the need to assuage primitive fears.

In the general furnishing of the rooms of a house with objects large and small, utilitarian and ornamental, the inventory is long, the possibilities endless. In looking at furniture I have endeavoured to illuminate those aspects of the subject, such as native woods, dressers and paint, that are peculiar to the smaller house, but I must acknowledge that much has been omitted such as clocks, wardrobes and writing desks. Clearly the presence of pottery in small houses was important but no space remains to describe the sgraffito ware of North Devon and Somerset, or the treen love-spoons of Wales, or the universal and ancient tradition of corn dollies made from ears and stems taken from the last wheatsheaf of the harvest and hung from the ceiling of the farmhouse for a year, perennial but enduring symbols of the 'staff of life'. All such objects contributed to the appearance of the home, to its spiritual and physical comforts.

201. Curfew, late thirteenth century, 18 in (45.7 cm) diameter, 9 in (22.9 cm) height. The earthenware *couvre-feu* or fire-cover was probably used at many social levels to both dampen down and retain a fire overnight, although this example may be a unique survival. Later, the apsidal curfew for wall (as opposed to central) hearths was made of repoussé brass for more elegant establishments. *Salisbury and South Wiltshire Museum*

Notes to Chapter 10

1. Robert Roberts, *The Classic Slum, Salford Life in the First Quarter of the Century*, Manchester University Press, 1971, p. 17.
2. Oliver Goldsmith, quoted by Geoffrey Wills, *English Furniture 1550–1760*, Guinness Superlatives, London, 1971, p. 17.
3. Loudon, p. 633.
4. Despite its Stone Age culture this remote site may be as late as 300 BC. V. Gordon Childe, *Official Guide to Skara Brae*, HMSO, Edinburgh, 1977 edition, p. 5.
5. In a house from Mule, Bordo, Faeröe Islands, now in the Frilandsmuseet, Copenhagen.
6. Evans, *Irish Folk Ways*, p. 93.
7. Usually from the same tree, as the grain will confirm.
8. *Stollen* means a supportive post or foot. See Gislind M. Ritz, *The Art of Painted Furniture*, Van Nostrand Reinhold Company, 1970, English language edition, New York, 1971, p. 9 and figs. 157–60.
9. An example of this can be seen at the American Embassy, London, where the mitre at the base of the stone revetment rising from the pavement is deteriorating rapidly.
10. Moxon, p. 85.
11. Wolsey and Luff, p. 44.
12. Emmison, p. 16.
13. Addy, pp. 76–7.
14. Smith, *Nollekens and His Times*, vol. II, p. 228 (see page 145, note 22).
15. Quoted by Wills, *English Furniture 1760–1900*, p. 113.
16. Evans, *Irish Folk Ways*, p. 88.

17. Moxon, p. 125.
18. This traditional term occurs in Robert Manwaring's *Cabinet and Chair Makers Real Friend and Companion*, London, 1765.
19. Thomas H. Ormsbee, *The Windsor Chair*, Deerfield Books, New York, 1962, p. 16. This book is primarily concerned with American Windsors.
20. Jane Toller, *Country Furniture*, David and Charles, Newton Abbot, 1973, pp. 38–9.
21. Information appended to the label in the British Museum by Mrs Bernard Croft-Murray together with a photograph of a William Webb chair. Therle Hughes in *Cottage Antiques*, Lutterworth Press, London, 1967, p. 23, quotes 'Stubb's Manufactory' which offered 'all sorts of Yew Tree, Gothic, and Windsor Chairs, Alcoves and rural Seats, Garden Machines, Dyed Chairs &c.' on a trade-card of 1790–1803.
22. The metamorphosis of the English Windsor into the American version may be attributed entirely to the use of different materials. In America the 'sticks' of the back were often made from hickory which permitted more elongated lines than was possible with the English ash. Furthermore, in America the seats were traditionally of pine or some other such softwood. The elm seats in England were strong enough if only $1\frac{1}{2}$ in (3.8 cm) thick but pine had to be at least 2 in (5 cm) thick and the point at which the legs entered the seat had to be kept well to the centre if splitting was to be avoided. To reduce their apparent thickness the seats of American examples were elaborately dished and chamfered. All these features resulted in the more elongated forms and exaggerated angles of the American Windsor. Occasionally such characteristics will be found in English Windsor chairs such as the mid-eighteenth-century example once owned by Oliver Goldsmith and now in the Victoria and Albert Museum (538–1872).
23. Helen Comstock (ed.), *Concise Encyclopedia of American Antiques*, Hawthorn Books, New York, 1958. Chapter on 'Windsor Chairs' by Marvin D. Schwartz, vol. I, pp. 59–61.
24. 'Correspondence', *Country Life*, 8 April 1976. An article by J. Geraint Jenkins, 'A Chiltern Chair Bodger', occurs in the same journal for 29 September 1955 giving details of manufacture.
25. Toller, p. 43.
26. Ormsbee, p. 191 (see note 19, above).
27. Loudon, p. 319.
28. Toller, p. 43.
29. Peter C. D. Brears, *The English Country Pottery*, David and Charles, Newton Abbot, 1971, p. 13.
30. Wills, *English Furniture 1550–1760*, p. 7. As we have seen, wheelwrights too were makers of Windsor chairs.
31. Iona and Peter Opie, *Oxford Dictionary of Nursery Rhymes*, Clarendon Press, Oxford, 1951.
32. Randle Holme, *The Academy of Armory*, written 1648–9, published in Chester, 1688, III, ch. 14, ill. 73.
33. Chairs of turners' work known to the author in Scandinavia, where birch was the wood most favoured, such as the example in Urnes Church, Norway, are rectangular on plan. The Low Countries are a more likely source of the type, as both chairs and stools of this kind occur in the work of artists like Jan Steen.
34. R. W. Symonds, 'The Craft of the English Turner', *Apollo*, London, May 1939, p. 223. See also accession card for a seventeenth-century turned chair in the Victoria and Albert Museum, W.24–1913.
35. In the collection of the Victoria and Albert Museum, P.51–1962.
36. Toller, pp. 45–6.
37. An example can be seen in the Dutch House at Newcastle, Delaware.
38. Evans, *Irish Folk Ways*, p. 85.
39. Ibid., p. 93, quoting W(illiam) M(offat), *The Western Isle*, 1724, Canto 2.
40. Loudon, p. 317.
41. Ibid., p. 317. The word 'jib' may be a verb meaning 'to swing' as in the jib of a crane. Nicholson refers to a 'jibb' or 'jib door' which he defines as one 'which is flush with the surface of the wall, being generally papered over, the same as the room, the design being to conceal the door as much as possible, in order to preserve the symmetry . . . of the room'. Nicholson, p. 183 and Plate L.

42. An example may be seen in The American Museum in Britain at Bath. John Fraser describes them in his *Canadian Pen and Ink Sketches*, Montreal, 1910, and says that 'they are to be found in every house, more particularly the French and Scotch farmhouses . . . [they] are always nicely painted.' See the magazine *Antiques*, New York City, March 1968, p. 345. I have found no examples of these settles in Scotland and it is likely that Fraser is referring to the 'Scotch-Irish'. See Russell Hawes Kettle, *The Pine Furniture of Early New England*, Dover, NYC, 1929, ill. 69, and Ralph and Terry Kovel, *American Country Furniture 1780–1875*, Crown, NYC, 1965, p. 13.

43. George S. Knocker, 'The Jersey Kitchen. La Tchuisinne Jerriaise', *Société Jersiaise Bulletin*, 1932, p. 27.

44. Harrison, II, p. 240.

45. Wills, p. 32.

46. Grant, p. 169.

47. Loudon, pl. 1291.

48. Excavations on Fyfield Down in Wiltshire revealed a long-house with a bed outshot associated with twelfth-century pottery. Mercer, *English Vernacular Houses*, p. 35.

49. Desmond McCourt and Emyr Estyn Evans, 'A Late 17th Century Farmhouse at Shantallow near Londonderry', *Ulster Folklife*, vol. 14, 1968, pp. 14–23. 'Though the outshot (on the ground floor) projects only 3 ft [91.4 cm] externally it has been given an internal depth of 3 ft 6 in [106.7 cm] by reducing the width of the outside wall to 18 in [45.7 cm] as compared with the thickness of 2 ft [61 cm] in the rest of the house.'

50. Marie Hartley and Joan Ingilby, *Life and Tradition in the Yorkshire Dales*, Dent, London, 1968, p. 6.

51. A number of highly sophisticated mediaeval food cupboards survive with pierced tracery panels.

52. Wolsey and Luff, p. 36.

53. Toller, pp. 65–9.

54. A very late manifestation that did not occur until families lived on board the boats, after the decline of the canals with the advent of the railways.

55. Eric Mercer, *Furniture 700–1700*, Weidenfeld and Nicholson, London, 1969, pp. 30, 43. A number of examples of fairly complete painted mediaeval furniture survive. Harvey, p. 155, cites documentary evidence (of 1483) for early joiners having painting equipment in their workshops. Apparently these craftsmen also made saddle-bows which like the furniture would be painted.

56. Joan Liversidge, *Furniture in Roman Britain*, Tiranti, London, 1955, p. 16.

57. Grant, p. 207.

58. Loudon, p. 347.

59. Evans, *Irish Folk Ways*, p. 93.

60. Peate, *Tradition and Folk Life*, p. 51.

61. *Oxford English Dictionary*.

62. Moxon, p. 105.

63. Stalker and Parker, p. 70.

64. *The Practical Carver and Gilder's Guide*, printed by Simpkin, Marshall and Co. for Brodie and Middleton, c. 1880, pp. 145–6.

65. Drawing of Samuel Pepys's library at York Buildings, London, c. 1693, reproduced by Cornforth, p. 88.

66. Morris (ed.), *The Journeys of Celia Fiennes*, p. 85, written in 1697.

67. *The Practical Carver and Gilder's Guide*, p. 168 (see note 64, above).

68. Ibid., p. 167.

69. Ibid., p. 165.

70. Quoted by Bea Howe, 'Pottery Toys of the Image Maker', *Country Life*, 26 April 1962.

71. George S. and Helen McKearin, *American Glass*, Crown Publishers, New York, 1941, 15th printing, 1963, p. 179.

Glossary

Arch A method of spanning the space between two points by means of a curve or curves. In the true arch this curve is composed of a series of individual stones known as voussoirs. Where an arch is cut from a monolithic block it is not a true arch and is structurally the same as a lintel. The single-centred arch is a characteristic of the Romanesque tradition. Mediaeval architecture used, and indeed was based upon the use of, the two- and later four-centred arch.

Architrave The lowest member of an entablature. The word is also applied to a door, window or fireplace surround.

Ark A chest with a barrel or curved top made by arkwrights.

Arris The sharp edge where two planes meet.

Astragal Narrow semicircular moulding. On a large scale this moulding is known as a torus. A characteristic location for the astragal is the glazing bars of windows or bookcases.

Aumbry The early name for a built-in cupboard with a door. The early cupboard was simply an open shelf.

Baluster A species of small column (or pier). Usually found in groups as in the balusters which support the handrail of a staircase.

Bay One or several uniform divisions of a building often defined by structural features such as columns or piers. In timber-frame buildings the bay is often 16 ft (4.9 m) but may be as little as 9 ft (2.7 m).

Bead A narrow moulding of convex form.

Bed The natural way that stone lies in the quarry is referred to as 'the bed'. So that stone may 'weather' well it should be laid 'on bed' by the mason.

Bed-cupboard A bed enclosed by cupboard doors.

Bob-tail The dove-tailed extension sometimes found at the back of the seat of a Windsor chair to hold two additional sticks to provide extra support to the back.

Bodger A name given to the turners who used pole lathes in the Buckinghamshire beech woods where the legs of Windsor chairs were turned.

Bolection moulding A projecting moulding of ogee section often used to surround panels and connecting a higher plane to a lower one.

Boss A feature used in both stone and wood to mask the intersections of ribs in vaulting or ceilings. The term is also used more generally to describe a decorative protuberance.

Bressumer or **breast summer** A horizontal structural beam built into the face of a wall to support a considerable load above a void as over a shop window.

Buffet A sideboard or a three-legged 'turned' or 'thrown' stool (also Tuffet). A three-legged 'thrown' chair was known as a 'buffet chair'.

Buttery A service room used for the storage of drink.

Cames Slender rods of cast lead having grooves along their sides designed to take glass in a 'leaded' window.

Carcase The 'body of a piece of 'case' furniture.

Chamfer The narrow surface or bevel produced by planing off the arris on timber or masonry.

Chimney board or **fire board** A board designed to fit into a fireplace opening to seal it in summer. They were usually decorated.

Cill or **sill** The lowest horizontal timber into which the studs of a timber-frame building are morticed. Also the horizontal member at the base of a window—window cill.

Cloam oven A type of bread oven made of earthenware (from the seventeenth to the early twentieth century) in Devon and Somerset.

Cob A clay or a mixture of marl or chalk, gravel, dung and straw used for building walls. Known as 'wichert' in Buckinghamshire.

Collar A beam which 'ties' two principal rafters half way up their length.

Corbel A projecting stone or timber used as a support for a structural member or sculptural feature.

Court cupboard At first a two-tiered buffet or side table which was later enclosed by doors but retaining vestigal traces of the original form.

Cove A wide concave surface.

Cruck A timber used in pairs providing the principal members of roof and wall. Such timbers were often arched and employed the natural curves of chosen trees. In early examples the whole diameter of the log was used. 'Full crucks' have been located in the north and west of England and in Wales. Eric Mercer has identified and defined 'base', 'jointed', 'middle', 'raised' and 'upper' crucks which widens their distribution.

Dais The raised platform for 'the high table' in a mediaeval hall. Such a feature was once common in quite small houses.

Daub Plaster (or to plaster) with cob or clay as in wattle and daub.

Distemper Whitewash or colour wash mixed with water and bound with size.

Dog-legged stair A stair rising in two or more straight flights united by a landing and either without a 'well' or with a very narrow one.

Dormer window A window which rises vertically through a roof and is usually provided with its own pitched roof (once also known as 'lucans' as they are still so termed in East Anglia).

Dragon beam The diagonal beam supporting the joists in a building having a jetty on two adjacent sides. Also the diagonal tie beam of a hipped roof.

Entablature The whole of the parts (in effect, the beam) of an order above a column. These parts comprise the architrave, the frieze and the cornice.

Feather edge A tapering of the edge of a board—a feature which is not appropriate to stone.

Fielded panel A panel with raised central area or field—an effect often produced by bevelling the surrounding edges of the panel.

Figure The decorative grain in wood.

Flag stone A paving stone.

Floor cloth also **oil cloth** A canvas floor covering prepared with oil paint, plain or decorated. They were common before the introduction of linoleum in 1860. The use of oil cloth on kitchen tables persisted until it was displaced by plastics in recent years.

Frog (in bricks) An indentation on the larger face or faces of a brick.

Gablet A small gable in a hipped roof devised (when open) to permit smoke to escape from the central hearth in the hall.

Gallet A chip of stone as produced when 'pitching'.

Gambrel roof, also **curb roof** A roof which is pitched in two sections, that is to say a roof with two angles of slope on each side of the ridge.

Gibb door or **jibb door** A door which is fitted flush with the wall and without an architrave and decorated so as to be all but invisible. The word jibb or gibb occurs in a number of contexts as in a jibb bracket (one that swings), the jib of a crane or the jib sail of a boat. From the Danish *gibbe*.

Grip floor A 'plaster' floor made of a mixture of lime and ash.

Gudgeon A 'hook' on which a strap hinge turns (also known as a pintle).

Guilloche A band of decoration (classical in origin) consisting of a series of interlacing circles.

Hall The principal and often only room in a house of mediaeval type.

Harr A primitive type of hinge where one side of a door projects providing a pair of 'horns' on which a door (or gate) swings.

Heck A short internal wall separating a fireplace from an entrance and often supporting a manteltree and fire-hood..

Hooked rug Made of rags or coarse wool pulled through a coarse canvas backing. In Northumberland and Durham they are known as 'hookies and proddies', in Cumbria as 'stobbie rugs' and in Scotland as 'clootie rugs'.

Interstices The narrow spaces, quirks, grooves or veins such as are found in carved work.

Jamb An upright flanking a door, window or fireplace.

Jerkin-head An end wall which is half gabled beneath a roof which is half hipped — a type common to thatch. Despite the use of this feature in Britain the term is almost obsolete here although in current usage in America.

Jetty In a timber-frame house the projection supported on the floor joists.

Joggle A tenon in stone.

Joiner A craftsman whose skills are employed at the bench and generally in a workshop, in contrast to the carpenter who works on buildings *in situ*.

Kidderminster carpet A decorative carpet without a pile popular in the first half of the nineteenth century. In effect the different colours in these carpets are in separate although interlocking layers of fabric. 'Scotch ingrain' is similar to Kidderminster.

King post or **crown post** The centre truss post that supports the tie beam and the rafters of the roof. These posts were often treated decoratively. When used in pairs they are known as queen posts.

Knee A piece of timber forming a near right angle by natural growth and deriving strength from that fact.

Lintel or **lintol** A horizontal member bridging a void as over a doorway or window.

List carpet A coarse carpet without a pile. Typical examples are striped in different colours.

Long house A building combining a home for man and his animals, the 'house part' being separated from the byre by a cross passage. The byre is often one step lower than the 'house part'.

Mason's mitre The form made when two mouldings cut out of the solid meet at an angle.

Medullary ray The 'flash' that occurs in some woods such as oak.

Mendlesham chair A chair the design of which incorporated turned balls. Most examples were made in fruitwood and date from the first quarter of the nineteenth century. Named after Mendlesham in Suffolk where the chief makers (Daniel and Richard Day) were located.

Mitre A joint or junction of two similar members each cut to the same angle which for a right angle would be 45 degrees.

Mortice A sinking in wood (or sometimes stone) designed to receive a tenon (or joggle).

Mullion The vertical division of a window composed of two or more 'lights'.

Newel The vertical post or posts in a stair which bear one end of the stairs or one end of the string and handrail.

Outshut or **outshot** An extension or lean-to formed along the side of a house and roofed over by extending one slope of the main roof down to the pole-plate of the extension.

Pamments A name given in East Anglia to earthenware floor tiles.

Parlour A private room into which members of the family could retreat. These rooms were generally without a fireplace until the seventeenth century.

Paterae A small rondel or rosette popular as a result of the Classical Revival — originally referred to the round flat dish used to receive a sacrificial libation.

Pennant A hard blue grit stone used for flooring or paving in and around Bristol and in South Wales.

Pess A drum-like hassock of rushes.

Piano nobile An Italian term referring to the principal or first floor of a Palladian house.

Pintle A 'hook' on which a strap hinge turns (also known as a gudgeon).

Pitched stone By the use of a pitching hammer and pitcher a mason 'roughed out' his work by the removal of large gallets. These gallets could be used for paving. The pitching hammer is of steel rather than iron and is long and narrow, two features that produce a harsher knock. The pitcher is not sharpened (to cut) but is near square ended in section to split the stone.

Plank and stud A type of early panelling often found used in screens and composed of a series of vertical studs alternating with planks.

Rail Horizontal timber in framed buildings and horizontal boards in panelling or panelled furniture.

Rebate (pronounced 'rabbit' and spelt thus in early references) An angle worked in a section of wood so as to receive a panel or similar element in a construction.

Riser The vertical faces of stairs or steps.

Scantling The dimensions to which large timber is reduced to be useful for a given purpose.

Scarf The joint (of which there are many variations) by means of which a timber may be lengthened.

Scumbling The achievement of broken colour effects by removing or texturing a wet coat to expose part of the coat beneath it.

Seise A type of settle common in Scotland.

Settle bed A type of settle found in Ulster and in north-east North America. The seat folds forward to form a bed.

Shieling Summer dwelling.

Shippon A byre or cow house.

Smoke hood The precursor of the chimney being a funnel (often of wattle and daub and even paper!) corbelled out over the fire. Early references to chimneys often allude to 'funnels'.

Spere or **spur** A short fixed screen running at right angles to an outside wall. Various dialect and regional terms are also used for this feature.

Spline A thin narrow strip of wood which serves the same function between boards as the tongue in tongue-and-groove boards.

Stile An upright member in framed panelling.

String A raking board into which the treads and risers of a staircase are 'housed'. Such boards take two forms, the 'close string' and the 'open string'.

String course A decorative, usually projecting, thin course of brick or stone. Usually only found in grand interiors where it is often executed in plaster. Common on external elevations.

Stop As in 'chamfer stop', the feature which terminates the chamfer.

Studs All vertical timbers in a timber-framed wall.

Summer beam The principal beam which supports the joists. The word although archaic in Britain (where the cumbersome term bridging beam is used) is current in America.

Tenon A horn or protrusion in wood designed to fit into a mortice. In stone a tenon is termed a joggle.

Transom or **transome** A horizontal member as in the transom (or transoms) of a mullioned window. This feature occurs between the lintel and the cill dividing the window horizontally into one or more parts. Also the horizontal member between a lunette and a door.

Trennell or **tree nail** An alternative word for a dowel.

Tridarn A Welsh term for a three-tiered court cupboard.

Trunk A chest 'dug out' of a log. Later used to describe a travelling trunk or chest.

Tuffet See Buffet.

Vernacular Native language or idiom. A word that has become much associated with building as in vernacular architecture. (From the Latin *verna*, a home-born slave.)

Wainscot A term used for panelling or panelled furniture and originally referring specifically to oak.

Wattle Woven timber often made of oak posts with split ash or hazel strips woven into them.

Wichert See Cob.

Bibliography

The study of vernacular architecture has generated a great many books some of which are listed below. However, very few publications have appeared that are exclusively concerned with vernacular interiors. The most relevant publications are identified thus *. The presence of a number of books on aspects of American interiors is due to the paucity of published work on smaller domestic interiors in Britain.

Vernacular Architecture and General

*S. O. Addy, *The Evolution of the English House*, George Allen & Unwin, 1898, 1933 edition.

Arts Council of Great Britain exhibition catalogue, *The Idea of the Village*, 1976.

Arts Council of Great Britain exhibition catalogue, *English Cottages and Small Farmhouses*, Paul Oliver, 1975.

*James Ayres, *British Folk Art*, Barrie & Jenkins, London, 1977 (Overlook Press, New York, 1977).

* M. W. Barley, *The English Farmhouse and Cottage*, Routledge & Kegan Paul, London, 1961.

M. W. Barley, *The House and Home*, Vista Books, London, 1963.

*Harry Batsford and Charles Fry, *The English Cottage*, Batsford, London, 1938.

B. Anthony Bax, *The English Parsonage*, John Murray, London, 1964.

*Hugh Braun, *The Story of the English House*, Batsford, London, 1940.

A. T. Broadbent and A. Minoprio, *The Minor Domestic Architecture of Gloucestershire*, Tiranti, London, 1931.

*R. W. Brunskill, *Illustrated Handbook of Vernacular Architecture*, Faber & Faber, London, 1971.

Abbott Lowell Cummings, *The Framed Houses of Massachusetts Bay, 1625–1725*, Harvard University Press, Boston, 1979.

*W. Galsworthy Davie and W. Curtis Greene, *Old Cottages and Farmhouses in Surrey*, Batsford, London, 1908.

*E. Guy Dawber and W. Galsworthy Davie, *Cottages and Farmhouses in the Cotswolds*, Batsford, London, 1905.

F. G. Emmison, *Elizabethan Life*, Essex County Council, Chelmsford, 1976.

*Emyr Estyn Evans, *Irish Folk Ways*, Routledge & Kegan Paul, London, 1957.

Alexander Fenton, *The Island Black House*, HMSO, Edinburgh, 1978.

*Alexander Fenton, *Scottish Country Life*, John Donald, Edinburgh, 1976.

Alan Gailey, Victor Kelly and James Paul, *Rural Housing in Ulster in the Nineteenth Century*, HMSO, Belfast, 1974.

Anthony N. B. Garvan, *Architecture and Town Planning in Colonial Connecticut*, Yale University Press, New Haven, 1951.

*I. F. Grant, *Highland Folk Ways*, Routledge & Kegan Paul, London, 1961.

*Joseph Gwilt, *Encyclopaedia of Architecture*, revised by Wyatt Papworth, London, 1876.

*Robert de Zouche Hall, *A Bibliography of Vernacular Architecture*, David & Charles, Newton Abbot, 1972.

*William Halfpenny, *Twelve Beautiful Designs for Farm Houses*, London, 1774.

Richard Harris, *Discovering Timber Frame Houses*, Shire Publications, Princes Risborough, 1978.

*William Harrison, *Description of England*, London, 1577, F. J. Furnival edition, 1877.

W. G. Hoskins, *Provincial England*, Macmillan, London, 1964.

William Howitt, *The Rural Life of England*, London, 1837, 1840 edition.

*C. F. Innocent, *The Development of English Building Construction* (Cambridge University Press, 1916), David & Charles, Newton Abbot, 1971.

David Iredale, *Discovering Your Old House*, Shire Publications, Princes Risborough, 1978.

*Gertrude Jekyll, *Old English Household Life*, Batsford, London, 1925, republished 1975.

S. R. Jones, *The Village Homes of England*, Studio, London, 1912.

Batty Langley, *The Builder's Jewel*, London, 1754.

*Nathaniel Lloyd, *A History of the English House* (London, 1931), The Architectural Press, London, 1975.

Norah Lofts, *Domestic Life in England*, Weidenfeld & Nicholson, London, 1976.

*J. C. Loudon, *Encyclopaedia of Cottage, Farm and Villa Architecture*, London, 1836, 1842 edition.

*R. T. Mason, *Framed Buildings of the Weald*, Coach Publishing House, Horsham, 1964.

*Eric Mercer, *English Vernacular Houses*, HMSO, London, 1975.

Christopher Morris (ed.), *The Journeys of Celia Fiennes*, Cresset Press, London, 1947.

*Richard Neve, *The City and Country Purchaser*, London, 1726.

Ralph Nevill, *Old Cottages and Domestic Architecture in South West Surrey*, Guildford, 1889.

*Peter Nicholson, *The New Practical Builder*, London, 1823–5.

*Basil Oliver, *Old Houses and Building in East Anglia*, Batsford, London, 1912.

Paul Oliver, see Arts Council of Great Britain.

Crispin Paine and John Rhodes, *The Working Home: Small Houses in Oxfordshire through Three Centuries*, Oxfordshire County Museums, Woodstock, 1979.

Vanessa Parker, *The English House in the Nineteenth Century*, Historical Association, London, 1970.

*Iorwerth, C. Peate, *Tradition and Folk Life, A Welsh View*, Faber & Faber, London, 1972.

*Iorwerth C. Peate, *The Welsh House*, Hugh Evans & Sons, Liverpool, 1940.

*L. F. Salzman, *Building in England down to 1540*, Clarendon Press, Oxford, 1952.

T. Hudson Turner, *Some Account of Domestic Architecture*, London, 1877, 2nd edition.

Isaac Ware, *The Complete Body of Architecture*, T. Osborne and J. Shipton, London, 1756.

*C. Henry Warren, *English Cottages and Farmhouses*, Collins, London, 1948.

*B. Weinreb Architectural Books Ltd. (edited by Priscilla Wrightson), *The Small English House* (A Catalogue of Books), B. Weinreb Architectural Books Ltd., London, 1977.

Margaret Wood, *The English Mediaeval House*, Phoenix House, London, 1965.

*John Woodforde, *Georgian Houses for All*, Routledge & Kegan Paul, London, 1978.

John Woodforde, *The Truth about Cottages*, Routledge & Kegan Paul, London, 1969 (paperback 1979).

Interiors

*William Bardwell, *Healthy Homes and How To Make Them*, London, 1854.
John Cornforth, *English Interiors 1790–1848*, Barrie & Jenkins, London, 1978.
Ralph Dutton, *The English Interior 1500–1900*, Batsford, London, 1948.
Ralph Dutton, *The Victorian Home*, Batsford, London, 1954.
Charles L. Eastlake, *Hints on Household Taste*, London, 1868, revised 1872.
*John Fowler and John Cornforth, *English Decoration in the 18th Century*, Barrie & Jenkins, London, 1974, 1978 edition.
*Caroline Halsted, *Investigations or Travels in the Boudoir*, London, 1837.
Margaret Jourdain, *English Interior Decoration 1500–1830*, Batsford, London, 1950.
*Russell Hawes Kettel (ed.), *Early American Rooms 1650–1858* (Southworth-Anthoensen Press, 1936), Dover, New York, 1967.
*Peter Thornton, *17th Century Interior Decoration in England, France and Holland*, Yale University Press, New Haven, Connecticut, 1978.
Arthur Stratton, *The English Interior*, Batsford, London, 1920.

Furniture, Crafts and Details

*Peter C. D. Brears, *The English Country Pottery*, David & Charles, Newton Abbot, 1971.
*Douglas Falkland Cary, *Colour Mixing and Paint Work*, Lockwoods Trade Manuals, London, 1925.
Edward Croft-Murray, *Decorative Painting in England 1537–1837*, Country Life, London, 1962.
Robbert Dossie, *The Handmaid to the Arts*, London, 1758.
E. A. Entwisle, *The Book of Wallpaper* (1954), Kingsmead Reprints, Bath, 1970.
John Harvey, *Mediaeval Craftsmen*, Batsford, London, 1975.
*A. S. Jennings and G. C. Rothery, *The Modern Painter and Decorator*, Caxton Publishing Company, London, 1920.
*Wilfred Kemp, *The Practical Plasterer*, London, 1893, Crosby Lockwood and Son, 1926.
*J. Seymour Lindsay, *Iron and Brass Implements of the English House* (Medici Society, London, 1927), Tiranti, London, 1964.
*Nina Fletcher Little, *American Decorative Wall Painting 1700–1850* (Sturbridge, Massachusetts, 1952), Dutton, New York, 1972.
Nina Fletcher Little, *Country Arts in Early American Homes*, Dutton, New York, 1975.
Eric Mercer, *Furniture 700–1700*, Weidenfeld & Nicholson, London, 1969.
Joseph Moxon, *Mechanick Exercises or the Doctrine of Handy-Works*, London, 1677.
*E. H. Pinto, *Treen and Other Wooden Bygones*, Bell & Sons, London, 1969.
*Rodris Roth, *Floor Coverings in 18th Century America*, Smithsonian Press, Washington DC, 1967.
William Salmon, *Polygraphice Or the Arts of Drawing, Engraving, Etching, Limning, Painting, Vernishing, Japanning and Gilding &c*, London, 1672.
John Smith, *The Art of Painting in Oyl*, 1676 (and many other editions).
J. S. Stalker and G. Parker, *A Treatise of Japaning and Varnishing*, Oxford, 1688, Tiranti reprint, London, 1971.

*Jane Toller, *Country Furniture*, David & Charles, Newton Abbot, 1973.
*Nathaniel Whittock, *The Decorative Painters' and Glaziers' Guide*, London, 1827.
Geoffrey Wills, *English Furniture 1550–1760*, Guinness Superlatives, London, 1971.
S. W. Wolsey and R. W. P. Luff, *Furniture in England, The Age of the Joiner*, Arthur Barker, London, 1968.

Many of the Museums listed in the Gazetteer publish helpful guides. Among them are the following: The Weald and Downland Museum, the Welsh Folk Museum, the Museum of Lakeland Life and Industry, Avoncroft Museum of Buildings and the Ulster Folk and Transport Museum.

Acknowledgements

Relatively few books have been published on interior decoration in England. In those that have appeared the country house is the primary concern. They refer to the large and elegant houses of the rich who, until the Industrial Revolution, were necessarily landed. A possible exception to such an exclusive view is Sir Osbert Lancaster's *Homes Sweet Homes* which, in both line and word, bestows the 'common touch' with such an imperiously sure hand. There is no such prejudice against the smaller house in the United States and I must therefore express my gratitude to a number of American scholars and institutions. Until the emergence of the barons of industry in late nineteenth-century America, no large houses were built there. By English standards Mount Vernon and Monticello are modest manor houses. As a result, organizations such as the Society for the Preservation of New England Antiquities and the Henry Francis du Pont Museum, as well as individuals like Mr and Mrs Bertram Little and John Sweeney have perforce done much to show us in Britain how to look at our vernacular interiors. It is their published research over the years as well as their personal advice that has proved invaluable to me in the preparation of this book. I am indebted to Mrs Little's *American Decorative Wall Painting*, for without it I doubt that I would have discovered examples of early nineteenth-century stencilled wall decoration in this country. Similarly, had Rodris Roth not published her research on *Early American Floor Coverings* it is unlikely that the great importance of oil cloths in the eighteenth century would have occurred to me. Such points are not only clearly but also beautifully demonstrated at the American Museum in Britain. I owe a considerable debt of gratitude to the Fulbright Commission, the Ford Foundation, the Museum School, Boston, and the Institute of International Education for without the munificence of these institutions my experience of America would have remained that of the tourist.

In their turn the Americans owe much to the first open air museums in Scandinavia of which the earliest was Skansen, near Stockholm, opened in 1891. Just as American vernacular architecture shows us what became of the British tradition when transported to the west, so some of our traditions originated to the east of the North Sea. I therefore acknowledge the assistance of the Norsk Folkemuseum, Oslo, the Frilandsmuseet, Copenhagen, and my Danish mother.

All writers on any aspect of vernacular architecture in Britain must salute S. O. Addy and C. F. Innocent for their pioneer studies which contain interesting descriptions of details of small domestic interiors. In recent years research has been more concerned with statistical matters of the distribution of house types. Nevertheless, the work of scholars like M. W. Barley provide an indispensable matrix for the study of interiors, whilst folklorists like E. Estyn Evans, I. F. Grant and Iorwerth C. Peate have written on the use of interiors.

In travelling around the British Isles it is remarkable to discover how many of our folk museums are recently founded or, like the Agricultural Museum at the Royal Highland Showgrounds, Ingliston, about to open. One of the first and finest of these institutions is the Welsh Folk Museum (founded in 1946) at St. Fagans and I am especially indebted to J. Geraint Jenkins and Derick Jenkins for their help and advice. Another inspiring establishment is the Folk and Transport Museum, Holywood, Northern Ireland and, after the most fruitful and enjoyable days spent there, I would like to thank the Director, G. B. Thompson OBE, Joan Morris and Dr Philip Robinson. My gratitude is also due to Alan Graham of Queen's University, Belfast; Wendy Osbourne of the Ulster Museum and the staff of the Department of Post Mediaeval Antiquities of the National Museum of Ireland, Dublin. In Scotland my research was eased with great generosity by Gavin Sprott of the National Museum of Antiquities, Edinburgh; R. Ross Noble of the Highland Folk Museum, Kingussie; J. Hugh M. Leichman, the National Trust for Scotland; Andrea Kerr, Kirkcaldy Museum and Art Gallery; Angela Weight, Aberdeen Art Gallery and Museum, and the Scottish Women's Rural Institute.

In England numerous organizations and individuals were kind enough to enter into the spirit of my enquiries and give of their time and knowledge. I would like to thank the staff of all those institutions listed in the gazetteer and in particular to acknowledge the help of the staff of Bath Public Library (Reference Department), the British Library and its Department of Manuscripts, and the Photographic Library of the Royal Commission on Historical Monuments. I gratefully acknowledge the assistance of Ashley Barker (GLC Historic Buildings Council), Martyn Brown (Somerset Museum of Rural Life, Glastonbury), Anthony Davis and Ron Clarke (Coventry City Museum and Art Gallery), John Gere (Department of Prints and Drawings, British Museum), John Hardy (Department of Woodwork, Victoria and Albert Museum), John Harris (Drawings Collection, Royal Institute of British Architects), R. W. Higginbottom (St. Helier Museum, Jersey), Tiffany Hunt (Salisbury and South Wiltshire Museum), Michael Middleton (Civic Trust), John Renton (Museum of Lakeland Life), John Rhodes (Oxfordshire County Museum), Peter Robshaw (Civic Trust), Dr Sadie Ward (Museum of Rural Life, Reading), Group Captain W. R. Williams OBE DFC (Landmark Trust), and Cleo Witt and Katherine Eustace (Bristol City Museum and Art Gallery). In addition, essential help has been provided by the Avoncroft Museum of Buildings, Worcestershire, the Bath Preservation Trust, Beamish Open Air Museum, the Bradford-on-Avon Preservation Trust, the Museum of East Anglian Life, Suffolk, and the Weald and Downland Museum, Sussex. I would also like to pay tribute to the National Trust who own a number of small properties for their architectural importance (such as the Priest's House, Muchelney) or literary associations (as with Beatrix Potter's house in the Lake District).

Among the individuals whose advice has been invaluable as well as those who were kind enough to show me their houses I would like to thank Ian Bristow, Jeanne Courtauld, Dr and Mrs Andrew Crowther, Anthony Dale, Mrs C. L. du Pre, Sir John Eardley-Wilmot, Commander and Mrs Colin Ellum, the Hon. Desmond Guinness, the Revd Terry Hampton, Morrison Heckscher, Anthony Herbert, Martin Holmes, Stanley Jones, Francesca Jordan, Mr and Mrs Stanley Lewis, Dr A. T. Lucas, Ian McCallum, Mrs M. Maurin, Mr and Mrs Kenneth Monkman, Dr Dallas Pratt, Mr and Mrs M. F. Pratt, Mrs Polly Rogers, Mr and Mrs Charles

Smith, Gordon H. Smith, Sir Robert Spencer-Nairn, Lisa van Gruisen, David Whitcombe and Robin Wyatt. The correspondence generated by this book was capably handled by Sarah Trevatt.

To my father I owe an early upbringing in the building crafts which I hope has brought to the book a physical understanding of the timeless skills that wood and stone demand. To my wife who not merely translated my illegible hand into typescript and assisted with the editorial process but has also, over the years, lived this book night and day, I owe the greatest debt of all.

Gazetteer

As can be seen from the sources of the photographs in this book, many museums contain items of relevance to small or vernacular interiors, but for some of these institutions such material is of prime importance. They fall into two categories: those that show the basic internal construction and those that also house the more fugitive elements from such interiors. National Trust properties are identified by the initials 'NT', and Landmark Trust properties by 'LT' (Landmark Trust properties are not open to the public but are accessible on application to the Trust, Shottesbrooke, Maidenhead, Berkshire).

England

Map Reference

AVON
2 and 2a Abbey Green (NT)   1
  Bath
BERKSHIRE
Museum of English Rural Life   2
  University of Reading
  White Knights Park
  Reading

BUCKINGHAMSHIRE
The Chilton Open Air Museum   3
  Newlands Park
  Chalfont St. Giles
High Wycombe Art Gallery and Museum   4
  Castle Hill
  High Wycombe
Milton's Cottage   3
  Chalfont St. Giles

CAMBRIDGESHIRE
Cambridge and County Folk Museum   5
  2 and 3 Castle Street
  Cambridge

CHESHIRE
Quarry Bank Mill (NT)   6
  Styal

CORNWALL
Four Houses (LT)   7
  Combe
  Morwenstow
  Bude
Lawrence House (NT)   8
  Castle Street
  Launceston
Old Mill House   9
  Zennor
  St. Ives
Old Post Office (NT)   10
  Tintagel

CUMBRIA
Beatrix Potter's House (NT)   11
  Hill Top
  Sawrey
Courthouse Museum (NT)   12
  Hawkshead
Museum of Lakeland Life and Industry   13
  Abbot Hall
  Kendal
Townend (NT)   14
  Troutbeck

Index

Numbers and letters in italics refer to illustrations